WEST FARGO PUBLIC LIBRARY
109 3rd Street East
West Fargo, ND 58078

Prairie Voices

An Oral History of Scandinavian Americans in the Upper Midwest

by

Gerald D. Anderson

©2014 Gerald Anderson

All rights reserved.

ISBN-13: 978-1503354586
Cover design by Karl Anderson

BOOKS BY GERALD ANDERSON

Fiction

The Uffda Trial

Saving England

One and a Half Stone of Stories

Palmer Knutson Mystery Series:

    Death Before Dinner

    Murder Under the Loon

    Pecked to Death ... or ... Murder Under the Prairie Chicken

    Murder in Bemidji ... or ... Paul's Bloody Trousers

    The Unicorn Murder ... or ... Victoria's Revenge

Nonfiction

Fascists, Communists, and the National Government

Study Guide: The Western Perspective, Volumes I and II

Contents

Introduction 1

Chapter I: Patterns of Scandinavian Immigration 19

Chapter II: "I Worked So Damn Hard!" THE OLD COUNTRY 41

Chapter III: "I Got the Fever to Come" THE GREAT MIGRATION 61

Chapter IV: "Foot Your Own Canoe" THE FIRST SETTLEMENT 101

Chapter V: "It Helps Sometimes to Know Who Your People Are" SCANDINAVIAN ETHNICITY AND THE FRONTIER 155

Chapter VI: "It Was Wheat, Oats, and Barley" WORKING IN THE NEW WORLD 189

Chapter VII: "Talk English Now!" SCANDINAVIANS AND THE AMERICAN SCHOOL 213

Chapter VIII: "They Were Fussy about Religion" THE SCANDINAVIAN CHURCH IN AMERICA 243

Chapter IX: "Everybody Had *Decorah Posten*" NEWS FOR SCANDINAVIANS 289

Chapter X: "'Democrat' Was a Word for Something We Didn't Like" THE POLITICS OF THE NEW AMERICANS 311

Chapter XI: "Now Speak Norwegian!" HOME LIFE IN TOWN AND COUNTRY 331

Chapter XII: "They Pert'near Kicked the Ceiling" SCANDINAVIAN-AMERICAN ENTERTAINMENT 365

Chapter XIII: "It Grows on You" SCANDINAVIAN FOOD ON AMERICAN PLATES 391

Chapter XIV: "It Was a Day to Live For" THE SCANDINAVIAN-AMERICAN CHRISTMAS 409

Chapter XV: "We Got to Be More United" THE ETHNIC WATERSHED: WORLD WAR I 436

Chapter XVI: "That's What America Is!" SCANDINAVIAN-AMERICAN VALUES 451

BIBLIOGRAPHY: THE PRAIRIE VOICES 461

SELECTED BIBLIOGRAPHY 467

Introduction

Oral history is nothing less than the voice of the people. If we are to accept the premise that the voice of the people is important, it is incumbent upon us to preserve it. Throughout the Upper Midwest there is a vast reservoir of living witnesses who represent historical data from the grass roots. Yet, of the impressions and memories of those who have lived our histories, little will ever be written down for future use.

The use of oral history is hardly a new idea. Herodotus used oral sources for his account of the Persian Wars and Thucydides used carefully selected oral accounts for his history of the Peloponnesian War. Nevertheless, the use of oral sources presents a number of problems to the historian, some of which perhaps can never be completely overcome. Both the process and the product must continually be examined in light of existing knowledge whenever possible. Yet, as Alice Kessler Harris has noted, oral history can offer "a glimpse into the life styles, belief systems and values of ordinary people. ... Because at its best it posits answers in terms of a dialectical relationship between changing consciousness and social, political and economic movements, such materials deserve far more analysis and criticism than they have so far received."[1]

---

[1] Alice Kessler Harris, "Introduction," *Envelopes of Sound* (Chicago: Precedent Publishing Company, 1975), p. 3.

The historian must always critically examine his historical evidence. Whether documents are written or oral they "derive from humans who have biases and prejudices, selective perceptions and memories, incomplete and limited powers of observation, and fallible memories. Furthermore, people undergo changes over time and are subject to external influences and manipulation and, as such, are mirrors of their time and environment."[2] All of these problems are evident in the oral histories examined in this study. One subject, for instance, reported that her father had emigrated from Norway on a steamship in the 1890s and had been on the ocean for nine weeks. The listener may assume that the captain of the ship was not lost and that the subject really meant to say "nine days." Yet, she did not mean nine days, she meant nine weeks. Obviously she had accepted this item of family history and had never considered the unlikelihood that her father's trip to the New World had taken longer than that of Columbus. Nevertheless, the total acceptance of her father's immigration story as she understood it does reveal something about the subject and her significance as an historical source.

The people interviewed for this study were all "ordinary people." There are no congressmen or college presidents included, but there are many farmers, farm wives, builders, teachers, pastors, and even a retired milkman. Yet, the voices of these ordinary people can serve to provide a shared sense of their society and their history. Ronald J. Grele, who called oral history "a

---

[2] Gary Y. Okihiro, "Oral History and the Writing of Ethnic History: A Reconnaissance into Method and Theory," *The Oral History Review* (Volume 9, 1981), p. 31.

tool to democratize the study of history,"[3] maintained that the aim of oral history was to "transform an individual story into a cultural narrative, and, thereby, to more fully understand what happened in the past."[4]

According to Gary Y. Okihiro, the collection and interpretation of oral history reveals several implications for American ethnic history.

> Oral history offers us an alternative way of conceptualizing history and a means by which to recover that past. And while oral history does not maintain that each individual's view of history is equally legitimate or that every voice must be heard, it does argue that by going directly to the people for historical documents, a more valid variety of history can be written. Oral history proposes that we rewrite our history to capture the human spirit of the people, to see how ethnic minorities solved or failed to solve particular problems, how they advanced or resisted change, and how they made or failed to make better lives for themselves and their children. In short, oral

---

[3] Ronald J. Grele, "It's Not the Song, It's the Singing," *Envelopes of Sound* (Chicago: Precedent Publishing, Inc., 1975), p. 87.
[4] Ronald J. Grele, "Movement Without Aim: Methodological and Thematic Problems in Oral History," *Envelopes of Sound* (Chicago: Precedent Publishing, Inc., 1975), p. 142.

history proposes nothing less than the writing of a people's history, liberated from myths and imbued with humanity.[5]

These were the general considerations that led to the development of the Scandinavian Oral History Project. Dr. I. Kenneth Smemo of Moorhead State University was the original director of the Northwest Minnesota Regional History Center. By the time I joined the center as Associate Director in 1975, Dr. Smemo had already amassed a significant oral history collection. He had also taught courses in oral history and had begun a file of potential interviewees. We decided that an oral history project that emphasized the uniqueness of the region could provide an added dimension to the holdings of the center.

In culture, tradition, language, genealogy, and state of mind, the Upper Midwest is overwhelmingly Scandinavian. "Uffda" is less of an epithet here than it is a philosophy of life. O. E. Rolvaag's *The American Letters* could describe the lives of hundreds of people still living in this area. We decided, therefore, that a collection of the voices of the first and second generation Scandinavian immigrants would be a natural and valuable addition to the Northwest Center.

It was not difficult to find interview subjects. As anyone who has done an oral history project knows, one of the best sources for potential

---

[5] Gary Y. Okhiro, *loc. cit.*, pp. 4546.

interview subjects is the recommendation of other subjects. By asking the interview subject for the names of people who would be able to provide us with additional information, we were able to widely expand our files of potential interviewees. In some cases the people came to us. I appeared on the local television "talk shows" and described our project and this publicity always resulted in additional names for our prospect list.

During the Spring Quarter of 1976 at Moorhead State University, Dr. Smemo offered a course in oral history. This presented us with a marvelous opportunity to combine the academic procedures of oral history with our existing project. The students usually had a favorite grandparent or knew of a hometown acquaintance that would substantially contribute to our project. Later courses at Moorhead State University and my own courses in Scandinavians in America at North Dakota State University significantly added to this collection.

The Scope of the Project: The major criteria used in the selection of a subject for inclusion in the project was that the person to be interviewed must be either a Scandinavian immigrant or of the first generation born of immigrant parents. This presented no particular problem, for Swedes and Norwegians abound throughout the region, and there are numerous pockets of Danes, Icelanders, and Finns as well.

Through a telephone contact with the subject, an appointment was made for a preliminary interview, generally in the subject's home. At this interview, rapport was established and the subject was given the usual assurances that the purpose of the project was legitimate and entirely benign. By this time, at least one cup of coffee had been consumed, and the subjects were not distressed to be given a general outline of the coming interview. The outline, to be discussed below, served to aid the subject in the process of remembering and gave all of the oral interviews a desired degree of organizational unity. An appointment for a taping session was usually made for about a week later in order to give the subject time to review the outline and to gather his or her recollections for the interview.

There were three general parts to the interview: biographical information, personal memories of the Scandinavian heritage, and the decline of the immigrant experience. Each of these areas will be discussed in terms of the questions asked and the meaning of the response.

Biographical Information: The interview began with the subject stating his name, address, and date and place of birth. The subject was also asked for biographical and genealogical information on his spouse (including names of parents, date of birth, date of wedding, etc.) and his or her children. The genealogical data was never meant to compete with that of the Latter Day Saints, but it did provide a meaningful reference point for understanding the subject. The subject was then asked to relate his or his parents' immigration experience. Among the information sought in this portion of the interview was: name in Scandinavia (if different), occupation in Scandinavia, when immigration occurred, how immigration occurred (a student interviewer is recorded as inquiring, "How did they come then? By boat?"), why immigration was necessary or desirable, and the area in Scandinavia from which they came. The responses to these questions did not produce any major surprises, although the number of immigrants who arrived in the United States by way of Halifax, Nova Scotia, was perhaps higher than might be expected. The overwhelming motive for immigration was, as one would expect, economic.

The subject was then asked to describe his or his ancestors' initial settlement in the New World. Among the answers sought were: Where did they originally settle? Why did they settle there? Were there any relatives or other Scandinavians already living there? How long did they stay there? When did they arrive at their current location if they had stayed for a time in older settlements? How did they acquire their land or business? Did their occupation remain constant? Did they immediately become citizens? Did the immigrating generation learn to speak English? Did they leave an account of their pioneer efforts? Did they ever return to Scandinavia to visit or to live? Did they keep in contact with relatives in Scandinavia? Did they join or form an "ethnic" church congregation?

The answers to these questions were very consistent with the accepted idea of Scandinavian immigration. In almost every case, among the earlier Norwegian immigrants for instance, the trip to the newer settlement areas had been interrupted by a stay of several months or years at an older settlement such as Winneshiek County, Iowa. Swedes and Danes tended to disperse to whatever opportunity awaited them, while Norwegians, Finns, and Icelanders tended to find areas where their erstwhile countrymen had already settled. First generation Norwegians were almost always rural, while first generation Swedes more often became urban residents and engaged in building trades. Most of the Scandinavian-Americans interviewed reported that they (or their parents) did remain constant in their occupations, did soon become citizens, did learn at least some English, did not keep an account of their pioneer efforts, and usually did not retain a great deal of contact with their relatives in Scandinavia. Most also found or started a church similar to that which they had known in the Old Country, whether that congregation were "high church" or "low church."

Personal Memories of the Scandinavian Heritage: The object of this part of the interview was to collect information on the extent to which Scandinavian customs were transported to America. Among the questions asked were: Did you or your parents receive Scandinavian language newspapers and read books in the Scandinavian language? What were these newspapers and books? Was there a definite Scandinavian influence in music or entertainment? Were there special Scandinavian foods in your home? Did you have a traditional Scandinavian Christmas? Approximately what percentage of your community was Scandinavian? Of this percentage, what percentage was Norwegian/Swedish/etc.? What other nationalities were represented in your community?

Answers to these questions were remarkably homogeneous. Almost all of the subjects reported that they had at least one Scandinavian language newspaper in their home. Among the Norwegians, the most popular newspaper, by far, was the *Decorah Posten*. Interestingly enough, many Swedes also took the *Decorah Posten*, although many also received the *Minneapolis Tidende* or the *Svenska Amerikaneren*, published in Chicago. Several women reported that they received the Norwegian language magazine, *Kvinden og Hjemmet* (Women and the Home). Virtually all Icelanders were acquainted with one of two Icelandic newspapers published in Winnipeg, while Finns usually reported reading either the *Raivaja* or the more radical *Industrialist*. Most Scandinavian language books seemed to be of the religious variety, although occasionally a history or a Scandinavian-American novel might be mentioned.

Descriptions of home entertainments frequently contained a nostalgic reference to the Hardanger fiddle or the Halling spring dance, the fun of Julebok ("Christmas fooling"—a unique blend of a masked ball and a charivari in which the host does not know he is the host until the guests arrive), or the glories and regenerative powers of the sauna. Scandinavian foods, it appears, rapidly disappeared from the table, to reappear only during Christmas or other festive occasions. While *grot, rullepolse,* and boiled potatoes remained a staple, lutefisk, lefse, *krumkake,* and Icelandic prune cake were usually reserved for a holiday treat. Christmas was celebrated in almost the same manner as it had been in the Old Country, complete with the early morning *Julotte* church service, and remains to this day the most retained part of the Scandinavian heritage.

The project was also concerned with the interaction of the various Scandinavian ethnic groups. To gather information on this topic, the subjects were asked to comment on how the various immigrant groups got along with each other. Were there, for instance, significant rivalries between Norwegians and Swedes? Did Scandinavians stick together against other ethnic groups and how was this rivalry, if any, expressed? Again, this portion of the interview tended to reflect most of the accepted notions on ethnic interaction. As a rule, it was found that ethnic rivalries tended to exist to a far greater degree in an urban environment than in a rural one. In the city of Moorhead, Minnesota, for instance, the Swedish and Norwegian populations tended to be far more cliquish than in the rural eastern part of Clay County, where these groups worked together in such activities as threshing crews or socialized together in school or community events. In like manner, the isolated Finn seemed to have interacted with other ethnic groups to a far greater extent than did those Finns who resided in the New York Mills, Minnesota, area. Such results were only to be expected, perhaps, but it was interesting to compare the subject's reaction to other ethnic groups in relation to his or her geographical circumstance.

The religious aspect was another notable element of Scandinavian diversity. The subject was asked to recount the existence of the churches in his community and the effect that they had on community life. Among the questions asked were: Did religious divisions parallel ethnic divisions? Did social activity parallel religious divisions? How did the passage of time lessen this division? In what language were the church services conducted? When did the church adopt the English language?

As was expected, the interviews revealed an ethnic-religion connection. Obviously the Norwegian would go to a church that featured the Norwegian language rather than a church featuring Swedish services, but the most significant aspect of this part of the study was the extent to which each group stayed with their ethnic congregation half a century beyond the time when the Scandinavian language was discontinued. In Moorhead, for instance, a great many of the early Swedish families are still members of Bethesda Lutheran Church, which was originally a congregation of the Swedish Augustana synod. Similarly, an equally large proportion of the descendants of the early Norwegian settlers still attend Trinity Lutheran

Church, originally a Norwegian Evangelical Church. It was also instructive to compare attitudes among Norwegian Lutherans themselves. In Rollag, Minnesota, for instance, two large Lutheran churches stand across the road from each other. Rollag, population about thirty, would not seem to need two such churches to fill the spiritual hunger of its citizens. Yet, in the 1880s, two churches were required to serve the Haugeans in their manner and the adherents of the *Synoda* church in theirs. Rollag continued to be blessed with two Norwegian language services until the latter part of the 1930s. The divisions that may have existed among these people are, however, extremely difficult to determine. Of the three Rollag residents who were interviewed, all maintained that there was no rivalry with or animosity toward members of the other church, but did admit that there was little socializing between them. There is, to this day, no merger of these two churches.

Although the subjects were often hesitant to talk about it, they were also asked about political affiliation. The responses varied from an unsolicited denunciation of Herbert Hoover to a flat statement of "We were all Republicans around here!" While some of the subjects detected a change in the political affiliations during the 1930s, most considered it an unimportant aspect of their community life.

<u>The Decline of the Impact of Immigration</u> In this portion of the interview, an attempt was made to gather information for the understanding of the process

by which the first and second generation immigrant lost the more pronounced aspects of his ethnicity. Among the questions asked of the subject were: Could you speak English when you came to America? Could you speak English when you started school? Could your teacher speak a Scandinavian language? Were you permitted to speak your Scandinavian language on the school grounds? Did your teacher ever discuss Scandinavian history or culture? What percentage, approximately, of your fellow students were Scandinavian? The responses to these questions varied considerably with the location of the school. In rural areas, a high percentage of the subjects reported that their teacher was Scandinavian and, while the Scandinavian language was never used in the classroom, there was a general usage of it on the playground. In urban areas, most incoming students already spoke English, the percentage of fellow ethnics was much lower, and little attention was paid to any form of Scandinavian culture.

The First World War is often considered to be a watershed in the decline of ethnicity in America. The interviews explored this theme by asking the following questions: Did you, or any member of your family, serve in the war? Do you remember bond sales or Red Cross drives in your community? Was there any pressure to become less "Norwegian" (or "Swedish," etc.) and more "American?" Was there more attention paid to American patriotism in the schools? The responses to these questions strongly indicated that ethnicity did suffer a marked decline during and immediately after the First World War, even in rural areas.

Finally, an attempt was made to gather responses to questions that would measure the ethnic presence that remains today. Among the questions asked were: Is the native language still heard in your community today? Are there occasional church services or other special events conducted in a Scandinavian language today? Have you ever visited the land of your ancestors? What old world customs or traditions do you retain in your family today? The responses to these questions revealed that the use of the Scandinavian language in everyday communication is common for those who were born before 1910, somewhat common for those who were born from 1910 to 1925, and quite rare for those born after this date. For the most part, Scandinavian languages are not used except for an occasional diamond jubilee or centennial church service. The number of Norwegians who had traveled to the land of their parents or grandparents was surprisingly high, especially when compared to other Scandinavian ethnic groups. Retention of old world customs and traditions varied widely among individuals as well as among ethnic groups. In all cases, however, it was apparent that the one common remaining vestige of Scandinavian tradition was in the Christmas experience.

Voice inflections and tonal subtleties are extremely difficult to capture in the printed word. In the selections included in this oral history, this has caused some problems in punctuation. The responses included in the following chapters are not strictly *verbatim* in that vocal hesitations, the "ers" and the "ums," have been edited out. Periods, commas, and exclamation points have been inserted in such a manner as to portray, as accurately as possible, the tone and meaning of the response. Furthermore, there are some passages that include information or observations that may not be germane to the topic of the chapter, but are included to retain the context of the response.

Some of the interviewees had, as may be expected, a very thick Scandinavian brogue. For the most part, I have avoided an attempt to reproduce this accent phonetically, but in some cases a heavily accented word becomes part of the message and has been reproduced to the best of my ability. In addition, the Scandinavian "yah" for "yes" is so ubiquitous as to be an accepted part of English speech in the Upper Midwest. Finally, there has been no alteration of word order. Those who are not familiar with Upper Midwest speech patterns may find some of the word orders to be unusual because sometimes they reflect the word patterns of the particular Scandinavian languages.

The responses to the interview questions have not been quantified. Written records, such as the subscription lists of the *Decorah Posten* might, perhaps, be more accurate in determining the reading habits of Norwegians than are the recollections of several dozen randomly chosen first and second generation Norwegian immigrants. Tax rolls, voting records, church records, school records, deeds, census data, etc., are in some cases more accurate than the memory of a ninety-year-old man. But the written word cannot capture the love of country in a man's voice as he speaks, as one of the subjects does, of serving in the Norwegian army as it patrolled the Swedish border in 1905. Nor can it capture the renewed suffering of an old woman as she speaks of the first years on the treeless North Dakota plain. The spontaneous humor of an event long forgotten but suddenly remembered, be it accurate or not, is a valid part of our cumulative heritage.

The following history is not, nor can it be, a comprehensive story of Scandinavians in the American Upper Midwest. It is rather a collage of experiences, with much that is left out and some that is unrepresentative. It is, however, the account of some Scandinavian-Americans as they view this history. From an individual standpoint, it is one person's evaluation of his family and friends and how they adjusted to new conditions, complete with his wisdom and ignorance, bias and sensitivity. From a collective standpoint, there emerges a picture of a courageous people, not always confident, who ached for their old land but learned to love the new. Like other ethnic groups in America, the Scandinavian-Americans met new challenges and opportunities and in this confrontation they transformed themselves into a new people. In the largely rural areas of the Upper Midwest, this would not be the sink-or-swim assimilation process that was found in America's urban environment, but a gradual, perhaps less painful, movement from being a

Scandinavian in America to a Scandinavian-American and finally to an American of Scandinavian descent.

Chapter I

Patterns of Scandinavian Immigration

The immigration experience of leaving one's home and creating a new life in America was not unique to Scandinavia. Each group of immigrants to America established its own pattern of settlement, determined by economic, political, social and historical factors. To a large degree, the concentration of Scandinavians in the Upper Midwest is explained by the fact that Scandinavian immigration peaked at the time that agricultural land in this area was opened to settlement. And yet, this is only part of the story. The following summary is not meant to be a comprehensive history of Scandinavian immigration to America. A general background of this development, however, may be useful in understanding the oral histories of the participants.

The first European contact with North America occurred in 981, when Eric the Red, of a prominent family in Iceland, was banished from the island for killing a man in a feud. Instead of sailing back to Norway, Eric sailed westward to an island that may have been sighted on a previous voyage. He found a hospitable land that was suitable for agriculture and here he apparently served out the three years of his banishment. In 985 he returned to Iceland, and by giving his island of exile the somewhat imaginative name of "Greenland," he was able to persuade a number of Icelandic countrymen to settle there.

Eric set up his estate in Brattahlid, in what would become the middle of a hundred-mile long stretch of homesteads. This would be the beginning of a vibrant European settlement that would last for almost five hundred years. Over the course of the next ten generations, Scandinavian Greenlanders would provide Europe with a variety of products ranging from furs to the horn of the narwhal, which was marketed in Europe as the unicorn's horn. Greenland would exist as the farthest outpost of Christianity when, in 1124, the king of Norway appointed a bishop for Greenland and a cathedral and a bishop's residence were constructed at Gardar.

There is very little in the way of written records concerning these first Scandinavian-Americans. There is, however, a treasury of oral history known as the Norse sagas, which were not consigned to a written form until decades after the events they describe. According to one such saga, Bjarni Herjulfson was the first to see America when, on a quest to find his father, he became lost at sea. He sighted land several times before he finally returned to Greenland. In another saga, Leif Ericson was blown off course and made the initial sighting. In both versions, however, it would be Leif Ericson who would make the first settlement in the newly discovered land. About 1002, according to this oral history, Leif Ericson set out with thirty-five men to the shores of North America. Here he found a land teeming with game and salmon, with grassy meadows and fine timber, and one of his men discovered wild grapes. The new land was therefore called Vinland.

Determining the precise location of Vinland indicates the problems involved in using oral history as a reliable source. The mention of grapes in the saga seemed to indicate that the site had to be at least as far south as New England. In 1960, however, Helge Ingstad, a Norwegian archaeologist, found the ruins of a Viking settlement at a place called *L'Anse aux Meadows* in Newfoundland. The topography of the site closely matched the description found in the sagas and some berries were found from which a wine could be made. The early Norse presence in North America is an established fact, and the *L'Anse aux Meadows* settlement may even be Leif Erickson's original colony.

In 1898, a quite different piece of archaeological "evidence" was discovered in Douglas County Minnesota near the village of Kensington. A large stone covered with runic carvings was unearthed by Olaf Ohman on his farm. The runes told of a voyage westward from Vinland by a party of eight Goths (Swedes) and twenty-two Norwegians and gave the date of the expedition as 1362. The stone was soon the center of controversy as experts pointed out obvious historical anachronisms in the runic characters while romantics insisted that the stone detailed the presence of Scandinavian-Americans in Minnesota 130 years before Columbus discovered the New World. A University of Wisconsin historian, Hjalmar Holand, set out to prove the authenticity of the stone and had soon put together a grand saga of his own. According to his theory, in 1354 Magnus Erickson, King of Norway, Sweden, and Skane, had commissioned Sir Paul Knutson to make an expedition to Greenland to investigate rumors that the western settlement had fallen away from the true faith. When he found the western settlement abandoned, Knutson continued on to Vinland and proceeded down through Hudson's Bay, the Nelson River, the Red River, and various other waterways until he reached the Kensington area.

In support of this theory, Holand cited "artifacts" found throughout the Red River Valley and Park Region districts of Minnesota, including such items as firesteels, halbeards, a Viking sword found near Ulen, Minnesota, and various "mooring stones." (A mooring stone was a large rock located near what someone with imagination could call a waterway and possessing a somewhat triangular hole about one and a quarter inches in diameter into which a mooring pin could be inserted. One such stone was, in fact, found on the author's family farm in eastern Clay County, Minnesota) In the course of several decades of work, Holand was able to add such circumstantial evidence as the reported existence of Native Americans with blonde hair and blue eyes, Native American religions that contained Christian themes, and another lost runestone. It made a good story, appealed to the imagination of Minnesota school children, and provided a needed tonic for the tourist industry of the Alexandria region.

Unfortunately, it was a hoax, albeit a brilliant one. In its Winter, 1976, issue, *Minnesota History* published relevant portions of a tape of a 1967 interview with a son and daughter of John P. Gran, a Douglas County neighbor of Olaf Ohman. In this interview the son, Walter, he reported that when his father mistakenly believe that he was on his deathbed, he had confessed that he had served as the left handed partner of the right-handed Ohman in carving the stone. The director of the Minnesota Historical Society, Russell W. Fridley concluded that the stone was a modern forgery, but that it was nevertheless a "monument to Scandinavian humor and the American frontier."

It was at the time of the aforementioned Paul Knutson expedition, however, that the Scandinavian presence in North America began to experience significant difficulties. In a relatively brief span of time there occurred a rather drastic change in the climate that shortened the growing season and made the already harsh climate more severe. European trading patterns began to change and ice began to choke Greenland's harbors. Finally, it may be assumed that Greenland did not escape the ravishes of the Black Death, a plague that took the lives of two out of every three Icelanders. The last bishop to reside in Gardar died in the 1370s, and although bishops to Greenland were continually appointed until 1540, none would actually reside in their see. By the middle of the fifteenth century, the first Scandinavian occupation of North America had ended.

By the seventeenth century, political conditions in Scandinavia had undergone considerable change. The Union of Kalmar, which had once united the thrones of Norway, Denmark, and Sweden, had been dissolved. Sweden, under the leadership of the house of Vasa, had become a European power. Under Christian IV, Denmark, which possessed Norway, had also become a significant European state, and in 1619 Jens Munk undertook a Danish expedition to Hudson's Bay in an attempt to find the Northwest Passage. In 1638, under the leadership of the Swedish chancellor, Axel Oxensterna, an attempt was made to establish a Swedish colony in the new world. In March of that year, a ship called *Kalmar Nyckel* (The Key of Kalmar) landed on the shores of the Delaware River. The new colony was called Christina, after the daughter of King Gustavus Adolphus. Over the course of the next seventeen years, several more settlements were established, but in 1655 a force of more than 600 troops equipped by the Dutch West India Company captured the Swedish forts and the territory became part of New Netherlands. Nine years later, as a result of a war between the Netherlands and England, the remaining American Swedes became subjects of the English king, Charles II. Nevertheless, the former Swedish colony would remain as a Swedish-speaking enclave in North America until well into the eighteenth century and Lutheran ministers were sent from Sweden until the 1770s. A descendent of one of the New Sweden colonists, John Morton of Delaware, cast the deciding vote in favor of the American Declaration of Independence.

Meanwhile, Danes and Norwegians were already living in the New World. It is estimated that by 1675 as many as one hundred Danes were living in New Amsterdam, including Jonas Bronck, who had arrived in 1629 and had purchased a large tract of land that would eventually be called the Bronx. In 1735, Danish converts to Moravian pietism established a mission at Bethlehem, Pennsylvania, and over the course of the next few decades Danes and Norwegians would travel in organized companies to join the predominantly German settlers in that area. Among the Norwegians living in New Amsterdam were Anneken Hendriksen, from Bergen, who married Jan van der Bilt, and Claes Carstensen, who served as an interpreter for the Dutch and the Indians in the Hudson River Valley.

Denmark was also concerned with a totally different part of the New World. The Danish West Indies Company acquired and occupied the island of St. Thomas in 1672, and in 1754 the crown took over the administration of the island and opened it to all Danish citizens, some of whom eventually established plantations for the cultivation of tobacco, sugar, and cotton. Throughout the eighteenth century, close ties existed between the Danish West Indies and the British colonies because of business connections, and several Danish planters sent their children to Philadelphia for their education.

When the Revolution began, several Danes fought on the colonial side, especially in the navy.

Other than the Moravian pietists, there was no mass migration of Scandinavians to North America until 1825. Individual Scandinavians had continued to arrive, however, among them Cleng Peerson, who had explored upper New York state and other areas in the early 1820s. Peerson, since called the "Norwegian Daniel Boone," had been born in Stavanger in 1783, and appears to have become dissatisfied with the church in Norway. On July 4th, 1825, a Peerson led expedition consisting of Quaker or Quaker adherents from Stavanger departed from Norway aboard a ship called *Restorationen*. They landed in New York on October 9th, a date observed since 1964 as Leif Ericson Day. It had been Peerson's plan to buy *Restaurationen* in Norway, fill it up with iron and passengers, and sell both ship and cargo in New York for a tidy profit. Unfortunately, they were sold at a loss, and the first Norwegian business enterprise in America was a failure. There would be others.

This first group of Norwegian immigrants, known as "the Sloopers," had for the most part forsaken the faith of their fathers and had left the state Lutheran church. Furthermore, by this time, the teachings of Hans Nielsen Hauge, which stressed a personal piety, a spiritual outlook on life, and a simple form of worship, had affected the religious attitudes of many Norwegians. A repressive state church thus became a significant "push factor" which would compel a large number of people to leave Norway. In the decades to come, freedom of religion would become a significant "pull factor" in drawing many Scandinavians to America.

The "Sloopers" first settled on the shores of Lake Ontario, about thirty-five miles east of Rochester in Kendal County, New York. Although most of the original immigrants did not stay there for long, this first settlement did provide an important "way station" for later settlers. For most of the Norwegian immigrants, land was too expensive in New York, and they were ready to follow the lead of Cleng Peerson, who now saw alluring possibilities in Illinois. All but a few of the Kendal County settlers traveled to La Salle County, Illinois, about seventy-five miles west of Chicago, to the Fox River settlement. This settlement would be the point of origin for almost all Norwegian concentrations over the next decade.

Beginning in 1838, settlers from the Fox River area began moving to the north and west into Wisconsin Territory. The end of the Black Hawk wars had reduced the Indian threat in that area and the Preemption Act of 1841 provided an added incentive. The first known Norwegian settler in Wisconsin was Ole Knudsen Nattestad of Jefferson Prairie, and by 1850, some four hundred and seven Norwegians lived there. About twenty-five miles southwest of Milwaukee, another settlement developed around Muskego, but it was Koshkonong, farther to the west, that became the center of the growing Norwegian community in Wisconsin.

One of the most influential people in the Norwegian settlement of the Upper Midwest was actually a Danish pastor, Claus Lauritsen Clausen. His contributions as a colonizer, newspaper editor, and Civil War chaplain mark him as one of the most influential Scandinavian-Americans. Clausen was influenced by the followers of Hans Nielsen Hauge while on a visit to Norway and eventually took ordination at the hands of a German Lutheran pastor. In 1850, Clausen and several of his followers explored southern Minnesota and Northern Iowa. Three years later, from the Rock Prairie community of Wisconsin, a caravan consisting of about seventy-five people in forty covered wagons and accompanied by about two-hundred head of cattle set out for Iowa. This trek may have been the largest of its kind in Norwegian experience, and thousands were to follow. By 1860 there were 4,207 Norwegians in Winneshiek County, Iowa, and its county seat, Decorah, was seen as a Norwegian-American capital. Indeed, a joke of the time featured a Norwegian immigrant disembarking from the ship in New York and saying, "If this is New York, can you imagine what Decorah must be like!"

Clausen had gone on to establish another settlement at St. Ansgar, Iowa. From there, and from the Winneshiek County settlement, Norwegian immigrants began to pour into Minnesota. An early Swedish visitor to Minnesota, the novelist Fredrika Bremer, had visited Minnesota in 1850 and had written "What a glorious new Scandinavia might not Minnesota become.

Here the Swede would find again his clear, romantic lakes, the plains of Skane rich in corn, and the valleys of Norrland; here the Norwegian would find his rapid rivers … the Danes might here pasture their flocks and herds, and lay out their farms on richer and less misty coasts than those of Denmark." By 1860, there were 11,893 Norwegians in Minnesota. Originally located in Houston, Fillmore, and Goodhue counties, they soon spread throughout the southern tier of Minnesota counties. By 1854, the railroad had reached Minnesota, and shortly after statehood in 1858, an official immigration commission was preparing information on Minnesota, written in Norwegian and Swedish. Within fifty years, Minneapolis would become one of the largest Norwegian cities and one of the largest Swedish cities in the world.

The first recorded Norwegians in Dakota Territory are reported to have arrived in 1858, advancing westward from Minnesota. The Sioux Indian wars of 1862 had a dampening effect on settlement, but by the early 1870s Norwegians began to populate the Red River Valley. In many cases they were the sons of the Iowa settlers and even grandsons of the Fox River immigrants. The Civil War was over and the Homestead Act of 1862, which provided the opportunity for free farms of 160 acres, was drawing Scandinavians to the prairie. Their struggle would be movingly described in Ole Rolvaag's *Giants in the Earth*. By the 1890s, solidly Norwegian communities were to be found throughout the Red River Valley and through the northern half of North Dakota. For many of the later immigrants, Minot became the new "Decorah."

The mass immigration of Swedes to America began about a generation later than that of the Norwegians, and did not follow the same pattern. There were, however, some earlier individual immigrants, among them Gustav Unonius, an Uppsala University student and unsuccessful author who settled in Pine Lake, Wisconsin in 1841, and Pehr Cassel, a farmer and master builder who led a group of farmers to the Skunk River area of Iowa where they founded a colony called New Sweden in 1845. Both Unonius and Cassel would popularize American immigration through "America letters" published in the Swedish press. In February of 1846 Cassell wrote from Iowa that "the ease of making a living here and the increasing prosperity of the farmers ... exceeds anything we anticipated. If only half of the work expanded on the soil in the fatherland were utilized here, the yield would reach the wildest imagination." A year later, Erik Jansson, a well-known religious dissenter who is often referred to as "the Prophet from Biskopskulla," led a group of his followers to western Illinois. There they established a communal society known as "Bishop's Hill," after Jansson's birthplace in Sweden, Biskopskulla.

The first significant wave of Swedish immigration occurred in the early 1850s, an experience perceptively described in Wilhelm Moberg's novel, *The Emigrants*. It was during this period that rural Swedish settlements were developed in western Illinois, eastern Wisconsin, central Iowa, and in northern Washington and southern Chicago counties in Minnesota. There were also centers of Swedish settlement in New York, Pennsylvania, and Texas. Following the Civil War, rural settlements in the Midwest grew rapidly, as Swedish communities were established in eastern Nebraska, and in the Lindsborg area of Kansas.

Minnesota would become the most "Swedish" of all of the states. In 1853, Hans Mattson and others founded a settlement in southeastern Minnesota that came to be known as the "Vasa" congregation. Mattson, who would go on to be the greatest Swedish promoter for Minnesota, was soon writing letters to Swedish newspapers extolling the virtues of Minnesota. Before the outbreak of the Civil War Swedes had populated large areas north and west of Minneapolis and by the 1870s were settling in the Red River Valley.

Swedish immigrants were also much more inclined than the Norwegians to settle in urban areas. Chicago became, for a time, the second largest Swedish city in the world and became an important distribution center for Swedes coming to America. Swedes made up an even larger proportion of the population of Minneapolis, Saint Paul, and Duluth, Minnesota. By 1910, about 665,000 Swedish born adults and approximately 700,000 Swedish born children lived in the United States. Over all, in the seventy years before World War I, about one-fourth of the population of Sweden would immigrate to America.

The major influx of Danes to America came later. It was not until 1788, after all, that the *Stavnsbaand* law was repealed. This remnant of a feudal ideal had prohibited the peasant farmer from leaving the estate of his birth. Although freed from such repressive laws, the Danish peasant still lacked the means to purchase sizable plots of land, and most Danish peasants remained as day laborers for the owners of the large estates. In the course of the nineteenth century, much of this would change as Denmark experienced a military defeat, lost forty percent of her territory, and saw the immigration of about 300,000 of her people.

Most of the Danish immigrants who came to America before the Civil War were single men who married women who had been born in the United States. The major exception was a group of Danish Mormons. The first missionaries of the Latter Day Saints arrived in Denmark from Utah in the 1850s, and until the 1890s Mormon missionaries were more successful in Denmark than in any European country except England. In all, about 17,000 Danish Mormons would emigrate, most of them to Utah. The first great wave of Danish immigrants other than the Mormons came to America as a result of the 1864 Danish-Prussian War. Denmark was defeated and forced to cede Schleswig and part of Holstein and an estimated 150,000 Danes were placed under German rule. Forced to use German as the official language and forced to serve in the German army, they fled their former homeland. It is estimated that as many as 50,000 Danes left Schleswig, with the majority of them going to America. Later in the century, "America Fever" infected Denmark in much the same manner as it had in Norway and Sweden.

At first, there were too few Danes on the frontier to form exclusively Danish settlements and they generally mingled with other immigrant groups, especially the Norwegians. In 1845, however, a Danish farming community was founded near Hartland, Wisconsin, and shortly thereafter other Danish communities were founded at New Denmark and Neenah. In the next two decades, Danish communities were also founded in Michigan, Illinois and Iowa. By 1890, Iowa was the most "Danish" of all the states. The first settlement in Iowa that was large enough to form a Danish congregation was at Cedar Falls in 1867, when Pastor C. L. Clausen, the Dane who founded the Norwegian settlement at St. Ansgar, formed the Scandinavian Church Society. The most prominent Danish settlement was at Elk Horn, where the Danish language predominated and which featured the most prominent folk school and several successful cooperatives.

The first Danish settlement in Minnesota occurred in 1861 in Freeborn County when Lars Jorgensen Hauge, a Baptist pastor, established a congregation in the Clark's Grove area. Beginning in the 1880s, Danish Lutheran ministers and other cultural leaders established connections with private land companies to develop over twenty rural settlements. The Danish

Folk Society, the *Dansk Folkesamfund*, sponsored a number of these settlements, including the 1885 settlement in Lincoln County, Minnesota. Within a few years this Tyler settlement could boast of the usual Danish community assets such as a folk school and a number of cooperatives. A third notable settlement in Minnesota was at Askov, southwest of Duluth, which was establish in 1906 through the efforts of the Danish People's society.

Danes moved into Dakota Territory soon after it was established. There were Danes in South Dakota in the Yankton area as early as 1864. A second major concentration of Danish settlement occurred in the east-central counties near Brookings. In North Dakota there were also two major areas of settlement, one completely separated from the Lutheran church and one founded as a result of the church. In eastern North Dakota, in Cass County, an influential newspaperman with socialist views, Christian Westergaard, took up land west of Fargo in 1878. Soon other Danes from Iowa joined him. In contrast to other Danish settlements, the Cass County settlement concentrated more on politics and did not organize a Lutheran church. In 1895, however, a Danish Lutheran pastor who lived in Hutchinson, Minnesota, H. Hanson, organized a colonization Committee. Out of this action would come a settlement in Ward County, near Kenmare, and by 1906 there were five congregations in that area. The Danish settlement in Montana was essentially a spillover from the North Dakota communities. The first

Danish congregation in Montana was founded in 1906 by members of the United Church on the border of North Dakota near the town of Westby. Other Montana communities with significant Danish populations included Dagmar, Reserve, Antelope, and Sidney.

The Danes, like the Swedes, were often inclined to settle in urban areas. Chicago attracted about one-tenth of all of the Danish immigrants, and there were significant numbers of Danish immigrants in Racine, Wisconsin (which for a time had a larger proportion of Danes than any other city in the United States), Omaha, Nebraska, and in the Twin Cities of Minnesota. The Danes, in fact, would go on to become one of the most widely and thinly spread of all of America's ethnic populations.

In direct contrast to the Danes, the Icelanders tended to be concentrated in a few specific areas. Located just below the Arctic Circle, Iceland has a climate that, while not harsh, can hardly be called pleasant. A treeless mass partly covered by glaciers, what useful land remains is basically suited only for grazing. Although settlement in Iceland has been continuous since 874, survival has seldom been easy, as the population occasionally experienced near extinction from plague, volcanoes, earthquakes, and famines. By 1800, the population of the entire island was only about 47,000 people. In the nineteenth century, the general growth of population, which was experienced throughout Europe, created particular hardships for Icelanders. When a large volcano, Hekla, blew its top in 1875, many Icelanders began to look to America. A significant number of Icelanders were also attracted to North America because of political conditions. Iceland had been forced to accept colonial status from Denmark and that government strictly controlled Iceland's commerce. Although Iceland was given a separate constitution in 1874 by the Danish king, political autonomy was still centered in Copenhagen.

As in the case of the Danes, the first major immigration of Icelanders consisted of Mormons, who came to Utah in 1855. Over the course of the next twenty years, they would be joined by a few Icelandic Lutherans and Presbyterians. In 1870, four Icelanders founded a small settlement on Washington Island, off the Green Bay Peninsula of Wisconsin, and over the next few years, some Icelanders created a secondary settlement in Lyon and Yellow Medicine counties in Minnesota. About the same time, a colony was established on the shores of Lake Winnipeg, called New Iceland, or Gimli. This settlement was established in a swamp and beset by smallpox and starvation. Such conditions forced about half of the settlers to migrate southward into Dakota Territory. There they joined another group of Icelanders who had been led to the area by an Icelandic Lutheran minister, Pal Thorlaksson. Thorlaksson, a remarkable "Icelandic Moses" who had passed through what would become Pembina County on his way to do missionary work at the New Iceland settlement, was impressed by the land around the Pembina Hills and urged his countrymen to settle there. In March of 1878, he and two of his companions chose the site that would become the center of the largest Icelandic community in the United States. By 1879, four small communities existed: Hallson, Akra, Mountain, and Gardar. Within a few years, Svold, Eyford, and Hensel would be founded as well. The Icelandic community prospered, and by the 1890s some Icelanders seeking additional land returned to Canada, while others founded a satellite community in McHenry County, along the Mouse River, centered around the village of Upham.

The Finns were the last of the Scandinavian immigrants to begin a mass movement to America. A number of Finns had been rather unwilling immigrants to the New Sweden colony in the late 1630s, but with the exception of a few individual immigrants, there was little in the way of Finnish immigration before the Civil War. Life in Finland was hard in the nineteenth century. Covered with forests, lakes and swamps (indeed, the Finnish word for their country is Suomi, probably derived from "Suo," which means "swampy"), only three percent of the land was tillable. Yet Finland, like the rest of Europe, experienced a population explosion in the nineteenth century. By 1900, seventy percent of the farms were smaller than twenty-two acres and thirty percent were smaller than five acres. Not surprisingly, the lure of land in America was strong.

In addition to the economic hardships, Finland was politically troubled. A part of Sweden until 1809, Finland had been acquired by Russia and had been created a Grand Duchy. During the last few decades of the century, however, the Tsars began a Russification program that resulted in growing cultural and political repression, capped by a government decree of 1899 providing that the Finns would be conscripted into the Russian army. Finnish migration to America was relatively late compared to that of other ethnic groups. Many of the Finns immigrated to Norway, and from there they eventually made their way to America. During the Civil War President Lincoln authorized the importation of workers for the copper mines of Northern Michigan. Many of the Finns were experienced miners and were actively recruited to help supply the North with copper. A Finnish settlement developed in the Upper Peninsula of Michigan in the Calumet and Hancock area. When the iron mines were developed in northeastern Minnesota, thousands of Finns migrated to the Iron Range. They also developed rural settlements in west-central Minnesota in the New York Mills region, and Brown County, South Dakota, and in Dickey county of North Dakota. Later Finnish communities were to be established in Walsh, Logan, Emmons, and Towner counties of North Dakota. Most of the Finns who settled in the prairie regions of Minnesota and North Dakota did not come directly from Finland, but from one of the earlier mining settlements. In these and other areas the Finns, like the Icelanders, clung tenaciously to their language and culture.

Although Scandinavian-Americans are now to be found everywhere in the United States, the greatest percentage of them are found in the states of the Upper Midwest. In thought, language, and state of mind, Minnesota and North Dakota, especially the Red River Valley region, are overwhelmingly Scandinavian. It is among the people here, in New Scandinavia, that the most vivid recollections of their Old Country and of their pioneering settlements can be found.

Chapter II

"I Worked So Damn Hard!"

THE OLD COUNTRY

In the nineteenth century, Scandinavia was overwhelmingly rural and, with the exception of Copenhagen and Stockholm, the cities were quite small. In 1830, for example, the population of Oslo was only about 30,000 people. But Scandinavia, like the rest of Europe, was undergoing significant changes in politics, population, and economics. Following the end of the Napoleonic wars, there was a sustained period of peace and young men were no longer lost to war. Improved sanitary conditions and the development of vaccines produced healthier societies and, due to the widespread use of the potato, the people were better fed. As a result, there was a general population explosion across Europe. In Scandinavia the population almost tripled from 1750 to 1900 and not even the humble potato could feed them all. For many it was a bewildering time, as the growth of families created severe strains in traditional land holding relationships. For most families, this meant that either the land would be inherited by the eldest son, leaving the rest of the family landless, or the land would be sub-divided until the parcel was too small

to support them and their families. The social and political system made it almost impossible for the small landowners to share in the society.

Religious freedom was also constricted. In Sweden, a Conventicle Act had been passed in 1726, which prohibited all religious meetings, or "conventicles," outside the state church. The Swedish pietists, or *lasarna*, defied this act and were frequently prosecuted for doing so. The followers of Eric Jansson were just one example of such groups. Although the act was repealed in 1858, religious intolerance did not disappear for a long time. Meanwhile, immigrants to America wrote enthusiastic letters to their fellow dissenters in which they described with evangelical enthusiasm the religious freedom they found in the United States.

Many of the people interviewed who remembered the old country remembered these conditions, especially the intense pressures of large families and over-population.

"They didn't have room for all their kids on the farm, the farms were too small in Norway, you know, so unless you were the oldest, you got sent out." — Eloise Kromarek (Bowman, ND)

"There were sixteen kids altogether in my mother's family [back in Sweden], and that was quite a gang. And they all started from scratch over here." — Clara Furcht (Moorhead, MN)

"We were ten sisters and brothers. I was two years old when my mother died. My father was a widower for two years and then he married a woman who worked there and they had two boys, so that made twelve."
— Kristine Svidal (Starkweather, ND)

"The older son inherited everything and the rest of the family got nothing so I think the rest of the boys resented that. My dad's oldest brother was named John, and he was a judge, but my dad never spoke to him because the rest of the boys took off and left him [in Sweden]." — Roy Carlander (Moorhead, MN)

"The first son, John, who was born in Sweden, was born in a stable. … Grandma was a stable boss. The house was there, and the barn here, and during the time she was doing chores or taking care of the cattle, the time for delivery came and she reclined in the manger." — Lynn Anderson (Moorhead, MN)

"They came to America because they had no land and they had no way of feeding their family. And I think they had some bad years in Norway, too, and there just wasn't enough food for all of them. There were stories that there was free land they could get just by homesteading — they didn't need to inherit it. And the land was so plentiful it could feed everyone and there was prosperity everywhere." — Florence Fritz (Detroit Lakes, MN)

The primary motive for coming to America was economic betterment and employment opportunities. But for many it was more than a chance to get a job, it was a chance to change jobs. For some of the immigrants to America, their memory of Scandinavia consisted of little more than mind-numbing and backbreaking labor.

"It was between Oslo and Hamar. There was a lot of mountains in that area. I worked at home all the time then, you know. And there I was digging graves in the wintertime. My dad, he took care of the church and graves and everything. And I done that from the time I was twelve years old. I worked so damned hard. I was so tired I could hardly go home, just a few steps. There was no machinery, just pick-ax and shovel! The only fun I had was 'ski-yumping.'" — Arne Arneson (Fargo, ND)

"We were busy all the time and I decided, *This is not for me!* I could have married a farmer. [The women] had to do all the chores, the women did more work over there than the men. The men had time to go and play cards … but not the women. And in 1903, everybody wanted to go to America! And they went to America in droves, you know. And I'm really glad I was along." — Kristine Svidal (Starkweather, ND)

"To live on a farm [in Sweden] in them days you had to work. You had to walk through the snow to get to school, and then you came back and had to carry water for them cows and carry wood for the wood box and you didn't get to play ball in them days, you got a lot of exercise at home."

— Oscar Lindgren (Fargo, ND)

"My dad worked in the woods [in Sweden] in the wintertime, in the lumber camps, and I think they did a little farming. They had just a little plot, and in the summertime then they herded the cattle up into the mountains or someplace for the summer, so then somebody stayed up there and they did their haying up there. They brought their hay home in the fall and all their cheese and hard tack that they cooked and baked up there." — Amy Erickson (Moorhead, MN)

"My father was a fisherman [in Norway] from the time he was fourteen. Him and his brother went out with his father in a boat to fish when he was just a young boy and he remembered how he got so cold, his hands got so cold, well the water never froze, you know, but it was still cold. But that was their only livelihood." — Matilda Blumer (Hazelton, ND)

"In 1907, I hired out for three years to learn the blacksmith trade, and my wages was 100 Kroner the first year, 150 the second year, and 250 the third year, and board and room. … We made tools and did lots of horse shoeing. I worked at the blacksmith trade almost seven years in Sweden and trade was very poor and I seen that it would be very hard for me and would take a long time before I would be able to buy anything of my own. And then, besides that, I would have about four years of military training. And at this time I was only nineteen and I could leave Sweden anytime before twenty-one. So I decided that maybe, to better myself, that I would consider a trip to the United States. I talked it over with my father and mother when I was home at Christmas, and I asked them about their opinion and they told me they'd let me know in the morning. And in the morning my mother told me that they would not stand in my way. And she also said that in case I was short of money that they would help me a little bit. I met a friend, about the same age as me, at that time of Christmas, and he also said that he was interested in going to the United States. We looked in the daily paper, and in the paper we found the schedule of Cunnard lines leaving England."

— Henry Holmgren (Henning, MN)

"I came from Julstear, a fjord where we farmed, and we had cows and sheep and goats and one horse or two and a pig for Christmas. They butchered him just before Christmas and they would feed him mush so he would get real fat. And they used every bit of that pig. They scraped the feet and made headcheese and made use of the fat, everything! They lived off the farm. They wore clothes that they got from the sheep. They knew how to prepare the wool and how to prepare the cloth. It had to have a lot of preparation. They weaved it and they dyed it and they prepared it later to make it soft. And they wore those clothes, they were all wool and they fit nice. They made their own shoes out of leather. And they made wooden shoes, too, and they decorated them up and made them to fit and we never got wet feet. Those wooden shoes was nice to wear. Each father would know how to make these. They had some sort of instrument to dig it out of a wooden block. It was all in one, you know, and some of them could fit them so much nicer. We argued about who had the nicest wooden shoes. We lived right under a glacier and this river came from the glacier and was cold all summer and each farmer had a mill right along the river … and they ground their own flour. They always grew oats and they had some barley. It was too cold for wheat. If we wanted wheat flour, we had to buy it." — Kristine Svidal (Starkwather, ND)

"When I was fourteen I had to start working in the lumber camps in Sweden. My dad was a shoemaker and didn't make much money." — John Norman (Hawley, MN)

"My grandfather took apprenticeship as a locksmith and later he got to be locksmith for the royalty of Norway. It was kind of tough for my grandmother, after my grandfather left her. … She had a small coffee shop near a bridge in Gudbransdalen. When the boys came over here they got enough money to send for her and she lived in Byron until her death." — Art Waldon (Detroit Lakes, MN)

"They never went back. It seemed to me they were a little bitter because of the poor conditions over there [in Norway] when they left."
— Edwin Markestad (Maddock, ND)

"My grandfather went back to Sweden twice. I think he still loved it. And he wanted to take my grandmother back to Norway, too. But she wouldn't go. She said that all Norway ever was to her was hard work. She told of how she had to carry baskets of manure on her head up the steep mountainside. So here was Norway with all its beautiful mountains and that wasn't pretty to her. She liked North Dakota, where there wasn't a hill in sight." — Violet Anderson (Hitterdal, MN)

Much is made of the "push-pull" factors leading to the emigration of Scandinavians to America. One of the post powerful "pull" factors of America was that it offered the possibility of a better future. Conversely, one of the most significant "push" factors was that, for many, life in Scandinavian promised little.

"They were looking for a better way of life. They were peasants, you know, and they knew that there was a different way of making a living. They worked wherever they had a chance." — Mabel Enger (Oakes, ND)

"My dad was only seventeen, and [his brother-in-law] wanted to farm and my dad's sister was kind of hard to get along with, and so my dad wasn't happy at home at all. He had to be twenty-one before he could get a share, and his brother-in-law farmed the place so there wasn't much for him to do. His father didn't want him to go to America, but he said there really wasn't anything else to do. And with mother, she was in a family of eleven children and she was the youngest, and there wasn't much for girls to look forward to in Norway. They'd have to marry these fishermen who were just barely able to make a living. Mother had no skill, except she knew how to farm, and women did all the farming in those days. She knew how to milk cows and make butter and make cheese and even knew how to plant potatoes and vegetables. But this was forty miles north of the Arctic circle!" — Allen Erickson (Moorhead, MN)

"Conditions were pretty poor [in Norway] and [my parents] were just happy to get away and get to the United States because they heard it was going to be pretty good here, you know, and they could make money." — Alma Olson (Souris, ND)

"They were crofters. I think [they came] mainly for an opportunity for a better way of life. They were sharecroppers. They were tenants and somebody else owned the land. Grandpa sold his property to get passage to the United States. He was about twenty-eight at the time and had three children. This was in 1868 when they left Sweden." — Lynn Anderson (Moorhead, MN)

"My brother wrote that life was pretty good in America. He sent pictures and wrote letters and we all wanted to go. We went to the Minister and he had to give us a record of everything. And that's all we had to have, it seems like." — Kristine Svidal (Starkweather, ND)

"I decided to come to America when I was sixteen, because I had to give up my scholarship to the University of Oslo and I wanted to go to school and my father, we were poor, so he couldn't raise the money I needed to cash in on that scholarship. And I was so disappointed I went right into town and applied for a visa for the United States. I saw absolutely no future for a young man in Norway." — Rev. Sven Thompson (Willmar, MN)

"They felt there was no future in Norway, and the conditions were high unemployment and very little money. Their older brother was taking over the farm." — Edwin Markestad (Maddock, ND)

Politics, for most of the Scandinavians, probably played a minor role in the decision to emigrate. Nevertheless, with masses of people leaving the homeland, it became a vital political issue and on the national level emigration was solidly linked to political dissent. In the last quarter of the nineteenth century, the nations of Europe began military expansions that would eventually culminate in World War I. The countries of Scandinavia, especially Sweden, were not immune to this trend. Although Scandinavians made good soldiers, as was evidenced in their performance in Minnesota and Wisconsin regiments during the Civil War, they did like to have a choice in the matter. In Sweden there was considerable immigration to escape compulsory military service. There, a royal decree prohibiting the emigration of military conscripts was a significant obstacle to those who wished to leave the country. At first, permission to emigrate was rather routinely

granted, but by the end of the nineteenth century, permits were generally issued only to those who had completed their period of service. Such regulations led to a significant degree of illegal emigration, mostly by way of Copenhagen, Christiania, and Trondheim, and a thriving market developed for counterfeit emigration certificates.

"This military life dates back, and when this last one retired, [our] name had been in the Swedish army for over three-hundred years, fighting with many of the well-known kings and staying in Sweden. My dad, born in 1873, was the first one to come to the United States, and since that time, none of the family has served in the army in the United States or in Sweden." — Oscar Olson (Lake Park, MN)

"There was one thing about Sweden that was real bad in them days. You had to go in and be a soldier for a whole year and then go home for a month, and then go back for nine months, then home for three months, then you went back for three months. And we didn't get enough money for that. But me and a friend, we cooked for the other guys in the army—everybody had to eat—hard tack and American salt pork. I had learned to cook a little bit, I learned it from my mother. She had eight boys in the family and every one of her sons had to learn certain things they could cook, so we could make a meal if she got sick. I made enough money off that so I could come to America." — Oscar Lindgren (Fargo, ND)

"I didn't want to go into the [Swedish] army. There was three and a half years of duty and there was no pay there. You didn't hardly get enough to eat in them days over there. I think it was twelve cents a day you got! My brother left before me because he didn't want to go into the army either, because it took three and a half years of your best time for nothing." — John Norman (Hawley, MN)

"I was twenty-one when I came over. I traveled alone. My mother had married a man that didn't want to work. And he had nine children with him so they were pretty poor. So, when I was fourteen I got a job at the sawmill and started to help my mother that way. And I worked that way for seven years. When I was twenty-one I was drafted into the army. The pay in the army was five cents a day. So I knew then that I couldn't help my mother anymore and I had to leave her, and that was [1913] when I left Mother."— Andrew Lindgren (Moorhead, MN)

"Grandpa was from Lillehammar, and he was a soldier back in Norway, a king's soldier, and when he came to New York, they took him directly off the boat, and that's when Grandpa served in the Mexican War. That lasted two years and when he came back he was married and they settled in Minnesota." — Lloyd Westrum (Moorhead, MN)

"And over there, there was a rumor that they were going to be drafted into the army. Well, I don't believe that, because my dad wouldn't run from anything. I just think he came over because there was an incentive to it and there wasn't much going on in Sweden that he could see held a future for him." — Vic Anderson (Moorhead, MN)

"Another big migration was started in the late 1880s because the Russian tsar started to impress the Finnish people into the Russian army and send them out to Siberia for training. A lot of the young men went at that time; rather than go into the Russian army they came to the United States." — Russell Parta (New York Mills, MN)

Not all of the memories of the old country were of hardships and deprivations. Among those who spoke of their memories of Scandinavia there could be found love and nostalgia for times gone forever. The Atlantic Ocean, however, did more than divide the world geographically. For many, it represented a break from a life that could never be recreated in America. Social patterns, school, and work represented a way of life in the Old Country that could never be quite replicated in the New World.

"In Norway ... they had to be responsible to the overlord. It was a terrible system, because they weren't free to leave. Of course, they didn't have any place to go anyway. [The overlord] had a big area of land, and he had *husmen* to work the place and he made a contract each year—how much work they were going to do on the farm each year. And now he's got a small house and a few acres to live on. He could even have a cow and some chickens and hogs and things like that so they could always live on that little place. At the same time, the "Bull," he was always giving them so much food per year and, of course, the husman got his board when he worked. But at the same time it was almost impossible to [improve your lot] because you couldn't get any further with that. And well, then, a lot of people started to read the papers and got to know about things and they weren't satisfied with their status and they knew that there were other places where they could make a better living and get somewhere. Norway was a poor country. ... And people had started to come to America and they wrote back about this glorious land here and it stood with open arms to receive anyone who wanted to come. ... Nobody knew any English when we came over. I was thirteen then. I went to school in Norway. I always wore wooden shoes—just like in Holland. My father made wooden shoes and he made very good ones and I always wore them to school. It was three miles to walk, morning and evening. In the winter in Norway you know it was dark until ten o'clock in the morning and school started at nine. And of course we walked home from school in the dark." — John Klukken (Osakis, MN)

"My mother was a butter maker and my father was an overseer of [a farm in Denmark]. My mother's sister married a man who went to America and she came home and wanted her sister to come, but she wouldn't come, but my oldest brother went ... when he was sixteen. And then he came home when he was twenty and he talked my dad into selling his share of his shop and the farm and then we moved to town. And then he worked and was hurt, broken ribs, and he went to the doctor but the doctor didn't discover that his ribs were broke and infection set in and he died at the hospital. So then my brother had to go [back to America], otherwise he would have had to serve in the army when he was twenty-one, in Denmark. But he wouldn't go unless his younger sister went and she wouldn't go unless her younger brother went and so those three went over and [my mother and I] moved to Copenhagen."

— Tora Johnson (Brewster, MN)

"In school [in Norway] they taught us reading and writing—they were very fussy about that—but the religion was the most important. The commandments, Bible history … why, we knew it by heart, at least we were supposed to know it by heart! But we didn't know much about [politics]. We had a king, you know, that's all we knew. … There wasn't enough ground in Norway, just rocks, brush, and groves, and lakes. Of course it was beautiful … but there wasn't enough space for all those big families. My brother came with me. He was two years older than I. He wrote for tickets. There wasn't much money, well maybe a little, so he wrote to an older brother, who had come here and was situated by Starkweather, North Dakota, and John wrote to him, 'Could he work on his farm?' So he sent him the tickets and so I said 'You tell him he has a sister here too. She isn't married yet and she's working.' So here comes a ticket for him and he says to me, 'Are you ready to leave?' I almost forgot I ever said anything. And so we were through with Norway." — Kristine Svidal (Starkweather, MN)

"I went to school [in Sweden] and had a long way to walk, three English miles. I wasn't very big and I was the only girl and Oscar, my husband now, he used to come and wait for me every day … we went to school together." — Anna Lindgren (Fargo, ND)

"My father lived in Vigrestad, the eastern side of Norway. And they were very fair-complected people with blue eyes. And my mother's parents and grandparents lived at Vruflat, the western side of Norway and they were very dark-complected, very different from my father's side. A friend told me that was because one was on the sunny side of the mountain and one was on the dark side." — Florence Fritz (Detroit Lakes, MN)

"My grandparents were married in Sweden in 1872 and they immigrated to America two weeks later. They settled down in Goodhue County, Minnesota. They came to Moorhead in 1882. They had lived on a *kirkegaard* back in Sweden. This was the place where the pastor's family lived. My grandfather was a hired man there and my grandmother worked as a hired girl. So they met there and came to this country right after they were married." — Gladys Westrum (Moorhead, MN)

"My parents came to this country in 1882, when I was four and a half years old. My father had sailed for seven and a half years and he was tired of sailing and he didn't like to go into the army and he was exempt from the army as long as he was a sailor. We lived over towards Oslofjord. We had a little garden, and a few rods of rye and potatoes. A fellow came every spring and plowed a few rods for us. We lived right on the water and we had to fish for a living. We lived in the country on a little spot of land right by the ocean, as close to the ocean so the waves would splash up on the windows. My father was gone all the summer months and in the winter months he worked in the shipyards. He was a ships carpenter. I remember it most distinctly, I remember fishing in the ocean." — Ole Olson (Fargo, ND)

"Lars Christiansen came from Denmark along with a brother and they settled in South Dakota for a time, apparently in a community of fellow Danes. His wife, Louisa, joined him a year later, in 1889. Her father was of the landed gentry, I suppose you'd call it, Baron von Walters. So she was a member of what was, I suppose, the wealthy class. They lived in the province of Schleswig-Holstein and when that was taken over by Germany they had to get out and they lost a good share of their land and wealth at that time. She and Lars had a little scandal here, I suppose. She had a child in Denmark out of wedlock. Whether that was a problem of social class I don't know, but they didn't marry at that time. And the child died, and then Lars came to this country to better himself, I suppose, and acquire land. After he was established a little bit he sent for Louisa and she joined him and they were married over here in South Dakota." — Walter Christianson (Kenmare, ND)

"My mother said she worked so hard! She had to go out working. They were poor and she had to work on farms and work with cattle, and she said she worked so hard that she'd never go back to Norway, even to visit." — Alma Ramse (McIntosh, MN)

"In November of 1874, just about all the groups that came from Iceland were large groups that came in one ship. This was shortly after the Hekla [volcano] blew up, erupted, and ashes all over. There was such a shortage of food that they went up in the mountains in the spring of the year and gathered grass and made soup and porridge out of that." — Leo Hillman (Mountain, ND)

The oral history of Scandinavian-Americans in the Upper Midwest reveals a lingering sense of the "divided heart." For many, recollections of the Old Country involve drudgery and hardships from which escape was most welcome. And yet, for the most part, there remained an affection for the ancestral home to the extent that the hardships are presented almost as a justification for leaving the land that they loved. Once the decision was made to leave, however, the opportunities of America superseded the ingrained love for Scandinavia. While very few of the Scandinavians may have been reduced to eating "grass soup," social and economic conditions showed few signs of improvement. It is said that "hope makes a fine breakfast but a poor

supper," and many Scandinavians were getting figuratively and literally hungry. However much they loved their old country, they began to look to the new.

Chapter III

"I Got the Fever to Come"

THE GREAT MIGRATION

"America Letters" to the people back home and active promotion by the railroads made the rich farmlands of the Upper Midwest a badly kept secret. Between 1881 and 1890, 324,285 Swedes came to America, and in one year, 1883, over 28,000 Norwegians left the homeland. By this time, great steamers carried immigrants from Helsinki, Stockholm, Malmo, Copenhagen, Gothenburg, Oslo, Bergen, Trondheim, and Reykjavik. With their prized possessions carefully packed in a large trunk, often decorated with unique rosemaling, they embarked on a voyage not unlike that of their Viking ancestors. The made their way from Bergen to Hull, from Hull to Liverpool, from Liverpool to New York or Halifax, then to Chicago, Minneapolis, and on to the endless prairie.

Whether they emigrated because of religious persecution, to avoid military service, or to escape an unpleasant social situation, the choice was seldom easy. A Norwegian emigrant wrote, "Farewell Norway, and God bless thee. Stern and severe wert thou always, but as a mother I honor thee, even though thou skimped my bread. All things vanish. Grief and care sink down upon the heart; still the memory of thee refreshes the soul like the deep sleep of a child. Other lands offer me independence, and for my labor well-being to my children. These, oh Norway, thou didst not give me, for thou art a land of lords and slaves, where the great ones ruled and we obeyed. Once more, God bless thee; to the day of my death I will pray God to keep thee; for thou wert the keeper of my childhood and the joys of childhood thou gavest me. I will remember thee always, whatever life may bring, and I will pray, 'Throw off the chains that embittered my youth for me.'"

"Oh, [I came] because my sister was over here, and I heard so much about America. I seen so many of the Swedish people who had been in America a few years and had been working in New York or Boston or whatever, and had come home to visit and they had such nice clothes and everything. And when you are a little kid you see all those things and I thought, oh, well, America must be a wonderful country! They always used to tell us they could cut gold with knives, you know, and I was going to do the same thing, and find this gold and I was going to be rich, come to America and be rich! … And I left my boyfriend back home and he said 'I wish you wouldn't go.' He went with me on the train until I changed trains the first time. And, of course, I'll never forget that. And a fellow come and sold apples, and he bought one big apple, a great big one and he tossed it up to me and I caught it and he was crying. But I wasn't crying. I was pinned up with flowers, you know, when you leave Sweden, you know. I don't know if they do it now, but they did it then and I had flowers pinned all over me so that everybody knew that I was going to America. When girls went to America in them days, they put all those flowers and things on them. There was a young minister on the train, he was on the same train that I was after my boyfriend had thrown up that apple to me and he was crying, he was wiping his tears and he said, 'Well, how come you don't shed no tears?' 'Well, why should I shed tears?' I said. 'I'm going to America, I'm going to make lots of money, I'm going to be gone five years. and I'm going to come home and marry him.' That didn't work out that way ... I was nineteen and a half years old." — Anna Lindgren (Fargo, ND)

"When I learned [we were coming to America], I was thoroughly happy. I thought it was the most wonderful thing that had ever happened. I ran around telling all my friends that we were leaving, and they thought I was really quite important. I was fourteen. We really didn't know much about America ... I can remember every once in a while being at a party for people going to America, and I thought that was a lot of fun." — Anna Hanson (Moorhead, MN)

"They came because just previously there had been an eruption of a volcano in Iceland which covered a lot of land with lava and also ruined a lot of the fishing areas along the coastline. So there wasn't enough land or food gathering possibilities and so that's the reason they left Iceland." — Wayne E. Dinusson (Fargo, ND)

"Well I was in the [Norwegian] army then, you know, and I was stationed along the border there [with Sweden], and that was in 1905 and we didn't know if there was going to be a war or not. I had gone to military school and was doing my active service. So anyway, that was over and, well, it was like everyone else, [you came] to better yourself, because you had heard of this great country. And it has been a good country to me." — Louis Haugen (Crookston, MN)

"It was a difficult journey, because I wasn't allowed to leave Sweden because I [had been drafted] into the army. So in order to get out of Sweden I had to go to Norway. And when I got to Norway they asked me if I had killed anybody. I said no. Well, that's all they asked me. They let me go." — Andrew Lindgren (Moorhead, MN)

"My old man, he let my two brothers go to Dakota, one in 1903 and one in 1907, but he wasn't going to let me go. So I went to my brother, a sea captain. And he had money in the bank, I knew that. He wasn't married and he had good wages. So he went to the bank and borrowed me the money to come over. I worked when I got over here. I think the second month that I was here, then I sent it back so he got his money back. [My father] came to the depot, and he said, 'Oscar, put that trunk back and I'll give you everything I've got if you stay with me. Come back home.' 'No sir,' I said,

'I've worked for you for twenty years and now, by golly, I won't work another twenty years for you!' So then he gave me some money, I think it was two or three hundred kroners. He could have given that to me a week before and then I wouldn't have had to borrow from my brother. He didn't know where I got it. He asked me and I said, 'You don't want to know, but I'll tell you one thing, I'm going to be good to you, Dad. What I don't need to get to Dakota, I'm going to send that back to you." — Oscar Lindgren (Fargo, ND)

"I got the fever to come [to America] and the old man gave me money for the ticket and I sent him the money back the first year I was here. I also saved and sent my younger sister some money for her confirmation and she never thanked me for it. And I never wrote to her either. The hell with her!" — Arne Arneson (Fargo, ND)

"Why did I come over? Adventure!" — Marlene Lein (Wahpeton, ND)

"Why? Why did I come? Well, I suppose I liked to see the country, more than anything else. I was alone, of course, I didn't have any family at that time." — Marie Tverdahl (Abercrombie, ND)

"And I remember how my uncle Lawrence went down to the ship to say goodbye and to see that mother got settled right. And I remember that we saw a whale." — Tora Johnson (Brewster, MN)

For many immigrants, the decision to come to America was influenced by a friend or a relative who had gone before them. The "America Letters" seemed too good to be true, and sometimes they were. In some cases, the father went to America to work to earn passage for the rest of the family. In other cases, a brother or sister promised passage and security in a strange environment. These were the fortunate ones, because they didn't have to face the uncertainties of America all by themselves.

While some Scandinavians came to America as contract laborers, this was not widespread. Swedish law, for instance, forbade such a practice. A far more common practice was for Scandinavian-Americans to send prepaid tickets to friends and relatives back home. It is estimated that during the 1880s almost half of all Swedish emigrants came to America through such an arrangement, often in the form of transport credit in exchange for short time work as farm hands or household servants.

Sub-agents for steamship lines played a significant part in organizing immigration to America. The Larsson Brothers Company of Gothenburg, for instance, acted as agents for the Guion Line, and by 1882 the company had about 150 sub-agents. This meant that at least one or two sub-agents were operating in every single parish of southern and eastern Sweden. These sub-agents would receive a commission of at five to ten Swedish crowns per immigrant.

Throughout the period of the Great Migration, increased competition between the Atlantic shipping companies produced a great fluctuation in ticket prices. In 1869, a one-way ticket from Gothenburg to Chicago cost about forty-one dollars. During the 1880s the price averaged around twenty-eight dollars, and in the early 1900s the price was around forty-seven dollars. These, however were only the official prices, and actual prices, due to specials and incentives, were often much lower.

"One of his sisters, my aunt Lena, had come to the United States some time earlier and she was housekeeper for a man who had lost his wife, and he had three small children. This man was getting quite old and he needed help. He lived near Paynesville, Minnesota. So then Dad had a chance to come over. They would send him the money for his fare … but then the agreement was that he was to work for him until he had paid back this money. And so he did that. He worked there until he had saved enough money to send for mother and bring the three of us over." — Matilda Blumer (Hazelton, ND)

"He got a ticket, one was sent to him, to come over to Brainerd, Minnesota, in 1885. And he worked in Brainerd, in the woods, cutting trees in the wintertime and the rest of the season in the lumber mills, working for at least fifteen months until he could get enough money to send tickets for his two eldest sons. Then the three of them worked another year and a half and sometime in 1888 they sent tickets for my grandmother, my mother, and three younger sons." — Clarence Glasrud (Moorhead, MN)

"My father was over here from 1912 to 1914, and he got so homesick that he wanted the whole family to come over. But mother got so seasick when she went [from Kristiansund] to see her sister in Arendal that she decided not to make the trip, so he came back to Norway. … My older brother came over a year after I did. He said he got so lonesome he had to come across to get together with me." — Rev. Sven Thompson (Willmar, MN)

"Father went to South Dakota because there were relatives there, his brother, and some of their old friends were already here and were farming. My mother came a year later. They went to Nebraska for a while. My mother wanted to get a job so she could pay for her ticket. Her sister had bought her ticket from Norway and had paid sixty dollars for it. And so she got a job in Riverdale, Nebraska, as a maid. And she worked for this family for twelve dollars a month." — Solveig Johnson (Niagary, ND)

"It wasn't until 1905 that my mother came to this country, and by that time my aunt was living in Crookston. We don't know why she came, she was about twenty-five or twenty-six years old, and she had a job, she was a bookkeeper. Rumor has it that she had an unhappy love affair and it was much more exciting to come here. She had lived here a year when she married my father." — Ruth Dahl Erickson (Crookston, MN)

"My father came here first, to find a home for the rest of us. He settled in the Oakes, North Dakota, area. He worked there as a laborer, as a carpenter, a year before the rest of us [came over]." — Dagne Faust (Colfax, ND)

"He came here from Sweden when he was sixteen because of poverty. They didn't have food, they didn't have any means of making a living, so he decided to come over here to make a new start. He had a stepbrother that had homesteaded in Gheen, Minnesota and he had a logging business. So my grandfather was sent some money to come over to the United States and he started helping his half-brother with the logging business." — Judy Nelson (Hibbing, MN)

"My mother and dad both came over in the year 1893, and they both came to Quebec, for some reason or another. My mother had a sister who lived in Deer Park, Wisconsin, and she had been given her share of the farm by her father when she left home, so she had enough to get by pretty easily. There were eleven children in the family and she was the youngest of the eleven. And that was the custom in Norway at that time. The girls each got a little inheritance and they could get it earlier if they wanted. So it was easier for my mother because there was someone who had gone ahead." — Allan Erickson (Moorhead, MN)

"They were originally from Skane, Sweden. Father came to Iowa. He had some cousins who had come before, so that's why he came to Iowa. And he left mother in Sweden with five little children, ranging in ages nine to one. And then father was to work on this farm and make enough money so that he could send for mother. It was a year, and in the meantime, he had to be sending back money to mother so that she could take care of the children. Then in a year, mother came over." — Nina Oien (Moorhead, MN)

"My father must have fallen in love with America when he was here from 1890 to 1893, because he often talked about this great country. But it was not until he had trained four of his sons in music and formed a string quintet that he realized his dream which came about in the fall of 1912. This group consisted of himself—first violin; son Leif—second violin; Svetter—viola; Rolf—cello; and George—second cello and bass. Later, in 1913, my younger brother, Gunder, joined us as a trumpet player." — Leif I. Christianson (Moorhead, MN)

For the coastal fishermen of Scandinavia, the sea had no special terrors, but many of the inland farmers had never seen the ocean. For some, the passage to America would be an adventure; for others, an ordeal. Yet, they all shared a common experience watching their

homeland gradually fade from the horizon. As one immigrant reflected, "To thee, beloved land, I bid farewell. Soon I no longer shall view thy beauty nor hear the music of thy waterfalls. The snowcapped mountains will fade from sight and slowly thy coast will sink away in the mists, like a mother being lowered in the grave. No glimpse then of the tallest peaks, only a lonely sail on the boundless deep."

"They all came to America. My grandfather and great-grandfather were mining engineers in the copper mines near Roros in Norway, that's right in the center and east part of Norway. They got on a sailboat and they sailed and they sailed, and that ship would stand still some days, you know, there wasn't enough wind—it would back up even. And you know, they were running short of food and there was a lot of people on this boat. … So then they run short of food and they had to turn in all the food they had. They appointed a food administrator and they put the food in one place. Some had dried beef and some had flatbread and some had some potatoes. They all put it together and then one man would sit by this pile of food every day and he passed out just a little bit to each one so they would live until they got to America. My grandmother had a child on the way over and that died and it was buried in the ocean." — Clifford Hitterdal (Hitterdal, MN)

"In Sweden I guess there wasn't too much future for them at that time. When my dad came over here he was only twenty-one years old, and he didn't like the compulsory army training they had over in Sweden at the time so he came over here where they didn't have any. He got on a boat and hid until the boat was quite a few hundred miles out in the ocean before he ever came out of hiding. 'Course, then they couldn't just stop and set him off. He worked his way through on the boat after that. It was a freighter and it was a coal-fired boat, so he helped the fireman and he got into New York. He had a cousin who lived in Minnesota." — Louis Westling (Longville, MN)

"I was born in 1880 in Sweden. ... I left Sweden on November 29th, 1895, with my mother, my aunt, four brothers and one sister. We left Goteborg and sailed for England across the North Sea and arrived in Liverpool on December 2, where we spent five days, went sight-seeing, and had a chance to go to two large museums, a Seaman's mission one evening, and even an indoor circus." — Minnie Carlson (Fergus Falls, MN)

"When my father came, he came with his mother and his brother, and they packed all their belongings in this huge, beautiful trunk she had, and there was rosemaling inside of the trunk and on the outside. The most beautiful wooden trunk! It was six feet long so they packed food and everything else they needed on the way over here. They left Stavanger and they sailed to Northern England. There all their goods were loaded on high carts, about eight feet high, pulled by horses, and they were shocked when they saw those horses because they were so used to the small horses that they have in the fjordlands and those were so big in England. And then they were transported to Liverpool and from there they went to Quebec, Canada, and from there by train to Duluth where his father was waiting for him. The reason they went to Quebec was that Canada had suddenly realized that they could haul lumber to Europe and make money this way. So they would take lumber to Europe and take immigrants on the way back. So they paid forty-five dollars for each adult to come across to Quebec." — Florence Fritz (Detroit Lakes, MN)

"My father was a student in high school when he came from Norway and my mother had gone through eighth grade. They came in 1906. They went by a small boat from Stavanger, Norway. That's the closest large city from where they were born, and they went from there to Southampton, England, Where they boarded a larger boat. And that was a freighter that had several decks. There were animals on the lowest decks, and the immigrants were on the second deck." — Solveig Johnson (Niagara, ND)

"My uncle took us out in a rowboat to a coast steamer, a little boat named *Flinke*. And that coastal steamer took us to Kristiansund in Norway. Then we took a boat across the sea to Germany, to Hamburg, and then we took the train from Hamburg to Bremen and were going to sail from Bremen on a ship called *Amerika*. But when it came to load, that ship was overloaded and we couldn't get on so we had to stay in a hotel in Bremen for a week. Then we caught a ship to Baltimore. No rough weather, a real smooth trip all the way. Two weeks on the Atlantic, four weeks altogether, including the time spent in Baltimore for us kids to get smallpox vaccinations. All we had was a small trunk, each one [of us]. ... [On the ship] we were crowded into a room with several others. It was a family of three children with us, and there was another family of a boy and his mother. They furnished food, but it wasn't very good. We were all those weeks without any milk to drink, so we were pretty thirsty for milk. A couple of days after we came over, Dad brought home a cow. Mother was milking the cow—she had a milk pail with a strainer on it—and Brother and I stood there, each with a cup in our hand ready for the first milk that came out of that cow." — Ole Olson (Fargo, ND)

"My mother had these five little children tugging at her skirts. They had dried fish and dried meat and *Knikabröd* to eat on the boat. And it wasn't sanitary, and oh, my sister had the most beautiful black hair. Here she was, Scandinavian, and she had black hair. And the rest of us were quite fair and she had this hair and it was her pride and joy and it was Mother's, too. And she got so many lice on this boat that they had to cut off that hair and that really hurt my mother terribly bad that they had to cut that hair before she could see Dad. I think the children were sick, too, and Mother said there were some who were buried at sea. But Mother was a God fearing person and I think she spent a lot of time in prayer and I think she felt that they were all spared because she left it in the Lord's hands." — Nina Oien (Moorhead, MN)

"I was in Goteborg two days and then there was a lot of people who were leaving on the same boat that I was, so we was a big company, and we went to Christiania one day and one night in a hotel before the boat left. For the first time I was traveling all alone, but I met some people. I met one man … he had a wife back in this county, but she was so sick when she came over to this country she said, 'I'll never make that trip again,' so he made a trip back to Sweden alone. He was in the second class. Them days there was three classes on the boat. First, Second, and Third, and I came on the Third, you know, and he was on the Second, because that cost more money. He felt sorry for me 'cause he seen how sick I was. He seen me one day and the next day he didn't see me no more, and he had to find out what happened to that Swedish girl. He came down to my cabin, and there I was laying in my clothes. 'You can't lay like this,' he said. 'You got to come up.' So he helped me, picked me up, and he said 'I think I'm going to take you up to the bar and get you a glass of beer.' And I said 'But I don't drink,' but he said, 'That's going to help you.' Well I took one sip of that beer and got awful sick and so I said 'no more of that' and so he took me to the lady's lounge where they were serving coffee and I said 'Maybe I can have a little coffee.' So I have some coffee and he took me down to my cabin and the next day I wasn't quite so bad, and he picked me up again and he had some pickled herring and some smoked meat that he had brought with him from Sweden. It was salty and he said 'You've got to have something to eat. You can't be sad.

Eat this up. You're going to die before you get to New York,' he said. So he gave me some of that food that he had with him. He was a very nice man. And, of course, when we got to New York he was an American citizen, so he could get off the boat. Then I had to go to the Ellis Island. There we parted and I never got to see him anymore. … And was I ever sick. I lived with my clothes on for three days. I couldn't take them off I was that sick. 'Oh,' I said, 'Why did I start out on this trip?' But I made it and the last two days when we was closest to New York, then you were feeling just fine, then the trip was soon over, then you thought you had a good time." — Anna Lindgren (Fargo, ND)

"Well, the ship was new. It made its maiden voyage and the ballast was poor. So we rolled along with the waves and many things on the boat were smashed, many of the dishes, for example. The cooks were ill, many of us were as sick as we had ever been. But then, when it calmed, we had just a lovely trip across. It took ten days. We were very, very seasick. For about two days I can't even remember that I ever got out of my bunk. But once you got well again, you seemed to be just wonderfully well." — Anna Hanson (Moorhead, MN)

"We had to go from Oslo across the North Sea to England. We were on a bus after we got off the boat, and Mother had got down and I had got down and my little sister Andrea was getting down and a man stepped on her hand. And Mother told him off in no uncertain terms. Oh, no, she didn't speak English, I don't think anybody did. And I can remember on the ship that Mother was dreadfully sick. She could only eat oranges. But I never got sick." — Matilda Blumer (Hazelton, ND)

"The voyage was rough and the family was very ill." — Lynn Anderson (Moorhead, MN)

"Oh, it was rough! And I got seasick, too, boy!" — Arne Arneson (Fargo, ND)

"I was so seasick they could have thrown me overboard and I would have welcomed it. But I got over it." — Rev. Sven Thompson (Willmar, MN)

"My grandpa came over here, but he didn't like it over here. He only stayed a year and then he went back to Norway. My mother said she laid in the bunk all the way over, she was so seasick." — Borghild Overby (Moorhead, MN)

"Eleven days to cross the ocean from Christiania. I didn't get seasick, *men* there were a lot of them that was. The trip was supposed to take nine days, but we got into some wind. We must have had waves of thirty feet one night. And here's this big, big boat, you know, and every time we'd hit those waves, then the propeller would come up out of the water and the whole thing would go 'oohooh-aroooo.' Then we'd hit the water again, 'awooo-awooo.'" — Oscar Lindgren (Fargo, ND)

"We came over here because we always heard it was the land of good opportunity. We were very sick, it was very rough, but we managed quite well." — Elsie Gale (Clearbrook, MN)

"It wasn't a great ship, but I think it was some over seven hundred passengers. We did have some of mother's hardtack along, a great big bag, and butter you couldn't take because that would spoil on the sea. But we did have lingonberries that was cooked like a jam, and we ate that with our hardtack. But we had good meals on the boat. We came so cheap! My mother, my aunt, myself—six children in all! If I remember right, the whole thing from Goteborg to Minneapolis, was a hundred and thirty-five dollars." — Minnie Carlson (Fergus Falls, MN)

"When he left Sweden he carried a leg of lamb with him, called *stykke kjøtt* [piece of meat], and he claimed he survived on that leg of lamb. There wasn't too much food, you know. He always liked it. But he never went back to Sweden, he never cared to." — Hazel Monson Barker (Moorhead, MN)

"We started on the ship to the U.S.A. on May 8th, from Malmo to Copenhagen, laid there overnight, and the following morning went on the train, and part of the trip was on ferry. We went on a boat, for to cross the channel, on May 10th, late in the night, and arrived in England on May 12th. In the evening we went on a train to Liverpool. We stayed on the train at the depot overnight and went aboard *Laconia* the following morning. The boat made a short stop outside of Queenstown in Ireland, where about five hundred young girls and boys came on the boat. The whole trip was very good and no serious seasickness. We were told there was about 3,800 passengers on the boat." — Henry Holmgren (Henning, MN)

"It took my dad six weeks to come over on a sailboat. Six weeks! They had a big trunk! … All the newcomers from Norway brought a mutton leg or dried beef and every kind of cheese you can think of. And it had worms in it too. I remember mother washed it off with coffee." — Nels Overby (Moorhead, MN)

"I was born in Norway in 1887. … We started out in Trondheim and then to the southern part of Norway and then across to England, I think it's Hull, the name of the town. And then we crossed England by train and then we got a big boat there in Liverpool and across to Canada, Quebec. This took about fourteen days. Then we took a train down to Montreal and then into the United States, Detroit, I think it was, and then we took a train to St. Paul, and from St. Paul to Osakis. The whole trip took about three weeks, I think."
— John Klukken (Osakis, MN)

"Dad landed in Boston harbor and Mother's ship came to Quebec, in Canada. They were sailing ships, and it took quite a while to cross the ocean. They had to bring their own bedding and everything they could carry with them, a trunk or so, and the food that they ate, they had to bring that with them. They shared and got along." — Art Waldon (Detroit Lakes, MN)

"He was in his twenties when he first came. I know Dad said when he came across the North Sea there was such a storm he thought they would never make it." — Roy Carlander (Moorhead, MN)

"My mother came [from Sweden] in 1880 and my father came in 1882. My father had quite an experience on the Atlantic. His ship ran into an iceberg. The front part of the ship was stove in, but luckily the damage wasn't enough to sink the ship and after many, many days they limped into Halifax, Canada." — Carl Axel Anderson (Erhard, MN)

"My husband told of a comical incident he had aboard ship. The little boys were playing, wrestling, and running around like five-year-olds will, and one boy grabbed his hat and threw it overboard. He often laughed about this and he said, 'I had to come to America bareheaded.'" — Clara Hanson (Moorhead, MN)

"And there was a storm, and all the portholes were closed, and they were closing other things, and I went up some stairs to see what it was all about. The sailors were closing the doors but I slipped out and anyway they seen me and they grabbed me and put me under their arms and took me down again." — Tora Johnson (Brewster, MN)

"I came on old *Bergensfjord*. It should have taken nine days, but it took eleven because we ran into so much fog. It was one of the smaller ocean boats. When I came over there were seven hundred passengers. We came across Newfoundland and then we stopped at Halifax to unload some people,

people who didn't have a visa for the United States but they did for Canada. Then we came to New York." — Rev. Sven Thompson (Willmar, MN)

"My mother came to Quebec and then by rail and came into the United States at Soo Saint Marie, and then to Brainerd from there. It was not a pleasant trip and she never wanted to go back to Norway. She had no interest [in going back] and said it was just a miserable trip." — Clarence Glasrud (Moorhead, MN)

"And, while we were on the ship my mother, of course, had just enough money to reach North Dakota. And so one day, while she was out of her cabin all her money was stolen. She didn't have a cent when she got to the United States. But there was a good man there who lent her money so she could get to North Dakota." — Dagne Faust (Colfax, ND)

There were several ports of entry, including Boston, Baltimore, Halifax, and Quebec. But most of the immigrants came to New York, where until 1892 they were processed through Castle Garden. After that date, the Scandinavians joined the other "huddled masses" as they passed through Ellis Island.

"The voyage across the ocean was interesting because we were unusual for a family having four young boys and a father in a musical group, so we were kept busy every day. It took ten days. Arriving at the docks in

New York, we discovered that we were not as welcome by the customs as we were led to believe. They thought surely these young kids can't play these instruments, so they thought that my father was an importer of valuable instruments. And we had to unpack our instruments on the dock and play for them. But the captain of the ship had heard us several times … and he came down the gangplank and verified, in no uncertain terms, that the kids really can play!" — Leif Christianson (Moorhead, MN)

"We came to Castle Garden, and there was a lawyer that came from Denmark and his family, they were with us too. And we were at Castle Garden and we were quarantined for three days because somebody on the ship had measles. And I remember this lawyer's wife helped mother with us younger children. The oldest that mother had was thirteen and the youngest was a year old." — Tora Johnson (Brewster, MN)

"Well, it looked to me like there were a bunch of cattle over there, take a ferry and then you stand in line and you go from one doctor to another and they look at your eyes and then they look at your mouth and they ask you some questions. I had a crippled finger, very particular, you know—it was hurt when I was a little girl. I cut myself and I never took care of it like I should. When we were going through this thing, you had to lay your hands out like this, you know, on the table so the doctor could see your hands, see that they were OK, because they put OK on your paper. And I watched all of this and everybody did it and of course then I started crying to myself. I thought, 'Oh my! When my turn comes along to go over there he'll see my hand and send me back to Sweden and I don't want to go back, I want to go to America, I want to go see my sister, and I don't want him to send me back home.' And a younger couple was standing over there and he asked me what I was crying for. I said, 'See, I have a crippled hand and I see that you have to put your hands on the desk and,' I said, 'he looks at the hands and he's going to send me back, I know.' And then I started to pray that God would help me so that he wouldn't see this hand. When I came up to put my hand on the table I put my left hand on it and I held the other one back and he never asked for my right hand. And then that man stood over in the corner, looked, and said my eyes were just beaming like the sun. He come over to me and shook hands with me and he said, 'My, your prayers are wonderful. I saw you when you were praying.' And I meant it, I thought, 'No, I don't want them to send me back to Sweden. No, I want to come to America.' But after I got that stamp on, then I was safe. Then they couldn't do no more to me, I was accepted into the United States then, you know." — Anna Lindgren (Fargo, ND)

"We went directly to New York, and I'll tell you about how exciting that was. My mother got me up and said, 'We are going to land today.' And so I hurried and another girl and I got ourselves lined up to see the Statue of Liberty. And it took all day long to get into the harbor. And by that time we were exhausted. My mother had to account for everything we had along. And

I remember sitting on the dock, crying, eating some apple pie that I had bought that really wasn't very good, and I thought that this was a bad beginning. And they put us on a streetcar and we rode and we rode and we were exhausted before we landed at the station and were put on the train. My mother had a big trunk and another leather trunk … because she brought all her linen, and some clothes … and it was quite a responsibility to be sure that we had all our things. I brought a doll … but outside of that I don't believe I brought anything else." — Anna Hanson (Moorhead, MN)

"They came to New York [in 1880, from Sweden] with their four children, and to top it off there, why, my oldest brother was nine years old then, and he decided he wanted to take a look at America. He wandered off and got lost in New York and they had to hold up the train going west toward Minneapolis and Fargo for a whole hour. And when they found him he was just walking carelessly down the street looking around to see what America looked like. They were pretty brave venturing out into a new country, they didn't know anybody, and with a bunch of kids like that." — Frank Alm (Christine, ND)

"We landed at Ellis Island. And I'll never forget the screaming and the crying and I especially remember one poor, dear old soul, she was real old and feeble and she was crying, and I suppose she was one of the unlucky ones that they sent back. Your health had to be just right, you know, and you had to have a place to go and somebody to take care of you once you got here or they sent you back. And I remember when we came on the train. I remember Chicago—that big lake—and I remember when we got to Paynesville. I was so happy to see that green grass I just wanted to get out and pull it." — Matilda Blumer (Hazelton, ND)

"I landed at Halifax. I was going to New York, but these guys I was going with were going to Halifax, so I had to go with them, you see, so I could get company to Abercrombie [North Dakota], and that I did. My grandmother's brother and sister were already there so that's why I came there." — Marie Tverdal (Abercrombie, ND)

"On March 31, 1907, I came to New York. Well, there wasn't too much to [Ellis Island], just go through with lots of people. We had our tickets and I was treated all right." — Louis Haugen (Crookston, MN)

"[Immigration inspection] was a big joke. They just lined us up and said, 'Open your mouth,' and the captain announced 'you're going to be examined for lice.' And I said to the doctor, 'How can you see lice in my mouth?' He didn't even have one of these, what do you call it, to hold your tongue down. He just looked at us and said, 'OK.'" — Rev. Sven Thompson (Willmar, MN)

"Coming over from Sweden I had two bottles of cognac, because I knew Dad would like that. I had that in my suitcase. And so the inspector, in Halifax, opened up my suitcase and saw these two bottles. 'Oh,' I said, 'that's medicine.' 'All right,' he said." — Minnie Carlson (Fergus Falls, MN)

"We came by ship to New York. We had some money—I don't know if it was ten dollars or what—and we stood in front of this man at Ellis Island. And he asked us if we got money and if we had a place to go, and John told him everything, 'Yah, we got money. Yah, we got a place to go.' And then John turned around and handed me the money. That's all we had between the two of us. And I said the same thing. ... I'll never forget the Ellis Island because that man said, 'Ah, let 'em go.' We were healthy looking, I guess, and he figured we could look out for ourselves and we had someplace to go. We were not scared. We stayed together and we found people here and there who could speak Norwegian. And we knew where we were going and we had a ticket. ... When we got to America we had to work it out and pay it back." — Kristine Svidal (Starkweather, ND)

"No, I didn't have any trouble. They marked an 'E' on me. That was one doctor who put an 'E' on you. But he wouldn't put it on everyone. There were some that couldn't go through, and they got a free ride home to Sweden again. Then the other doctor come and he talked Swede to me. They were all Swedish or Norwegian talking doctors then, and there were different rooms. It was all sanitary and clean." — Oscar Lindgren (Fargo, ND)

"The first time I came over was in October of 1919, when I landed in the hospital in Brooklyn with a case of the Spanish flu. My ship, on which I was a member of the crew, left the port of New York and went on to their destination in Australia. But I was left behind, and of course when I got out of the hospital I had to shift for myself and that's when I got my first introduction to the United States. I stayed for about a month and then I went back to Sweden. I came back in 1924. My father was a sea captain for about forty years with the same shipping company in Sweden. [The sea] was in the blood of practically all my family." — Hartwig Johnard (Hawley, MN)

"We arrived at Boston on May 21st and we stayed on the boat for the following morning, the 22nd. We were told in Sweden that we were supposed to have fifteen dollars in cash money in order to land in the United States. When my partner and I came to check on our financial condition we found that we didn't have quite fifteen dollars apiece, you see, and we had to have it because at the bottom of the steps was the fellow that checked you and you had to show him you had fifteen dollars. So it was decided that I take fifteen dollars first and go down with it and then when I go down I would throw my pocketbook up to him and then he will use the same fifteen dollars to get down with. I got down in good shape and showed him the fifteen dollars and then I put quite a bit of change in my pocketbook, but the boat looked like a four story building and I didn't know if I could throw it over, but I tried and I cleared the railing by about four feet and in about a second or so I seen a smiling face over the railing so he come down with the same fifteen dollars as I did." — Henry Holmgren (Henning, MN)

"He was thirty-one when he came over in 1895, and went through immigration in New York. And he also had his first tomato in New York. He thought it was an apple so he had a real surprise when he bit into it."

— Alpha Bowersox (Wolford, ND)

Alone in their new country, the immigrants faced an uncertain future. They were prey to swindlers, pickpockets, hustlers, and charlatans. They had heard plenty of stories about the rich land that awaited them in the Upper Midwest, but they had also heard stories of the cold and the heat and the storms and had been warned about outlaws and Indians. But with an optimism born of desperation, they boarded the immigrant trains heading west.

And most of them knew where they were going. They had been urged to come to a specific place in the Upper Midwest by industries, railroads, land companies, and, of course, earlier Scandinavian immigrants. They were also urged to come by the governments of the young states that were eager to populate the empty prairie. Perhaps the most spectacular salesman for Minnesota was Hans Mattson, a former colonel in the Union Army, who established the Minnesota Board of Immigration in 1867. Mattson wrote a brochure for Scandinavians, published in Swedish and Norwegian, contributed articles to the Scandinavian press, and corresponded with clergymen and other prominent immigrants. In the immigrant press, Mattson wrote: "It is my belief that if the Swedish newspapers have any concern for the welfare of

their country's emigrants, they can perform no better service than to inform those destined for Minnesota of the arrangements our state has made on their behalf." One of his brochures was entitled "Minnesota and Its Advantages for the Immigrant, Containing a Description of the State's History, Geography, Government, Cities, Rivers, Lakes, Forests, Climate, Soil, Minerals, Railroads, Commerce, Industries, etc., Which Are of Importance for Those Seeking Their Homes in the West."

"Well, we'd stand there at the depot area, after Ellis Island, you know, waiting for the trains, and there was a guy selling 'shoe boxes,' they called them. And there was two cartons of cheese, a loaf of bread, and one long, hard sausage for a dollar. I bought one. We all bought one. In them days, each of the men had a pocket knife, and I used that to eat it with."
— Oscar Lindgren (Fargo, ND)

"When we got to Chicago we had to wait for a train. So I went to a restaurant, a Swedish restaurant, or at least the manager was Swedish, and he could tell that we were greenhorns. And he talked Swede to us, you know. And was that ever good! [My dad] had bought tickets for Princeton, but they were only made out for Minneapolis. So, of course, we had Swedish money and we had to buy a ticket to Princeton. And they accepted Swedish money [in Minneapolis]. People were always good and they always had someone who could talk to you. I was the oldest one in the family so I had to carry the burden. I was going on fifteen, but I had to be in charge when we were coming over." — Minnie Carlson (Fergus Falls, MN)

"We got into Chicago and I seen a cafe so I had doughnuts and coffee and I just took the money and laid it on the counter. I didn't understand the money—she could take what she wanted. I came out of the cafe and I was standing there by myself and I thought, 'Well, what do I do now?' Then I heard the bell was ringing and then I looked and then I saw where the train was and I started to run. It was just ready to leave, and the conductor he sure bawled me out 'cause I had the ticket on me. I shouldn't have left the train, you know, but I did. I thought I was going to move with the crowd, and I did. I got back up there again and I said 'I'll never go off this train again!' And I sat on that train all the way from Chicago until I got to Glendive, Montana, and I think it took maybe three or four days. Anyway, I'm sure it did because the trains, they wasn't so good as they are today, you know. And there was wooden seats on them and those old fashioned stoves to heat, that's where they heated the train, you know. Lots of immigrants, that was an immigrant train, that's what it was. And the porter come along with candy and fruit and stuff and I thought people was so good in this country—they were giving things away! Because I didn't know what he said. They just put it on my seat so I took it. Then one man come and said to me, 'He's going to make you pay for that!' I bought one of them [food boxes] too, but I didn't have a knife. So I just had to break off the bread. I looked in and I thought, 'My goodness, the poor people who come over here will starve to death!' A loaf of bread, a can of sardines, some summer sausage—I didn't eat much of it and of course there was no diner on the train them days. You could get cold water, so I guess I lived on water and some of that bread for three or four days. And I'd seen some beautiful depots, you know, when you come from Chicago, but this wasn't! And there was board sidewalks in front of the depot and then my sister didn't come to meet me but my brother-in-law came and my cousin and his wife came to meet me and I stepped off and I said, 'Boy, this don't look like America!' — Anna Lindgren (Fargo, ND)

"It took about three weeks from the time I left Oslo to the time I landed in Minneapolis. I come to Canada, Halifax, and stayed there for a day or two, and then [the train] took us to Montreal, and I stayed there for about a week, and there were so darned many people there! I didn't have much. I think the old man gave me about fifteen bucks. Of course, that was a lot of money too, you know, at that time. And that lasted me until I come to Minneapolis, then I bought a ticket for Arcadia, Wisconsin, near where my uncle lived." — Arne Arneson (Fargo, ND)

"They landed at Quebec. They took the train west and landed at Folk Lake, Wisconsin. The whole trip took fifty-four days. From there they went by train to Saint Cloud, that was as far as the train went in those days. At this point a team and wagon was hired to take them to Pope County, in the area of

Glenwood, Minnesota. I'm convinced they had relatives that had come over two or three years earlier." — Lynn Anderson (Moorhead, MN)

"It was a Cunard Line boat. Conditions on the boat were pretty good, but it took a long time. It took a whole month to go from Sweden before I got to Minnesota … I thought it was a wonderful country to come to, because after I come to this country I never thought I wouldn't have something to eat and that's more than you could say over in Sweden. There was undernourishment there. Terrible! Terrible! People were dying there from T.B. and a lack of food. Seven of my brothers and sisters died from that. … And my trip ended in Minneapolis. I didn't have a ticket for any further. And I had no place to go when I got there and I couldn't speak English. So I stood there at the station and I looked and I didn't know what to think. I saw a full-grown man trying to sell a newspaper and I thought this can't be the place for me. It must be awful hard to get work here. So I went up to Duluth, but there it was the same thing. But there I met some lumberjacks, you know, and some of them could talk Swede. So I got to mix with them and I worked in the woods then for three or four years to make my living." — Andrew Lindgren (Moorhead, MN)

"So my dad came to Minneapolis and he remembered getting off the train at the Union Depot and walking down Washington Avenue and feeling like he didn't have a friend in the world and he didn't know what on earth he was going to do. Here he was in this strange new land and he didn't know the language or anything. ... And all at once he heard some people speaking Swedish, and he said it was the sweetest sound he had ever heard in his life. And so he rushed over there and there were three fellows and he started talking to them and before they were through talking, they had lined him up a job working on the railroad, on the North Dakota line they were building westward from Grand Forks." — Allen Erickson (Moorhead, MN)

"They came to Canada and settled at Gimli on Lake Winnipeg. They were among the first settlers landing there—September 1, 1876. The journey from Winnipeg was made on barges down the Red River from the lake. I don't know how they made it when you think about it. The Lord must have been with them. ... We came over in the summer of 1889, the year of statehood. I was three and a half years old. My maternal grandmother, my mother, my father, my aunt, and four children came together. They wanted to better themselves. They had heard about this wonderful country and so many of their friends were leaving and that gets to be kind of an epidemic, you know. They came from the eastern part of Iceland. First we came to Pembina County, near Akra, we called it the sand ridges. We stayed there until 1894, when we moved to the Mouse River loop with quite a few other families. We went by horses and wagons and drove our stock and my father homesteaded there in McHenry County." — Anna Bjornson (Fargo, ND)

"We got to Minnesota, to Paynesville, in April, 1902, and then we were there until the next spring. And in the meantime, all this land out in

North Dakota had been opened up ... for homesteading. And, of course, they heard about that. They could come out here and, what do you call it, file on a homestead and you got 160 acres for nothing." — Matilda Blumer (Hazelton, ND)

"We just got on a train. And I don't remember very much about that part of the trip. It took us two days to get to Chicago. From there on, it was a little pleasanter. We stopped over in Minneapolis and a very nice fellow helped us. We got breakfast there, and we stayed overnight, and then we got on a Chicago, Milwaukee, and St. Paul train that just lumbered along very slowly and after a day and a couple of nights we landed in Christine [North Dakota]." — Anna Hanson (Moorhead, MN)

"Well, we got off there and were taken to where we had to get on the train. [My mother] was coming over here [from Denmark] to Nobles County, Minnesota, because that was where her sisters lived and where my brother would be when we came. And I remember Chicago, and that was dark, but they helped Mommy, with her children, over to the other train. I don't remember leaving St. Paul, or coming there, but I remember coming to Brewster, and that was at night. My aunt had said they had been looking for us every night." — Tora Johnson (Brewster, MN)

"As far as the climate is concerned, it wasn't that different. But I think it was about the most snow they ever had in Minnesota the year we came here. We had to stay in the depot until morning and then we took the

train to Minneapolis. We slept in the seats. We couldn't speak any English so there was not much else to do. And we had to stay there, and the only thing we could read on the menu was blueberry pie and milk and that's what we had for breakfast. My parents didn't speak any English, but if you didn't understand, [the immigration authorities] had someone that came around, if there was any problem, to talk to you so we weren't too unhappy with that."
— Elsie Gale (Clearbrook, MN)

"We landed at Halifax, after ten days voyage across the Atlantic, having been delayed for three days because of heavy fog. From Halifax, we went by train to Chicago, Minneapolis, and Princeton, our destination, where my father worked. He had been in the United States for two years previous. We arrived in Princeton on December 20th, just a few days before Christmas, and we didn't know anyone except Father." — Minnie Carlson (Fergus Falls, MN)

"I don't know what year my parents came over, but it was the same year as the Chicago fire. [My mother] came through Chicago and it was still burning." — Nels Overby (Moorhead, MN)

"They came to this area and filed a claim. [My parents] came to Kenmare on an immigrant train … and homesteaded in Montrail County in 1904." — Walter Christiansen (Kenmare, ND)

"My father brought my grandfather and grandmother with him when he came over, and I had a brother and two sisters who were born in Sweden.

The rest of us were born over here. My grandfather stayed with [my father] and helped him build a log home. They came in July to Fergus Falls and then they came out and lived in the log schoolhouse until they got their own log house built. That log school house must have been built in the 1870s."
— David Swedberg (Otter Tail Co., MN)

"My brother had left when I was only two years old and he came to Moorhead. I really didn't know him when I got here except by pictures."
— Marlene Lien (Wahpeton, ND)

"My brother met me at the depot at Grandin and they had a job for me and, by golly, the man I was going to work for was waiting for me. He had one hired man in the field already and he needed another one." — Oscar Lindgren (Fargo, ND)

"They had, when they came to this country, only twenty dollars, and five or six children." — Carl Elmquist (Moorhead, MN)

"We moved to Hillsboro [North Dakota] to be with my uncle and his family. This community accepted us whole-heartedly, because I have not seen any community that has so much Scandinavian heritage embedded. In almost every farm home you could find a violin hanging on the wall. For us, my brothers and me, every day there was something new to see and observe in this great land. My mother and sister and brother came to Hillsboro in the spring of 1913, but mother didn't like it at all. She had never been any farther than Oslo in her life, and the environment, and all the customs were unusual for her. So we decided then that, possibly, we should go back to Norway. But it took only a short time for my folks to realize that opportunities for a large family were so much greater in America. And so it was easy to make this second trip and in July of 1914 [after a stay of only seven months] we left Norway. And the coincidence is that the last person we saw, in the Bergen harbor, was Kaiser Wilhelm, who owned a beautiful estate outside of Bergen and spent every summer there. This time we left with the specific purpose of making ourselves Americans. We arrived in Hillsboro only a few days before World War I began." — Leif Christianson (Moorhead, MN)

"When they came to Fargo they heard that north of Abercrombie a ways there was supposed to be a settlement and a lot of Norwegian people were there. I am Swedish, you know, and my folks were, and there was a scattered few Swedes around too. ... So eventually they set out. Christine wasn't on the map then, that was before that was born, and no railroad here, so the only way they could come up here was by a trail. If it was an oxcart trail, I don't know, Dad never told me. But they came up here ... and I suppose it was just by chance that they did stop there and there was a Norwegian couple there and they offered my folks, if they wanted to settle right in the community, to house them until they could apply for a homestead right." — Frank Alm (Christine, ND)

"He landed at Hawley [Minnesota], and he had five cents in his pocket. That's all the money he had and he walked up and down the streets there. He didn't know just what to do. He didn't know anybody. He didn't know where to go and so he went into the store and he bought five cents worth of snuff for the last five cents he had in his pocket. And there he met my dad and then he decided that he would come here so my dad staked him and he came to our place that day." — Clifford Hitterdal (Hitterdal, MN)

"Well, one time I went into a restaurant to eat, you know, and of course it was when I first come and I didn't have much money. So I couldn't understand what they were saying but I looked at the price because I could understand that. I saw something was twenty cents and I thought that must be pretty good if I can eat for twenty cents here. I ordered it anyway. And then they came and gave me some of that stuff that Popeye ate, this green grass. And I thought 'I've been poor all my life, but I've never had to eat grass before.'" — Andrew Lindgren (Moorhead, MN)

"We left Boston on the train on May 22nd, and it took us to Chicago and we arrived in Minneapolis on May 26th. My friend had a brother who worked at Malvey, and we bought a ticket to Malvey and we arrived at Malvey just about at midnight. When we got there the whole town was dark, and also we seen a sign that said restaurant, but we didn't know if we should bother them. So we had seen an empty boxcar at the siding, and we decided to get in and sleep in the boxcar. We woke up in the morning about five o'clock and we found there was an empty stock tank down just below the railroad, but also a pump alongside of it. So we washed our face and hands there and dressed up, and we seen four fellows over on a hand car coming in and we kind of figured they maybe would come to town to eat, so we walked to town. They were just a few steps ahead of us when they walked into a restaurant and they all sat down at one table and we sat down at the other table. The waitress come in and she said something to them in English and one fellow said, 'Bacon and flapjacks.' And the next fellow said 'Bacon and flapjacks,' and the other one said 'Bacon and flapjacks,' and so did the fourth, 'Bacon and flapjacks.' And she stood in the door of the kitchen, and she said 'Four bacon and flapjacks.' Then she come over to us and she said something to us which we didn't understand, but we figured she was asking what we wanted for breakfast. So I said 'Bacon and flapjacks' and my partner said 'Bacon and flapjacks' and we didn't know what we was getting, but we figured it was something to eat anyway. We heard in the kitchen that they were talking the Swedish language and so we told the waitress that we were newcomers and that we would like to rent a bed and a room for a day or two until we got some work. She said 'We thought you were Americans because you ordered your breakfast in English.'" — Henry Holmgren (Henning, MN)

"'Oh, wonderful,' I thought, 'Oh, this is a wonderful country.' It was really beautiful, you know, and I seen it! I was sitting there and I thought, 'Oh, what a wonderful land to be in!'" — Anna Lindgren (Fargo, ND)

Not all of the immigrants felt that it was "a wonderful land to be in." They missed family and friends, and although many intended to return to Scandinavia "someday," arriving in a small Midwestern town gave a measure of finality to their decision to leave the Old Country. They may have feared, as Beret did in *Giants in the Earth*, that "here something was about to go wrong." But they had arrived, and they now had little choice but to pursue the dream that had lured them to America.

Chapter IV

"Foot Your Own Canoe"

THE FIRST SETTLEMENT

A large number of the first settlers in the Red River Valley and the first homesteaders in Dakota Territory were second generation Scandinavian-Americans. Many had been born in America and could speak the English language as well as their parent's native tongue. In several cases they could trace their American roots back to the Norwegian settlements along the Fox River in Illinois or the Koshkonong community in Wisconsin. By the 1880s, sons and daughters of the Swedish immigrants to western Illinois and the Chisago area of Minnesota were beginning to populate the plains. There was a significant Danish presence in Wisconsin, the Finns were beginning to spread out from the mining areas of northern Michigan, and the Icelanders were established on the shores of Lake Winnipeg. As the moved to the prairie, they were in a new land, but they were not necessarily in a new country.

In 1841, the United States government had enacted the Preemption Law, which stipulated that government land was to be sold at a stable price of $1.25 an acre. The Homestead Act of 1862 extended

the opportunities for agricultural immigrants even further by offering one hundred and sixty acres to any immigrant who notified the government of his intention to become a citizen. If they were able to work and live on the land for five years they received full title to that land. Merely acquiring the land, however, was not enough to create a successful farm. The homesteader still needed capital, perhaps as much as a thousand dollars for stock and machinery, before his farm could produce a profit. The Homestead Act wisely provided for this by allowing a homesteader to work away from his farm for up to six months a year during the first five years. The earlier Scandinavian settlements would provide the opportunity for acclimatization, acculturation, and the amassing of capital.

"My mother's ancestors on my grandfather's side came from Telemarken, Norway, and they came here in 1836. [My grandfather], together with his mother and three sisters, came by boat up the Mississippi. It took 'em four months! They had been chased by pirates on the sea. And they came up the Mississippi River and landed first at Galena, Illinois, and that's where they stayed for a couple of years to earn a little money and to see what was what here in this country. After that they moved into Wisconsin in the neighborhood of Whitewater, and towards LaCrosse. Then they moved into southern Minnesota, near Houston, Minnesota, living on different farms.

They sold and they bought farms and whether they bettered themselves or not I don't know, but they were there until 1874. My grandmother was born in Valdres, Norway. She came with her parents to Rock County, Wisconsin, in 1850. And then they moved to Houston County, Minnesota, where she met my grandfather." — Oscar Olson (Lake Park, MN)

"The three Yitterboe brothers, their parents died and they had no land and so they came to America, to Stoughton, Wisconsin, in 1852. The Opsahls came to Decorah, Iowa, in 1857. Then they all came up to Manchester, Minnesota." — Vern Fogelberg (New Rockford, ND)

"They landed in Canada and eventually they landed in Hesper, Iowa—north of Decorah, just south of the Minnesota border. They landed there in 1865 and they stayed there for quite a while. There was quite a bunch in my family, you know, there must have been three sons and four daughters in that Hitterdal family." — Clifford Hitterdal (Hitterdal, MN)

"My father was born in northern Finland, and immigrated to this country at the age of three. And the family settled in Calumet, Michigan. My grandfather worked in the copper mines there for a while, and my father worked with him in the copper mines, not as a young man, perhaps, but as a boy. At the age of about ten to fourteen he'd be out there, working as a drill boy in the copper mines, and he didn't like it, so he apprenticed himself to a newspaper in the community, a Finnish newspaper, and went into the newspaper business." — Russell Parta (New York Mills, MN)

"My father came over in 1892 ... and he went directly to Michigan, with all its logging, and he went there as a carpenter and he stayed about four years. Then, of course, he heard about the free land in Minnesota and it was quite an opportunity to get some land because acreage in Sweden was always small. And here they were entitled to 160 acres. Well, he must have been at the end of the free land era because he only got 120 acres. This was in Kittson County, in the northern part of the state. I don't think Lancaster was founded in 1896, I think Hallock as the closest town at that time." — Myrtle Rundquist (Moorhead, MN)

"I had some great-uncles who left Numedal, Norway, back in 1839. They went to Jefferson County, Rock Prairie, Wisconsin, and bought some land there and established a community there. They had lived in a place called Rollag in Numedal. They were what they called 'husmen.' They didn't own the place where they lived on. The particular place where my relatives lived belonged to the Rollag church. My paternal grandparents came later, in 1870, and stayed with those uncles in Wisconsin for four years and then they came up here to Parke Township, near Rollag. They all left Norway to try to better their condition." — William Nelson (Rollag, MN)

"They came from Norway with several other Norwegian families and settled near Rochester, Minnesota in about 1876, when my father was just a baby. I was just a baby when we moved to North Dakota." — Mabel Fynskov (Osakis, MN)

"My father's family came originally to Dane County, Wisconsin, and then to the northern tier of Iowa, Winnesheik County. But by 1855 they had gone to southern Minnesota, Houston County, near Caledonia or Spring Grove, only six miles from Iowa and not much further from Wisconsin … And my father was born there. My father left there when he was twenty-one years old in 1878, and came up [to the Red River Valley] because there was land available for homesteading. He dug, or built, a sod house." — Clarence Glasrud (Moorhead, MN)

"My brother and I and my dad and mother, we landed at Boston in 1903 and from Boston, my mother had a sister who lived in Fargo, so we came straight to Fargo and stayed there for two months. My dad had a brother who lived in New Richland, Wisconsin, and we stayed there until 1909, when my dad moved up to the iron range. My dad worked at one of the biggest white pine mills there was and most of the workers were Finnish."
— Borghild Overby (Moorhead, MN)

"I came over in diapers. I was only a month old. I was baptized in Norway. Dad was over here before, you know, and then he went home and married Ma and then came back over here. That's when I came the first time. And then they went back home again when I was about four or five. I don't know nothing of them days, I don't even remember even the town we lived in. I suppose it was in Trempello County, Wisconsin, down near Winona someplace. We went back to Norway to take over the farm when my grandpa died, took over the home farm. There were nine kids in the family altogether." — Arne Arneson (Fargo, ND)

"They settled in Wisconsin because they had this immigration officer from Wisconsin in New York at Ellis Island, and he would encourage them to come there and he would also even give them some money." — Florence Fritz (Detroit Lakes, MN)

"My mother came to Fillmore County in 1868, directly from Norway, and stayed until 1869 when their first child was born. Then they came up here [rural Underwood, Minnesota]. Everybody came to that same place, and then they got scattered around later." — Clara Johnson (Underwood, ND)

"They came to Red Wing. People from their locality had come to Red Wing before, so they knew they would find Norwegians there. They both worked and managed to earn enough to send for their parents, my maternal grandparents, and they settled on a place next to ours." — Mabel Enger (Oakes, ND)

"They settled just south of Emmons, Minnesota, in northern Iowa. One time [in 1862] they say they hid down in the well to escape the Indians when they plundered the farmhouse ... they were down in the well when my grandfather was gone in the army." — Wilferd Anderson (Hitterdal, MN)

By the 1870s, Minnesota was well on its way to becoming the New Scandinavia as proclaimed by Fredrika Bremer. Norwegians were

moving along the entire southern border of the state and on into the Park Region of west-central Minnesota. Swedes came directly to Minnesota and began to take farms to the west and north of Minneapolis, or began to work in the forests of Northern Minnesota. A few Danes began to move into southwest Minnesota. Measured in the span of years, this pioneer period of log cabins and grubbing out stumps was remarkably short, but measured in the day-to-day struggle to survive it must have seemed much longer. This struggle would leave an indelible impression on the hearts and minds of the pioneers.

"If I would have had the money I would have gone back the second week, I think. I didn't like it one bit! I was homesick and I couldn't understand the language and that's no fun, to listen to somebody talk in English and you don't know what they are talking about." — Marlene Lien (Wahpeton, ND)

"It isn't easy for an immigrant, I will admit that. It wasn't easy because you're classified. 'Better not talk to him, he's Norwegian! He just came here!'" — Leif Christianson (Moorhead, MN)

"Then we bought some bows and some sheeting and covered the wagons and moved with these covered wagons to Morris, Minnesota, where my dad got a quarter of land, and he did well there, he farmed there for twenty-three years. That was pretty much a Norwegian settlement. My mother could go to ladies aid and to church and she loved being in Minnesota. We had two Norwegian churches near us, and all the kids in school spoke Norwegian." — Ole Olson (Fargo, ND)

"My dad came to America in 1881. They homesteaded at Stanchfield, Minnesota. Times were hard in Sweden at this time. They were being overpopulated and so the fact that they had the Homestead Act, that was another thing. You could get land here for nothing as long as you stayed on it for five years and make all the improvements and it would be yours. So that was one of the reasons why they came, free land, as much as they wanted. There wasn't a job for everyone in Sweden. Times were hard and farms were small and if you did have a farm, that was divided by the children and the next generation divided it again until you had only a potato patch and a house left. So, something had to give. The climate was very much like the climate in Sweden. And Minnesota was pretty much the same as it was in Sweden. It always looked the same, the layout of the land and the hay, they wanted hay for their cattle. And it seemed like everybody who came from Sweden, they had that scene picked out, to look the same as in Sweden, that they had left. And they always wanted a patch of wood somewhere that they could cut wood for firewood in the wintertime. Another reason was that they always settled where there were other Swedes. Around Malmo [Minnesota], where my mother came, there was nothing but Swedes there for a while. They took the name 'Malmo' from Malmo in Sweden." — Amy Erickson (Moorhead, MN)

"[My father] came to this country in 1884, and the reason he came to this country was that the girl to whom he was engaged had come ... some years before and she sent him the ticket money to come over. But when he came to this country, she had married somebody else, so he lived with an uncle in Wisconsin for a while and then he came to St. James, where an uncle of mine was living—this uncle had married a girl from Bergen—and with them came my mother. She came over in 1885. And my father came there and he was a painter and a paper hanger. They met at my uncle's farm and they were married in 1892. Where they settled in St. James, well, that was heavily Norwegian, and when they moved to Minneapolis they moved into the Scandinavian enclave, too, so it was pretty much the same thing." — Carl Narveson (Moorhead, MN)

"My mother's parents also came across from Norway, after my mother. My mother's parents lived with us for twenty years afterward. Some of their children had already settled in Minnesota. My mother's sister came when she was eight and a half years old and she lived with relatives that were here. Mom was about eighteen when she came. The whole bunch came. She had eleven brothers and sisters and they all came to the United States. But they went back to Norway, one or two of them, and went back and forth."
— Alma Olson (Souris, ND)

"My grandfather, Eric Gustav Anderson, and my grandmother, were charter members of the West Union Church in Carver County. He was in the Civil War and he served as a flag bearer. He walked the whole distance to Saint Paul for his mustering-out pay. He was wounded in the leg and I can remember that he always had a limp." — Gale Iverson (Hitterdal, MN)

"My mother's parents came from Skane [Sweden] in 1871, with two small children, and they first came to Sauk Centre, which seemed to be sort of a terminal. … Grandpa worked on the railroad there for about six weeks, and from there he went to Parkers Prairie. He had first planned to go to Battle Lake, where quite a few Skaningers lived already. Father came when he was twenty-two years old, in 1889. He had at least one sister who lived in Parkers Prairie already. I think he worked in a lumber camp for a while in Minnesota. Shortly after he landed in America, father said he overheard people talking another language, and he thought, 'Hmmm, if that's English I should be able to learn that.' It turned out it was German." — Lillie Strandness (Fargo, ND)

"We moved from Byron in 1899, when I was ten, and settled on a timber farm near Bertha, Minnesota. We developed that farm and it got to be a paying proposition." — Art Waldon (Detroit Lakes, MN)

"[My mother] was married when she came over. They was only in Minnesota just a short time before her husband died, and then my dad and her got married and started a little dairy farm. They had relations in the country where they went. Her first husband homesteaded a hundred and sixty acres, a lot of good timber on the land, that's what they were looking for. [My dad] homesteaded and said that he had to look straight up in order to see the sky—the timber was that thick! He said the first acre he had cleared he hired some of his neighbors to clear for him. He paid fifty cents a day for labor for clearing, and he said 'It cost me a hundred and fifty dollars to get that first acre cleared.' I remember some of those pine stumps. Some of them were three feet across." — Louis Westling (Longville, MN)

"They lived in a cave house cut into a hillside, like a root cellar or a log cabin built in a hillside, air conditioned year around, you know. This was the winter of '68–'69, close to Lake Johanna in the Starbuck area. With a man named Hicks he went on foot to Alexandria to file a homestead claim. From there they rode to the Red River Valley with a man who filed a claim to a homestead where the Fargo courthouse now stands. Then, with Ole Hicks, grandfather walked to Detroit Lakes, at that time the recording seat, to get a patent on their land. The fellow that came to Fargo to file, well his wife wouldn't come along for fear of Indians, there had been an uprising just a few years before. In the spring of 1870, Grandpa and this man named Hicks came to the claim and seeded land, then went back and came with the family on July 5th. It was wheat. The wheat was cut with a cradle and threshed and then taken to the mill in Alexandria." — Lynn Anderson (Moorhead, MN)

"The first-comers from our part of the country [Trondhiem] came here [Osakis, Minnesota]. And then we came here to people my parents knew and who had made it in the first place. And it was easier that way and I think it was a good way. And they stayed here [ever since]. At the time there was no homestead land left, so [my father] bought a small piece of land to start with, forty acres." — John Klukken (Osakis, MN)

"My mother moved to Douglas County, near Alexandria … in 1878 she came there. And she would tell stories about the Chippewas. They never bothered them. And people never locked their doors when they went to bed at night, and the Chippewas would come in and help themselves to milk and cheese … and they didn't have money but they would leave something that they had carved out of stone, and there were no problems." — Hazel Monson Barker (Moorhead, MN)

"My grandfather came to America first in the early 1880s. Most of the good land in this particular area [Underwood, Minnesota] had been taken but he came to this area because of other people from Hedemarken, Norway, who had settled in the area. He didn't have much luck in finding what he wanted, but he went back to Norway to sell his family on the idea of coming to America. So he came back a second time bringing his eldest daughter with him—my mother. Then he bought up the homestead rights on thirty-four acres on the north shore of the lake, two miles east of Underwood. And he went back to Norway again to get the rest of the family and they arrived in 1882. My mother had remained in America so grandfather went back alone. And the very day they came back, the fifteenth of September, 1882, when they arrived in Fergus Falls, was my mother's and father's wedding day. Father left Norway because of reaching the age of being inducted into the Norwegian army. Dad was the youngest of eleven children, and he was the only one of his family to come to America." — John Gronner (Underwood, MN)

"My father came from Sweden in 1882. He didn't homestead the land, he bought it from Ole Torkel. He paid eight hundred dollars for it, for the one hundred sixty acres. At that time there was not more than eight acres open up in field, so my father had to grub out practically all of it. When we grew up, we started out pretty young to grub. We just used a grub-ax. He hired out for some help in grubbing, and we maybe cleared eight acres a year. He donated one acre for the church, which was built in 1904." — David Swedberg (Otter Tail Co., MN)

"They lived in the side of a hill, in a cellar, that was their first home. They dug into a hill, and he was called 'Cellar Lars.' They built a house later on, a house and a barn and a granary, sheds, machine shops, blacksmith shop. Grandpa was very good!" — Ellen Abraham (Villard, MN)

"They came over [from Sweden] and they went up the Saint Lawrence. They landed, I suppose, in the area of Quebec and from there they were able to take the train to Minnesota. My mother settled in Fergus Falls. My grandfather right away got a job in a sash and door factory because he designed this so-called gingerbread on these old houses. That's what he had learned to do, and he was sort of an artist. My father's parents settled in Garfield, and he became a farmer, but now he had never farmed in Sweden so I think it was rather hard for them. But they came to that area because it was definitely a Swedish community." — Catherine Fossay (Moorhead, MN)

"The area to the northeast of Erhard was an area almost entirely settled by Swedish immigrants and now once in a while we refer to it as Swede Hollow just for the fun of it. The people who came from Norway preferred to settle on the west side of the Pelican River which was prairie country and all they had to do was to get the tall grass cleared off and start in with a breaking plow whereas on the east side of the river it was a matter of getting the ax and the crosscut saw and the grub hoe to work. … They went to work and grubbed out and they got a patch and in went blue stem wheat. And blue stem wheat was great stuff—long heads and the kernels were almost the size of garden peas, beautiful stuff! But there was one thing that they always had to keep an eye on, and that was the grasshopper. There was one instance where Johnson and Larson were neighbors. One day Larson went over to visit with Johnson and when he went over there—there were several acres grubbed out then—there stood the grain waving like an ocean and as he walked along, Mr. Larson looked up at the sky and he thought it was just a wonderful day. But they had talked with the Indians, and the Indians said the grasshoppers were coming from the west. But nevertheless, just at noon he came over to Johnson's and he found Mr. Johnson at home and as they were talking the bright sunshine became dulled and they looked up and lo and behold here were the locusts, or the grasshoppers. They got the children and Mrs. Johnson into the house, closed the windows and the doors, and down came what they called the grasshoppers, which were the locusts, and settled on everything. Some of these people had come from southern Minnesota and they had brought homestead tobacco. And Mr. Larson had a patch which he tended himself and Mr. Johnson also had a patch. The grasshoppers came down and they stayed for about twenty minutes. Everything was covered with grasshoppers. Then for some reason or other they took off and never a bite was taken out of anything at Johnson's. So when the grasshoppers took off and were gone, the first thing Johnson thought about was his tobacco patch and he went up there to see how things were and, lo and behold, there was the tobacco patch absolutely secure, not a leaf was touched. And Larson said, 'Oh, well, they haven't bothered yours, and I know mine is safe because I wrapped them up in old coats. Then they went to see Mr. Larson's tobacco patch and now then, lo and behold, the whole patch was black, there was nothing left but a few stakes standing upright and a buckle and a button lying here and there. The grasshoppers had devoured his tobacco, with the clothing that he had wrapped it in, completely. Mr. Johnson said, 'Don't worry, I have twice the amount of tobacco that I need, you can have half of mine.' And that settled the matter."

— Carl Anderson (Erhart, MN)

"It was so isolated out there, twenty miles north of Detroit Lakes, and it took too long to go to town, especially if you just had a pair of oxen. You'd go to town one day and come back the next. There was one woman out there who hadn't been to town for twenty years." — Charles Westerholm (Moorhead, MN)

"My grandfather bought the land out by Bagley from a real shyster. It was supposed to be farmland, but it was all full of rocks, very poor farmland. They never got over the fact that this man had cheated them. However, Grandfather was thrilled because now he was a landowner. They used my grandfather's homestead rights to get this eighty acres of virgin woods, virgin trees that would measure six and seven feet across. They were farming until they came up to Bagley and started the lumber mill and that proved to be a very lucrative business at that time." — Florence Fritz (Detroit Lakes, MN)

"Mrs. Nelson was the doctor for the early settlers [in the Erhard, Minnesota, area]. One day she came back carrying a young calf over her shoulders, which was pay for nursing a man that had been sick for a period of time. Mr. Nelson was amazed. He said, 'What's the idea of bringing home this calf? You know we don't have any milk for it.' 'Oh,' she said, 'I'll take care of that.' She tied the calf to a bush and went down to the creek bed with her hatchet and cut down willows and in no time she had formed a fishing basket. She deposited the basket in the stream and in about an hour or so it was full of minnows. She then took this big basket of minnows up to her iron kettle where she had her fire going and dumped the minnows in and boiled them to the texture of milk. When it cooled off she strained it thoroughly and presented it to the calf and the calf drank. The calf was a heifer and that heifer became the mother cow for a good many of the herds in the community." — Carl Anderson (Erhart, MN)

The Red River of North Dakota and Minnesota contains some of the best agricultural land in the world. The effect of leaving the wooded hills of Minnesota and coming upon a vast, treeless ocean of grass must have been startling for the first pioneers. Here, in what was once the bed of the ancient glacial Lake Agassiz, it was discovered that wheat could grow as well as prairie grass. For later arrivals who did not wish to homestead at the very edge of civilization, there was still plenty of opportunity to buy land from speculators or the railroad. Ironically, many of the Scandinavian settlers preferred not to settle on the open prairie where the land was usually richer and tended to assume that if there were no trees in sight there had to be something wrong with the soil. Nevertheless, after the Northern Pacific Railroad reached Moorhead in 1871, within ten years Scandinavian settlements were established throughout the valley.

"Dad met somebody who recommended a place near Doran. So he lived there and then he spent five winters working in the woods, chopping down trees, and in the summer he would farm. And he saved his money and then he bought this farm the same year I was born. They had a child each year for the first four years. My dad didn't like anything about Sweden, so he didn't have any Swedish friends. But Doran was a Norwegian community, and still is. He could write Swedish, but he couldn't write English. But he didn't like Swedish so that he would never allow Swedish or Norwegian in our home." — Allan Erickson (Moorhead, MN)

"My uncle learned the building business back in Sweden when he was just a young fellow, but he started building here [in Moorhead] and he became successful. He brought his brothers and sisters over and finally even brought his parents over. He went to work for the Northern Pacific Railroad and the Great Northern Railroad and he built bridges all the way out to Montana. He built the first penitentiary in Bismarck, when it was just cowboys and Indians out there. My dad and my mother both worked for him out there. They said the country was pretty wild at this time. It was in the early Eighties then." — Roy Carlander (Moorhead, MN)

"When they came up here my grandparents were both farmers. They took land. I know my Grandfather Pearson took what they called a tree claim. The lived north of Moorhead in an area called Swedetown because everybody up there talked Swedish." — Gladys Westrum (Moorhead, MN)

"My dad came directly from Vestergotland ... directly to Moorhead and he settled here in 1882, and my mother came about two years later. He was kind of a sharecropper; he rented his land. We had to go to the river to get water for our cattle. We had to go down to the Red River, cut a hole in the ice, and my dad had kind of a sleigh with three big barrels on it. We used to take that water and that would last us maybe a week." — Vic Anderson (Moorhead, MN)

"My uncle, John Berquist, established himself in a home where the high-rise is in Moorhead now. And most Swedes came to his place—I had heard him say that—that most of them came to his place to get sort of settled. You now, when a person comes to a new spot you just feel lost. He came to America eight years before the rest of them came, in 1872! None of them ever went back to Sweden that I know. My father had two sisters left in Sweden and I saw them later." — Robert Carlander (Moorhead, MN)

"My maternal grandfather came from an area near Oslo to Rollag in 1883 and my grandmother and my mother with her seven brothers came to Rollag a year later. Many from the same region had already settled here so they felt among friends. They learned to speak English, all right, because my grandfather who came from Norway in 1870, he was a little over forty years old at the time, and then years later he was appointed postmaster and the post office was established in his home and naturally, because he came from Rollag, Norway, he called the post office 'Rollag.' It wasn't easy, in 1872 there was smallpox. Two girls, one four and the other ten months, died the same day and had to be buried at night as everyone was fearful of smallpox. Fathers died, mothers died, children died, very many in the two years 1882 and 1883. Twenty-four children from the age of fourteen and down died here in Parke township." — William Nelson (Rollag, MN)

"My dad was the youngest one of eleven children. And he came over [in 1885] from Norway to his cousin in Carlyle, that's in Otter Tail County, not too far from Fergus Falls. Evidently his cousin had sent him money for the fare. He worked on the railroad when they built the railroad out to Devil's Lake. He married in 1889. My mother's folks had come from Norway in 1868 or thereabouts. Her brother, the oldest one in the family, had been on the Atlantic crossing. They came up here [in the Rollag, Minnesota, area] in 1892 and bought a quarter of land in Parke Township. The quarter that he bought was darned near all covered with timber. They had only cleared 12 acres. There was a fairly good-sized log house on the place, and a granary. The Norwegians took over the township of Parke because it was a wooded area. It was a damn thrill to live out here on the Dauner prairie where there wasn't a bush or a fence post or a damn thing anyplace. And on top of that, some of the Norwegians looked at that timber and saw there was already a crop there. They had to be where they could get their own fence posts. They had to be where they could get logs to build a house than if they lived way heck and gone out on the prairie there. I've thought about that a lot. My dad could have got land out here by Silver Lake, all flat, no stones. That land sold for eight dollars an acre. Dad paid ten dollars an acre [in Parke Township]." — Oscar Bratlien (Hawley, MN)

"Grandpa Bjorndalen came over to this country in 1876. He thought black smithing was too hard work, the younger fellows didn't like to work as an apprentice, you see, and he thought he'd like to make his living in America. There were relatives of his here. That's why he came to Hawley. He started in farming the next year, renting some land north of Rollag. He had seven acres of oats that was hailed out that first year before it was harvested so that was kind of tough." — Nilmer Bjorndahl (Hawley, MN)

"My father's folks, they came with oxen from Northfield up to Hitterdal. It was in the seventies, I don't know exactly when. They came from Sagedal in Norway. My mother's folks settled first near Bricelyn, Minnesota, before they came up here. My grandparents never learned English, at least I never heard them talk it. We always talked Norwegian, you know. They had a lot of Indians around here then, when they moved up here, but they were all friendly. You'd just have to give them a little bit now and then. They got along fine. Towards White Earth there were more of them." — Henry Jacobson (Ulen, MN)

"They decided in the spring of '71 they were going to move up here [to Hitterdal, Minnesota]. So they had a covered wagon and some oxen and some horses and the whole gang came up this way. It was so dry when they came up here everything was bone dry, there was no slough, no lake, everything was bone dry, and so then they had to look for water. So they had to dig a well in the deepest part of the lake here, about thirty feet deep, with spades ... and they had to get the water out with buckets, see, and they had made troughs, long troughs out of boards, and then if one farmer was there already watering his stock, then the other guy had to hold his cattle until this first guy was through. And they had about forty acres of woods up there by Twin Valley, and they used to go there and take lot of food along and stay, oh, for quite a while, and they used to cut wood there, haul it into Twin Valley, and load it on a flat car and ship it into Hitterdal, and then they would unload it here again and divide the wood. If they wanted to grind flour they had to go to Alexandria, Minnesota, and that's quite a little ways. They had to go there by oxcart or my folks were fairly lucky, they had a span of mules, so they got around a little better. My dad and Berndt Hitterdal had the first threshing outfit around here, a horsepower outfit. They threshed once on January 12, 1877. They had four teams, I understand, and they would go around and around and there was a shaft that run from the horsepower outfit to the threshing machine, and they all had stacks them years, there was no shock run, you know. ... And they got real sick and the doctors didn't know beans about it, you know. Kids died from diphtheria, scarlet fever, and all this, you know, and then [the doctor] would tell them, 'Now put them to bed and keep them warm, I'll be back tomorrow.' Whether he came back tomorrow or not didn't make any difference. They didn't know any more about it than you or I did, you know. And [my mother] said one place there was three kids in one bed, one was already dead. And then when they died, she said, they took them down and buried them in the cemetery and then they put a wooden cross on these graves, you know. And in two, three years or so the cross rotted and got covered with dirt. No one, she said, has any idea who is buried in that cemetery." — Clifford Hitterdal (Hitterdal, MN)

"[Mama] walked from Grandpa Bjerknes' place, right on the north side of Ulen, and they used to get together and walk to Lake Park for confirmation class. There was no church in Ulen or Hitterdal in 1881. They used to leave early in the morning. It would be a two day trip. Isn't that awful? The railroad didn't come through Ulen until 1886, but there were people there before that." — Anna Gregorson (Ulen, MN)

"At first, when [my father] came here [in 1888], he got work on the section, and that is how he learned to speak English, because the section boss was an Englishman named Doyle. He used the English language, naturally, and that is how my father learned to speak English, although all his life his language remained peppered with Norwegian. He learned to read English, but he never learned to write it. He was about thirty-seven when he came. Uncle Ole came [in 1882] and settled on a farm one mile south of Ulen. There was no village there at the time. Father bought a farm four miles southeast of Ulen after he married. There was no transportation, except by skis during the winter when they had those heavy snows. When they finally got the team of horses, after they moved out on the farm, they got a single buggy, and they finally built a little sled on their own." — Clara Hanson (Moorhead, MN)

"[When they came to America] there were boxcars ready to take them west but grandfather said they were not cattle. They took the train to Eau Claire, Wisconsin. In the early spring of 1871 they set out with a team of horses, which they traded in St. Paul for oxen. After traveling a month and four days over bad roads, heavy snow, they arrived at the homestead on April 4, 1871. They migrated to Lake Park Township, the northwest corner, section six. It reminded me of the home place, when I saw that back in Sweden. In 1892 Grandfather visited Sweden and he couldn't realize how small the farms were. He walked it out measuring. Grandmother refused to cross the ocean again." — Amy Erickson (Moorhead, MN)

"My dad come here from Sweden in 1892, by steamboat and railroad, to Lake Park, Minnesota. He got this job to work on the [Becker] County Farm in the spring of 1892 and worked through the summer season until November. From there he went to an uncle of his by marriage and cut cordwood for him during the winter and he repeated this, working on farms in the summer months. He worked on a farm in Absaraka, North Dakota, for three consecutive summers and came back to Lake Park in the wintertime. Others from the same area, from Appelbo, Sweden, had come here before, you know, which led him here, too, and in his time led many others to this area and that's how the Swedes got settled here among all the Norwegians. The Swedes who came here felt right at home, because when they come here they were not lost—they had places to go and visit and the ones that were here always found it interesting to visit with the newcomers to get more news from the old country, and in this way they got to know a lot of things that happened since they left Sweden. ... My grandfather then came up into the Valley to visit the Levi Thortvedt family who first come from Norway to the Red River Valley in 1870. In his visitation with the Thortvedts he got into discussing lands and looking over lands in the area, he finally bought four hundred and eighty acres, which got to be the Grover farmstead right across the river from the Thortvedts, in Moland Township, four hundred eighty acres for sixteen hundred dollars, which makes it three and a third dollars per acre. When he bought this, he hired a man to build a shack on the farm and he went back to Houston County. Then he moved his family up the following year, in 1874. Yes, it was virgin prairie at that time. At that time my mother was less than a year old so they had two wagons and Grover drove one and [his wife] drove the other wagon holding my mother on her lap most of the way from Houston County to just north of Glyndon, Minnesota. So she grew up there, attended the local schools and attended the teachers college in Moorhead and she was a teacher at the time my dad met her. And they got married in the spring of 1898, and settled near Lake Park." — Oscar Olson (Lake Park, MN)

"Grandma had a brother here, and he told her that everything was so much better than there, so they decided to come. Dad was only eight and a half years old when he come here. So they come to this minister's place and they stayed there for a while and they decided to have a homestead. That was my grandmother's brother, the first Lutheran minister in Fargo, Reverend Christian Wold. The homestead was in Moland Township in Clay County [Minnesota]. The first thing they built was a small frame house with a small lean-to as a kitchen, which was too cold to use in the winter. Then they did some fieldwork and got a little grain and then he had to build a granary. Well, they had to have a place to keep the stock so he built what they called stables in them days. And there was a partition in the center. In the rear of it they had hay, and the cows were on one side and the horses were on the other side. … I can remember [when we moved from there] very well. It was in October of 1901. My mother drove one team of horses and she had her flowers in the front [of the wagon], but Minnie and I thought it was fun to sit up there and swing our feet from this spring seat. Ma got after us about it, but you know how anxious we were to go to a new home. That was going to be something! She had a bed in the back of the wagon because my father had a crippled man that he took care of." — Clara Kragnes (Felton, MN)

"[My father] originally settled near Averill, Minnesota in 1873, but then he bought eighty acres in Oakpark Township, north of Moorhead. He farmed all his life there. He spoke good English, but he spoke sort of half and half, Norwegian and English. He would write to his sisters back in Norway and would even send them money once in a while. … In 1898 there was a big flood when the Buffalo River, the Red River, and the Sheyenne River came together. They said there were quite a few who stayed at my grandfather's because it was one of the highest places in the country. And to get to [Fargo], they went by boat to the railroad and then walked into town, sometimes carrying one hundred pound sacks of flour back home." — Lela Hegland (Moorhead, MN)

"When the family was coming from Pope County, they had sheep which they drove along side of them, and they had a little crate of chickens, and one chicken would get motion sickness and lay down and regurgitate and carry on when the ox-cart got to moving. And then when they stopped for a rest or whatever, they put the crate down and let the chickens out. After all, they were pets, you know. And the thing would be lying there and after a while it would shake its head and start to flop its wings and pretty soon it would be just as happy as happy could be, you know. And as soon as they got rolling again it would be laid out, deathly sick again. I thought that was so humorous that the chicken got motion sickness. … John Johnson was a friend and a distant relative, and he came out here, and I think it was him who helped build the house. This was in the summer of 1870. Three years later they built the larger cabin. In the eighties there were three families living in this house. It was four good-sized rooms, two up and two down. It was the first white settlement in this township [Holy Cross Township, Clay County, Minnesota]. It was a copy of the situation in Sweden except on a smaller scale." — Lynn Anderson (Moorhead, MN)

"When my dad first came to the place up here [near Perley, Minnesota], he had oxen. We had to go to town so he took the first section of a bob-sleigh and made a box on there and he started out for Moorhead. He had a few sacks of wheat on there that he was going to change for groceries. He started about four in the morning and by the time he came to Moorhead they were just lighting up for the night. So he stayed overnight. It took him all day to go one way and all day to go home again. … In the flood of 1897, I was nine years old then, one of my neighbors came over to my dad, and my dad had a new grain tank and they fixed it up for a boat. And the both of them rowed across the field in the wagon box, and when they got there, they had a small calf that had been in the barn that they took to the house. My mother's relatives fixed up a real boat and fixed up a sail and sailed right across the field all the way to where the Red River was. Then they took a hayrack, of some kind, and they made a bridge so they could take the cattle up to the second floor of the barn so they could get them out of the water."
— George Jacobson (Perley, MN)

"The very first time he came, he came alone, to seek work. And he stayed in this country approximately three years. And then he went back to Norway and brought my mother and two sisters back with him to live. They originally settled near Hendrum, Minnesota, because they had friends there and they were able to get a home or establish a home. Everybody was Scandinavian. That would be in 1892. He acquired a few acres of land and put up a house. He was a day laborer most of his life. He was a shoemaker and during the winter he fixed harnesses for practically all of the neighbors." — Alva Letness Hest (Perley, MN)

"We moved into Minnesota in 1916. I was nine years old. They shipped us right on into Detroit Lakes. And it was my mother and seven kids and then we slept right on the floor and they kept us there until nine o'clock the next morning when we got on a train up to Thief River Falls and from there we got on a Soo Line train for Clearbrook, Minnesota." — Lloyd Westrum (Moorhead, MN)

"When the Lysnes came, Gary and Twin Valley had already been established. The railroad had come through. But when the Schulstads came, those towns were not established. Instead, you had outposts, and some of them are still there, like Flom and Faith, and some of those places. And Lake Park, because it was on the main line of the Northern Pacific, was quite a jumping-off place; a lot of them came to Lake Park and then went north. The Lysne family and the Schulstad family lived in southeastern Waukon

Township [Norman County, Minnesota] and I believe that my mother did as so many other girls did at that time, she worked as a hired girl. And that's how my parents happened to meet. At the time they met my father was already renting land from her father." — Rev. Christian Schulstad (Dawson, MN)

"My dad slept many a time in the straw stacks out on the Crookston prairies, because it took them a day to get to Crookston, and then to come back, so they slept in the straw stack. They walked. They had oxen, but they got so sore footed that they couldn't take them on long trips. ... The Indians used to have their route from the White Earth reservation to the Red Lake reservation and that came right by us. They'd come by in covered wagons, and mother would always give them what they wanted. They would come up and say 'Chippewa' and that meant that they were friendly. We were always kind of afraid of the Sioux. And they came right by our schoolhouse, and we were kind of scared, well, we liked the white people the best, but we were taught never to be afraid of the Indians and always to be good to them. There was an Indian medicine doctor that came around [the McIntosh, Minnesota, area]. And he would show them how to make medicine out of the bark of trees and the roots of plants. My mother used one of his medicines to the very last. And that was from the popple bark, from the popple tree, took the outside bark off and then the next bark you take and boil and make tea out of it. It was very bitter, but it sure helped colds! ... The stagecoach would come

in with the mail. And then my uncle had to pick up the mail and he walked to McIntosh with it, to the place where you got mail then. He walked once a week. He had enough mail so he would just carry it in his hip pocket, and then walk back. And for that he got seven dollars for thirteen months."
— Alma Ramse (McIntosh, MN)

"My mom came through Canada when she came, from Halifax. And then they got there with a team of horses and took them across the line to North Dakota. They heard it was supposed to be good here. Some of them had already settled in Minnesota and they kept in touch with them and they heard it was good in Dakota. … One of Dad's brothers even went back to Norway because his wife was so afraid of the thunderstorms. She was so afraid that she didn't want to live here so they went back to Norway."
— Alma Olson (Souris, ND)

"My dad's name was Karl Nelson, but I took my grandpa's name, Arneson, when I got to this country. I can't say there was hard times [in Enderlin, North Dakota]. We all lived good. A lot of rich farmers down there. There were six brothers there—I know they had a half section apiece! They were neighbors to our place in Norway, but I didn't know them. They were over here and married before I was born." — Arne Arneson (Fargo, ND)

"My father, when he came from Norway, it was Ole Grangaard. But he had a brother who was named Ole also, so it was Big Ole and Little Ole. But the father's name was Ole also. The two Oles and a brother Tollef came across at the same time, and their name was Grangaard when they came to Spring Grove, Minnesota. After they moved here to Kindred there were so many Grangaards that their mail was mixed up. So they changed it. So my father's oldest brother was kind of a lawyer so they changed it to Grant. Tollef was the lawyer-type man and he changed the name. I was born in Kindred and we had a midwife come out. … My father had a sister in Spring Grove, that's why he went there. He only stayed there a short time, a month, maybe. But they all wanted to move, to the Kindred area, because there was a Norwegian settlement there. They homesteaded there. They traveled by horse and wagon to Kindred, and they brought their chickens along. They had a compartment nailed under a hayrack and that's where they kept their chickens." — Gunhild Laske (Kindred, ND)

"In Norway my dad was apprenticed out at the age of sixteen to be a shoemaker. I don't think he particularly cared about it, because when he came to this country he never practiced the trade at all. He went out to lumber camps and things like that, and at home he repaired shoes but he never worked as a shoemaker. He became a carpenter and built a lot of houses and barns in the [Abercrombie, North Dakota] neighborhood. And then he married a farmer's daughter and acquired a farm that way and became a farmer." — Palmer Tverdal (Abercrombie, ND)

"That was in 1880 [when he came to Fargo]. He was handy with the hammer and saw so he did all his own carpenter work. And there he built the house right in the quarter of that corner. They came from a place where there wasn't very much land to be gotten, but they were even stingy on the land. He was gonna conserve that. Then he built a barn too, and he acquired a rake to rake hay with, and then a mower, because he acquired a couple of oxen to start with. They must have gotten a hold of a breaking plow because they went to work and started breaking the ground so that they could start raising the crops and all that was done in the first few years after 1880. ... Then the old Milwaukee Railroad came along. It came out of Fargo and south of Christine. It went past Fort Abercrombie and then into Wahpeton. ... [When the] railroad came along it offered them work. It went right between the house and the barn, so it was handy. When it came they had to move the house and the barn, an extra expense. That's where the same homestead is standing, where I was born." — Frank Alm (Christine, ND)

"In 1878 he homesteaded land south of Fargo, but he lost his claim by somebody jumping his claim. They were looking for a place to settle after they moved up from Decorah, Iowa, where he had worked on a farm since he had come over. Then he worked as a carpenter and a millwright in Fargo."
— Lela Hegland (Moorhead, MN)

"They were so poor [in Norway]. Dad was poorly and he couldn't go out and work hard, so he had to go out and be a baby sitter for a while and do things like that so in that way he could get his living because they were so poor at home. My dad came to this country in June on 1880. He happened to come to Grand Forks and he walked around Grand Forks all day on a Sunday. His first Sunday in [Dakota Territory] he said he'd never forget. The bridge over the Red River was being finished and there were workers all around. Some worked, some played cards, some fought, and most of them were drinking. He said 'If I'd have had the money I would have bought a ticket back to Norway on Monday.' 'That summer,' Dad wrote, 'the railroad was built to Devil's Lake. People who grew up in these days can never imagine what it was like in the Red River Valley at that time. Such drinking and irreligion was a terrible thing to think of. … My brother had come here from Decorah, Iowa, the year before and had a homestead fifteen miles north of Grand Forks near the Turtle River. What I thought when I saw these homesteads words cannot describe! I thought I had come to the world's end. The country was just a wild prairie, houses looked like ant hills, and little shanties with sod roofs, and many lived in cellars!' There were no horses in those days, only oxen … he had to farm with oxen for fifteen years. [My father] worked near the Turtle River for about two years. He even started a farm there, but he was hailed out for two straight years so he didn't want to stay there. So he went to Grand Forks and from there they walked. And he met some neighbors and they wanted to come here. It was all wilderness around here. And they decided to take land just south of McIntosh. In the fall they came back and then he had to build a cabin and this cabin is still standing today and that was built in 1883. Mother came [from Decorah,

Iowa] in 1887 and they were married there. They had grown up together and had been confirmed together in Norway. And they spent their fiftieth anniversary in that log cabin." — Alma Ramse (McIntosh, MN)

"In fact, I spoke real English, as spoken in England, so when I came to Larimore [North Dakota], people laughed at me. That's the way I was taught it. I had an aunt who was married to a man there and I could get a job. He had a nursery and a farm, so I had to do some of the planting and set out trees in rows to separate the sections. He had broncos, but I didn't like them, I was afraid of them. I wasn't used to horses. So then I went to work on a section crew in Manville, [North Dakota]. The foreman was a Norwegian, and he was hard-boiled. He stood over me and looked at me and I worked like everything." — Louis Haugen (Crookston, MN)

"They had heard about this rich farming land in North Dakota, so two of the male members of the family went to investigate. They went back to Nebraska to move their families and possessions. They rented two railroad cars, freight cars, and they moved to North Dakota in 1912. There were three married men with families and two bachelors. And they rented land near Niagara, North Dakota, and all of them stayed with farming all of their lives. In 1916 they moved to Larimore, and they stayed there the rest of their lives." — Solveig Johnson (Niagara, ND)

"I recall my mother telling about how, when they were married, about two years after my father took a homestead [in Kittson County, Minnesota], about the quiet long days when she was alone, when dad wasn't home. And I know that there were days when, she said, she actually climbed up on the roof of the house, a shanty type of house, and from there she could see neighbor's houses, so she knew that she was not alone in the area." — Myrtle Rundquist (Moorhead, MN)

The Red River Valley also drew Icelanders. Pembina County, in the extreme northeast part of North Dakota, would become the home of the largest and most vibrant Icelandic settlement in North America. From a small Icelandic settlement in southern Minnesota and from a larger settlement called New Iceland in Manitoba, within a few years the Icelandic-Americans were settled in Hallson, Akra, Mountain, Gardar, Svold, Eyford, and Hensel.

"My father's people came from Iceland in 1873, and they came to Wisconsin where they were permitted to live in a vacant farmhouse and they worked for the farmer who owned the farm. Of course, at that time they could not homestead in Wisconsin because the land was all taken and they had no money to buy land. So after a number of years they moved to Minnesota, Minnesota, in Lincoln County, and they rented land there. One day an Icelandic minister named Pal Thorlaksson came by, and he was organizing Icelanders to go to Dakota and form a community. There was land to be had for homesteading in Pembina County. They moved to North Dakota in 1880, in the early part of the summer, on Whitsunday. That first summer they started building their log cabins. While they were doing this, they lived in their covered wagons. They didn't have much of anything, maybe two, three cows and a few chickens and that's about it. They came from the northern part of Iceland, both sides of my family came from that part of Iceland. My mother's folks came later, in 1888, and they came to Winnipeg. There were quite a few Icelanders there. My grandmother had two sisters who were living in Mountain, in Pembina County, so that is where they headed when they came. My father's people lived farther south, in Gardar. Rev. Thorlaksson organized [all of those communities] and worked to get them settled there. He has been called the father of the settlements there. Life was not easy, but they were so happy, and hopeful, that they just didn't feel too much the burdens that were theirs, because now they felt, 'We have land! And we can work it and we can get along,' and they were just delighted." — Kathy Thordarson (Fargo, ND)

"After Hekla, the largest volcano of Iceland, erupted, grass and other vegetation was killed and sheep had little fodder. There was much talk about providing a better living in America. They came to Canada and settled at Gimli, on Lake Winnipeg. They were among the first settlers landing there, September 1st, 1876. They built a log cabin immediately on the shore of the lake. That winter a smallpox epidemic broke out among the settlers and many died. The following spring Harkriemer left for Dakota Territory where many of his friends had taken homesteads. The trip was made by ox team to St. Vincent. The Red River was crossed by ferry to Pembina then they walked most of the way to Gardar." — Rosa Campbell (Moorhead, MN)

"In North Dakota they settled north of Hallson, the first store in the community, that's about ten or eleven miles north of Cavalier. They homesteaded the land there. Rev. Pal Thorlaksson had scouted the area and suggested that it would be a good place for the Icelanders to settle because they had come over in rather large numbers. My father's parents came first to New Iceland, around the Gimli area, and then went to Winnipeg and then came south to North Dakota. On my mother's side, her parents had stopped at Nova Scotia for six years and then came to Duluth and from Duluth to North Dakota. … There were three ways to acquire land—a tree claim, homestead, or a quit-claim deed, but they got theirs by homesteading. They were farmers for as long as they were there, although my grandfather was a lay doctor, if you want to call him that, and did assist with childbirth as a mid-wife and also with some of the minor diseases that he had a knowledge of and the medicine that he could use." — Wayne E. Dinusson (Fargo, ND)

"My dad came from Iceland when he was nineteen or twenty, in 1876, and came to Gardar, North Dakota. From there they moved to Morten, Manitoba [in 1901]. I don't know how many years they were there, but from there they went out to Saskatchewan. He was a farmer and we were a big family, seven girls and three boys. My father had an uncle living in Gardar, and he sent for him. ... We lived in a home of a friend of ours while we were building our house. It was a log house. It was a two-story house. The logs were, well, you wouldn't know they were logs because they were plastered in between. We used calamine—like a whitewash. But it was crowded for all of us. There were three bedrooms upstairs [for a family of twelve], and a dining room and a parlor and my dad later built a lean-to for a kitchen. It was exciting to watch the house go up. ... It was cold. We had to thaw out the water to make coffee. The kitchen was so cold that we had to carry the milk and cream and stuff we didn't want to freeze into the living room." — Freda Bjornson (Moorhead, MN)

"They settled in Ontario to begin with, but the land was too poor there to make a living. They moved out of there and went to Halifax and started on a farm, but that was right in the woods and the topsoil was so thin, the soil so poor, that they couldn't even raise potatoes so they moved out of there. They had been working in Halifax as carpenters, though, so they got along. Then they moved to Gimli for a while and from there they went into Winnipeg. Finally my dad moved to Akra, in North Dakota. My dad was hired out to chop wood and mother was a cook. Then they decided to move to the Mouse River settlement [in North Dakota] and that's were they homesteaded on a quarter of land. Southeast of Kramer about three miles. There were eight of us children, one died in infancy. We had a house that

wasn't large. We had a kitchen, a front room, and three bedrooms upstairs."
— Leo Hillman (Mountain, ND)

"They came to Canada first … and then they came to North Dakota. It seems like most Icelanders came to Canada first. They settled in the Svold area, both families. That's where they each purchased land. The whole area—Svold, Akra, Hallson, Mountain, Gardar, Edinburg—that whole area is all Icelanders. The second generation learned to speak English, they all did. The first generation, no. They were all Icelanders so there was never any reason for them to learn English. These little towns all had their own stores, where they'd bring their cream and eggs and things, and the people who owned them were all Icelanders." — Diane Volrath (Hitterdal, MN)

Most of the Red River Valley land was taken by 1900, but in western North Dakota and Montana, land was still free. The United States government bet the settlers one hundred and sixty acres that they could not live on the prairie for five years. In some areas, there was enough timber to build a wooden claim shack or even a log house. In other areas, the prairie sod was cut and shaped to form blocks for a "temporary" house. The number of years between the "soddie" and the first frame house would depend on the weather, insects, grain prices, hail storms, and the ambition and faith of the homesteader.

"My mother and I came to America a year after my dad did. He had gone out and built a shanty. He came to South Dakota and filed a claim at Redfield [Dakota Territory]. He didn't know exactly where [his homestead] was, so he hired a man to haul his lumber out to build his shanty and, of course, he had to have his stove and all his kitchen utensils with him on that land so he started housekeeping. He was just by himself then, and he put up his shanty right in the middle of his claim because he didn't know where the lines were. His uncle had come there a year ahead of him, he lived about five miles from our place. His uncle had kept writing him about America. He was a carpenter too, and he got a job with his uncle building houses. He hired a man with a team of mules to break up ten acres, which was required by the homestead law. You had to break up ten acres the first year you had it. Then after a while he bought a team of horses, and done his own plowing. Wheat was the main thing we sold, he didn't sell anything else. We tried to grow a little corn, but it all dried up." — Ole Olson (Fargo, ND)

"[My grandfather] and his brother married these two sisters and they all came together to Valley City. And then they took homesteads and that's where they settled down and then all of his brothers owned land around there. ... I think it was a little hard for my mother to get used to [the North Dakota Prairie]. I think mother used to get a little lonesome. She never said anything about it, but I think she would have liked to go back to Norway."

— Dagne Faust (Colfax, ND)

"Five of my uncles, brothers of my mother, homesteaded in Dakota territory. Even my grandfather homesteaded out there later on. Some went to Rock lake, or Perth, or Knox, and then Grandfather and the youngest son went all the way out to Divide County and descendants are still living there." — William Nelson (Rollag, MN)

"Turtle Lake, at that time, was at the end of the line. My mother and some of the women were in the caboose of the freight train that brought the cattle up, but several of them came by horse and wagon. Several families from Rochester, six or eight families, heard about the boom out in North Dakota and that land was real cheap and that they could go out there and homestead. So these people all went out there and took a homestead. They were all Scandinavian, all Norwegians in that area. There was one German man, and he had a grocery store about a mile away from us. I don't remember any Swedes out in that part of the country." — Mabel Fynskov (Osakis, MN)

"When they came out to Turtle Lake to take their homestead [in 1900], it was in the month of March, and the snow was so deep that they had to drive a sleigh from Washburn to Turtle Lake, forty miles from Washburn. There were no roads so they had to drive the railroad track to Turtle Lake and from there they went to the homestead, twelve miles north of Turtle Lake. And then Dad had to build up a house there with scrap lumber he picked up from along the railroad. And then they made a sod house out of it by cutting sod out of the ground and piling it like bricks. And they had to live there until they got enough together to make a farm home. They had four horses to start with and two pigs and two cows." — Lloyd Westrum (Moorhead, MN)

"There was quite a few. Several of the neighbors from down there had come from Norway and banded together and they came up here to file of these homesteads. So they did that in the spring and then they hurried and got lumber and got these shacks, they called 'em, you know, the first house. And then we, mother and us kids, came in June, because they had these buildings built by the time we got up here. And we came on the Soo Line to Braddock, that's where we lived, and Dad met us there. We lived about ten miles from Hazelton, in what they called the Buchanan Valley. All the Norwegians tried get as close together as they possibly could. In 1914, the folks sold the homestead and moved up closer to McKensie. It was so isolated around where we were and this was closer to Bismarck. And it was awfully unhandy when they didn't have cars and mother had to come up to Bismarck to see the doctor sometimes. She had T.B. They had to take the train up one day and come back the next, stay overnight in Bismarck. So that's why they bought the place by McKensie." — Matilda Blumer (Hazelton, ND)

"He originally settled in Fillmore County, Minnesota. He went by train from New York to Fillmore County, and he knew about this before he left Norway. … And that's where he met his wife. It was in 1898 that he went from there to North Dakota. He got as far as Devil's Lake by train, and then he walked up to another little town of Knox, and his land was about eleven miles north of Knox. One of the requirements was that he had to live on this land for five years and put buildings on it. He built a barn, I don't know how large it was, but above the barn, above the stalls, he built a loft, and that was his home. He went back in 1902 and got married in Harmony, Minnesota, and came back to North Dakota. He live in this loft until he got married and then they built a home. [The house] was like two rooms, a living room and a bedroom, I suppose, and the living room was a living room, that's where everything was! The kitchen and the living room, and then there were two rooms up above and they had a hole in the ceiling with a ladder and that's how you got to these rooms. And years later they built on one big room, which was the dining area and kitchen, and pantry and two big porches." — Alpha Bowersox (Wolford, ND)

"My folks were married in the spring of 1901 and moved out to North Dakota in the spring of 1905. They homesteaded about twelve miles north of Balfour, North Dakota. I remember the first time I went to Balfour. I was just five years old and there was just one tree on the prairie between there and Balfour. We just had a claim shanty that first summer, but they built a house that fall, I think it was twelve by fourteen. They started a sod house, but they decided they better make it wooden. I think they left North Dakota because Dad liked to go hunting and fishing, for his sake, and she was kind of homesick for her folks. … Between Balfour and us it was all Scandinavian, but to the southeast there were Germans. It seemed like they all got along together great out there." — Nilmer Bjorndal (Hawley, MN)

"My dad started the homestead with four horses, some cows, chickens, a cat and a dog, a walking breaking plow, a drag, a drill, and some lumber. He built a frame shack and put sod all around it and on the roof, and made a sod barn and a sod chicken coop and then he built a wood granary. I think he loaded everything on the wagon that he needed when he came down from Dickenson. When he built the sod barn, he went out to the Badlands where he cut poles for the roof. Then, netting over that and then straw on top of that for a roof, a nice warm barn. And a nice warm house, and Mama had those windows just full of plants that blossomed all the time. And it was cool in the summer. The walls was only two and a half foot thick!" — Ralph Simonson (Bowman, ND)

"They settled in Wisconsin—Independence—and there they farmed. I think there were a lot of Norwegian settlers there at the time. Dakota wasn't even a territory then. Dad came out [to Bowman, North Dakota] in 1904, picked out his quarter, and went back to Wisconsin, and came back out here and homesteaded in 1906. They took an immigrant train out to Dickenson, North Dakota, loaded everything on a wagon, and then came on down. It took him two days to get down here, about eight miles south of Buffalo Springs, a little town that doesn't exist anymore. They made thirty miles a day with a team, pretty good. … I was born the twenty-seventh of

September, 1915, and I weighed less than three pounds. My folks wrapped me in cotton batting and put me in my dad's shoebox and set me on the oven door to keep warm. And the midwife that was there when I was born said, 'Oh, there's no use bothering with that thing. She won't live anyhow!' And my mother had no more use for her." — Eloise Kromarek (Boman, ND)

"He built a small sod house, and then he moved another small board house over from North Dakota. I think it took sixteen horses to move this house. They put it on timbers and moved it twenty miles across the prairie. They borrowed the horses from the neighbors, because he farmed with oxen the first couple of years. ... There were no trees out there, but my father started a grove and it did quite well until a terrible hailstorm hit in 1916, and that killed almost all the trees." — Louise Anderson (Fargo, ND)

"When the Golden Valley opened up, near Beech, they all went out there. There must have been fifteen or twenty families from Hitterdal alone. They all went out there to homestead. There was this one guy from Hitterdal ... and he was a band leader and he was a ballplayer. So when he got out there he had enough experienced ball players and band members that he started his own band and his own ball team. Near Carlyle is where they homesteaded, south of Beech, thirty miles. And he built a little store and that's where they had their band and their ball diamond. It's still remaining and I have a picture of it. ... [When I went out there] they just put [the shacks] up temporary, to get along. Well, I made it a little bit bigger so I had a twenty-six foot shack and it was only a one-board shack, you know. But after we had been there for a little while, we had church at our place one Sunday. They brought stuff for dinner, potluck, you know ... **[Where did you stay until you built the place?]** Where did I stay? In the wagon box, right out on the prairie. I had a new wagon. I had an older wagon and Pa had what they called a mountain wagon—four-inch tires! So when I was going to leave for Montana he traded wagons with me. He gave me the best end of the deal. Ten and a half feet long, three feet wide! I was out there all alone. My cousin was with me, of course. [My wife] was in Ulen at the time. She came a while afterwards. **[At this point, Mrs. Gregorson interrupted: 'I was out there before Thanksgiving! You said if I didn't come out there you were coming back.']** Well, she was raised in a good home. So was I. She had a profession—she was a schoolteacher—where I didn't have anything, only labor. I'd never gone to school much or anything. But that was the situation. This was fourteen miles into Montana, near the divide between North and South Dakota. You could 'prove up' after a year and a half with money, $1.25 an acre. But you had to have water, so much fence and so much of this, so many acres plowed and so long as you had that, why you get your patent, the same as a deed now, from the government, but you had to pay them $1.25 an acre for this transaction. But if you didn't want to do that, you could live on it five years and then you got it free. I paid for it. ... It was tough to take, you know. You crawl in a boxcar and leave home and you've never been away from home and go right out into the open and foot your own canoe. The same with her. Why, she was raised in a good home and here I bring her out on the prairie in Montana in a shack, sixteen by twenty-six, one wall. Nothing on the floor except the board, wallboards and all these things, you know. It was hard to cope. It was hard, but it wasn't any harder for us than it was for anybody else, you see. This was a common thing, it was just starting out. People didn't live like that later on, they started farming, you know. We worked to beat the devil the first year we was there because, you see, I plowed ten acres for another man that first summer and we had fifty-one acres broke on our own homestead. Four horses pulling a single bottom plow. The land had never been plowed, all virgin. … I said to Ma one day, 'I'm going to go down to this rancher and get acquainted with him.' When I got down there he was standing on his knees fixing on this old horse disc. He had his little boy with him. He hated me because I was a homesteader, sodbuster, oh yah! So I rode up to him and stuck out my hand and greeted him and said, 'Can you tell me where the southwest corner of my quarter is here in your pasture?' I was kind of snotty, too, you know. You had to be. He says, 'It's right up there on that side hill where you see them white stones.' In the meantime, they had put a dam in there in a little creek that ran between us and my other neighbor from the southeast. It was a dry creek and the only water that run there was when it was an overflow. But, you see, the ranchers had made this little lake, with a dam, so they had water for their cattle, and it was on our land. That's what he was scared of, that he was going to lose his water. So he says, 'Are you going to fence your place?' 'No, I hadn't thought about that. But I'll tell you one thing before you go any further,' I said, 'I'm from Minnesota, and from the area we come from, we're human beings and I know what's the matter with you. You think you're going to lose this water, but you're not! As long as we live here you're going to have that water for your cattle.' It didn't bother us a bit. It was good for me, too. He brightened right up and all the ranchers knew me from then on. Everyone was so nice and it all started out all on account of that little water in that pool. We got to be the best of friends." — Obert Gregorson (Ulen, MN)

"In that two years, I think I was into Baker [Montana—the nearest town] twice. Because we went to Baker to church. It was the closest church. We went there one Sunday, and we stayed at the home of Haugen. He was from Lake Park. He was the one that was sponsor to our oldest son. A hundred miles from the railroad and seventy miles from the doctor in an old homestead shack on the prairie. That's where my oldest boy was born. ... If they'd given me Montana—the north side to the south—I wouldn't have stayed there." — Anna Gregorson (Ulen, MN)

In the summer of 1912, the Gregorson's dreams were ruined by a hail storm that destroyed their flax crop.

"Things were getting tougher by the hour. We had a little boy now, you see. So we left and went back to Minnesota in 1912. When I left that homestead it was snowing a few little sprinkles, but I made it to Beech that night. Bareback horseback, seventy miles in one day! That's good riding. Hard to beat! I had sores all over my hinder. I didn't have no saddle, not at that time. We had to sell a few things, you know. We got eight hundred dollars for the land. I borrowed four hundred dollars on it, and of course, we put something into it. I think I had two hundred and fifty dollars left." **["Would you like to do it again, Mrs. Gregorson?"]** "Absolutely No! I would never do it!" **["Would you like to do it again, Mr. Gregorson?"]** "Well, I enjoyed it. For the simple reason that I got what I wanted. I was all for this trip and we started out on a wild goose chase and we made our own home, we had a few dollars, had our own horses. I was always more of a hobo type." — Obert Gregorson (Ulen, MN)

"I filed for my homestead [in Montana] in 1912. I believe it was the same day Wilson was elected. Land was getting scarce by that time. Most of it was taken. A fellow had taken the quarter I got but he had never moved on to it so he had to relinquish it. I got a lawyer to work the papers for me. It was good farmland, but it never rained there and a lot of us went broke. That's when I moved back to Fargo." — Ole Olson (Fargo, ND)

"I came in August, just the time when all the fruit was coming in, and my sister had this big box of peaches. I stayed with her for about three weeks and then I said 'I gotta go out and make some money so I can go home to Sweden again,' so I went out and got myself a job [housekeeping, in Glendive, Montana]. He was Norwegian, she was Danish, the children spoke English, and I spoke Swedish. Four different languages! I worked for those people for nine months, and I could speak a little English. But they had small children, and I wanted to be a little more free so I could be out in the evenings more. So I got a job with an American family and they had no children. I stopped to see them on Sunday and asked for the job and told her I was a girl from Sweden and she said 'That's the kind of people we want,' she said, 'because I've had Swedish girls before and they are very good workers,' and she said, 'Can you bake bread?' 'Oh yes,' I said, 'I can bake bread, but I can't speak very good English.' She said, 'You will learn.' I stayed there for two years, then." — Anna Lindgren (Fargo, ND)

"My father came from Denmark and went to Chicago, or Gary, Indiana, and the next spring they loaded up their possessions and went to the western part of North Dakota, but most of that was homesteaded at that time so they went across the border into Montana. So they built their home there and started to live as squatters until the government came out and surveyed the land so they could homestead. They went back to Denmark with the idea of staying. They bought a place in Denmark when they went back. But that life was sort of an illusion, I suppose. They felt everything would be wonderful if they could go back home, but coming back there, for the better part of a year, they both decided it was the wrong move. ... My father moved out to Montana in 1906. My grandfather worked for Mitchell's Wagon Factory in Racine, Wisconsin, which was a place where many Scandinavians, and especially the Danes, worked when they came over. One day Grandfather and his best friend were walking home from church and they took a short cut and walked on the railroad tracks and they were both killed. So Grandmother had four grown sons and two daughters and she decided it would be a good idea to take these boys out west, so they decided to go homesteading out there. My mother met my dad out there and shortly after that they were married. Mother never went back to Denmark, but Dad made two or three trips back, shortly after coming to this country, but afterward he just didn't seem to have any interest in going back. One of the advantages to coming to Montana was that it was a very arid country so they allowed them to take three hundred and twenty acres for homestead whereas across the line in North Dakota the limit was one hundred and sixty. But after they all started coming in there was more control and the ranchers had to fence what they claimed was their domain and keep their stock under control. ... The first house they had probably had to be, oh, forty-fifty miles from the nearest town, usually a two day trip. ... When my dad first came out there, he met a farmer one day that was a Norwegian not too far from the Danish settlement there. This Norwegian was a Mr. Quam that had come across from Canada and they got to be friends and they got to talking about what they were going to do and Dad said, 'I've planted a crop now, but I don't know what I'm going to do when the crop grows up and gets ready for harvest because I don't have a binder!' He looks at Pa and says, 'Well, that's very simple, I live so many miles northwest of here in Canada, so you just come up when you are ready to harvest, because we'll already have harvested and we'll load my binder on your lumber wagon and you just haul it home and you can cut your crop and your neighbor's crop as much as you want. So Dad made the trip up there and they loaded the binder on the lumber wagon and Dad said that was the most treacherous trip that he had ever made because the wagon got very top-heavy. … And that was the way we harvested that first crop. I would imagine the trip was about fifty miles. … Mother found it stark and desolate, especially having moved from Racine, Wisconsin, where everything was so beautiful and so many trees. It looked pretty barren, but we were all in the same fix. Most of the Danes had stopped for a while further east before they went to the homestead. … I was born in the sod shack. We didn't have any doctor out there and my older sister and I were both brought into the world without one." — Phillip Anderson (Fargo, ND)

If the nearest town were forty miles away, one might think that the least of one's worries would be how to get along with the neighbors. Yet, as is apparent from the preceding accounts, this was of primary importance. An agreement over water rights allowed for a symbiotic

relationship between a cattleman and a sodbuster. A binder was loaned by a Norwegian-Canadian to a Danish-American who had apparently planted his crop in the belief that "God would provide." Neighbors, Scandinavian or not, could come in handy, and the immigrants soon learned to adjust to them.

Chapter V

"It Helps Sometimes to Know Who Your People Are"

SCANDINAVIAN ETHNICITY AND THE FRONTIER

As the Scandinavian immigrants spread out across the Upper Midwest they came into contact with other ethnic groups. Many Norwegians had never met anyone outside of their own valley, but six weeks after they left the Old Country they might have an Irishman or a Pole for a neighbor and would have to depend on him. For the first immigrants, such an experience was both frustrating and isolating. As fellow Scandinavians and fellow countrymen arrived, however, the transition for these later arrivals was considerably easier. They found a familiar cultural landscape and made it into an even more familiar community until many of the settlements of the Upper Midwest appeared to be literal transplants from Scandinavia. Oslo, Minnesota, was founded by, named by, and settled by Norwegians, and Malmo, Minnesota, was founded by, named by, and settled by Swedes. But in many other places, such as Decorah, Iowa, and Hawley, Minnesota, and any number of towns that grew up around the railroad sidings of the Northern Pacific and the Great Northern railroads, Scandinavians took over an existing community and made it their own.

The Scandinavian Americans who were interviewed for this study were asked about the ethnic make-up of their home communities. The collective response indicated the extent of Scandinavian settlement in those communities, but it also revealed how the respondent viewed himself and other ethnic groups. One of the difficulties in dealing with oral history is that one is dealing with memories that can be partial or even creative. A statement that a community was one hundred percent Norwegian may come as a surprise to the five German families who lived there. In like manner, perhaps the Swedes, who made up only ten percent of the community, were so significant in the mind of the person being interviewed that he remembered his community as being "half Norwegian, half Swede." For the most part, the issue of ethnic awareness was related directly to the opportunity to interact with other ethnic groups. For many of the Scandinavian immigrants, that opportunity was not much greater in the Upper Midwest than it had been in the Old Country.

"I don't recall any [other ethnic groups]. I think they were all either Norwegians or Swedes in Hitterdal at that time. I don't recall any certain, any other family that wasn't. In all the public places you went into, most of the conversation carried on was in Scandinavian" — Wilferd Anderson (Hitterdal, MN)

"Everything was Swedish. There wasn't anything else in that whole community. We had one poor little guy there who was a Norwegian, one guy, the blacksmith. That's as solid as it was! He was a good blacksmith. Oh, solid! The whole community of Scania [Minnesota]. Everything was transacted in Swedish until I was probably eighteen years old, and then things started to change a little bit. I was confirmed in Swedish, but my brother, who was five years younger, had an option, and he got an English Bible. So things had started to change, but in my age, everything was Swedish." — Carl Elmquist (Moorhead, MN)

"There was an awful lot of Norwegians, you know, when a person from a certain community come, then there would be a lot of friends, you know, that would come from the same place so that way there were a lot of people who knew one another from the old country. It was 'pert-near' all Norwegians [near Underwood]." — Clara Johnson (Underwood, ND)

"In the first years, up to about 1875, it was about fifty-fifty Scandinavians and English-speaking people. The English-speaking people lived mostly in the eastern half of Parke Township [Clay County, Minnesota], while the Scandinavians lived in the western half. But when I was born, just after the turn of the century, I would imagine it was close to ninety-five percent Scandinavian. The others had moved away. Those that were left of the English-speaking people had learned to talk Norwegian. … We spoke all Norwegian in our home at that time when I grew up. But I suppose the Swedes did the same. But the Swedish boys who grew up in this area, they didn't talk Swedish. It was so overwhelming Norwegian that they talked Norwegian, too." — William Nelson (Rollag, MN)

"Hawley, in the early days, the first settlers were English people. But the Norwegians and Scandinavians took over, it was such that in a grocery store, if you wanted to come in there and get a job as a clerk, if you couldn't speak Norwegian, well, you'd be out of luck. With the exception of the hotels in town—they were English people—the Norwegians had taken over so completely that if you couldn't speak Norwegian, you couldn't get a job. … Parke Township was just about ninety-five percent Scandinavian. There was only one family in our school that wasn't, well his dad was Norwegian, but his mother was German. And they didn't use the Scandinavian language at all at home. But he was the only one. There was one family of Swedes and another family that was half Swede and half Norwegian." — Oscar Bratlien (Hawley, MN)

"[In eastern Clay County] in the earliest times I think it was mostly Scandinavian, Norwegian and Swedish. I can't remember anything else. There probably were others, but I don't remember them." — Bernice Herfindal (Lake Park, MN)

"There might have been some non-Norwegians in the Twin Valley area, but I never knew of them. There was no Swedish church or Danish church, just those three Norwegian synods." — Carl Narveson (Moorhead, MN)

"Clearbrook was about fifty-fifty, Swedes and Norwegians. They were all Scandinavians. I think we did [feel right at home]." — Elsie Gale (Clearbrook, MN)

"Everybody in Clearbrook spoke Norwegian [in 1916]. The hotel man who met us at the depot and everybody who met us was Norwegian and the banker was Norwegian. It was right at home for us. Clearbrook was ninety percent Scandinavian. There were a few Swedes, enough to have their own church." — Lloyd Westrum (Moorhead, MN)

"They didn't need to know the English language [in Garfield, Minnesota] at all, and they didn't learn it either. My father's mother and father never learned to speak the English language; Grandfather was eighty-seven when he died and Grandmother was eighty-nine. In Garfield, all their neighbors were Swedish and they would go into town and the people who had their business establishments—they were all Swedish." — Catherine Fossay (Moorhead, MN)

"Other groups, like the Norwegians and Swedes, had already kind of made a little niche for themselves and settled down, and worked themselves into the society. And the Finns came later, and there was a bigger society as they might have looked at it, and this is not against them, but established into the United States system. And they were a smaller group on the outside. The

Finns were rather a clannish group. They stuck together very closely. Basically, in Europe, and in Finland too, being governed by outsiders for so many years, they had a tendency to stick together for their own self-protection and progress. So when they came to this country, they carried much of the same feeling with them. ... When I came to New York Mills [Minnesota], the small children spoke Finnish to each other on the streets, and of course that's a thing of the past. And then of course, the second generation married Finnish people so they spoke Finnish at home."
— Russell Parta (New York Mills, MN)

"Between Balfour [North Dakota] and us it was all Scandinavian, but to the southeast there were Germans. It seemed like they all got along together great out there." — Nilmer Bjorndahl (Hawley, MN)

"Everybody spoke Norwegian. And when you went uptown in Kindred [North Dakota] they were all speaking it. That is, when I was a little girl. And by and by, well by the time that I graduated from high school in Kindred, you heard more English. It was only Norwegians who settled in Kindred ... one hundred percent! Oh, there were some Swedes around the Kindred area, too, I guess." — Gunhild Laske (Kindred, ND)

"In the Abercrombie [North Dakota] area, before 1900, I would say there were seventy-five to eighty percent Norwegians, but then, between 1900 and say, 1914, there was maybe ninety to ninety-five percent Norwegians. After that there were quite a few people who came up from the southern states and that cut down the Norwegian percentage." — Palmer Tverdal (Abercrombie, ND)

"Mother never learned to talk English. We lived in a group of Americans who couldn't talk any Norwegian, and she couldn't talk any English so she never associated with any of them. We were there seven years and never a woman came into our house from the Americans and my mother never went to their place. There was one family of Norwegians about half a mile from us. Dad learned a little English when he was sailing, so he could help himself in a way. A kid my age, we played with him so much that he taught us how to talk English." — Ole Olson (Fargo, ND)

"I was totally Americanized right away!" — Anna Lindgren (Fargo, ND)

Perhaps Anna Lindgren was right, if becoming "Americanized" meant adjusting to a multi-ethnic and multi-cultural society. For many immigrants, adjustment to America meant adopting at least some of the elements of the host culture and abandoning elements of their old culture. Whether the confrontation with other ethnic groups represented a challenge or an opportunity often depended on the individual and his perception of himself and his neighbor.

The Scandinavians had already formed certain negative opinions of other nationalities even before they left the Old Country. This is

indicated by the fact that by the early 1870s Swedish emigrant agents were promising in their advertising brochures that the Swedes "would not be thrown together with the Irish."

"We went to country school one term there [near Brewster, Minnesota] and after that we went to town school. ... There wasn't any other Danes there. It was a mixed community. So the only time we heard Danish was at home. So we must have picked English up quite easily, the younger ones of us, because we went over to the neighbors and played with the children and they came over to our place and played. ... We made raisin bread and rhubarb pudding. But when you live in a community [that had so few Danes] and have hired help—they didn't care for 'foreign' food so you didn't have much of it. After we moved up here we had none of it because everybody else was all Norwegian." — Tora Jeppesen Johnson (Brewster, MN)

"I'd estimate that at least fifty percent had a Finnish background. I would say that once they were in America, even though the Finns on the Iron Range were rather cliquish, they would stay on with their own things just as the Croatian people and the Italians. They all had their own halls, and a lot of their social activities went on that way with the first generation that came over. With the second generation all that was gone, but they became more American than Finnish." — Karen Kivi (Moorhead, MN)

"There weren't very many Swedes in that area [Douglas County, Minnesota], mostly Germans, so she learned to speak German almost as well as she spoke Swedish. At home they spoke Swedish, of course." — Hazel Monson Barker (Moorhead, MN)

"The [Osakis, Minnesota] area was mostly Norwegian, and most of them was from our area in Norway. And also a few Swedes mixed in, here and there, not too many. North of us there were a few more Swedes. There were a few other nationalities, but they were very good people, and they were good friends. They used these others as a source to learn English, because they could speak English already. My brother worked for one and he learned English that way." — John Klukken (Osakis, MN)

"In school, the German kids were nicer than we were because they never spoke German, but we'd get together and speak Swedish to beat the band. They were more civilized than we were, I'm sure. Probably they didn't know German. I think a little better than half of the kids were Swedish, the rest were German [in Scandia, Minnesota]." — Carl Elmquist (Moorhead, MN)

"The Norwegians didn't think of themselves as being inferior to the Americans. The Norwegians themselves, in that community [Doran, Minnesota] were very proud of their accomplishments and their background, and they felt that they were superior to a lot of the other immigrants."
— Allan Erickson (Moorhead, MN)

"I think they were all Norwegians in Terrace [Minnesota]. Swedes and Norwegians. Oh, there was one German family, but they never associated with us." — Ellen Abraham (Villard, MN)

"This particular area [Underwood, Minnesota] was constituted eighty percent Norwegian, ten percent Dane, five percent Swede, and another five percent for Germans and one Irish family. It was pretty much a little Norway for many, many years. This part of Ottertail County was similar to much of Norway because of the lakes and forest." — John Gronner (Underwood, MN)

"Other than the Norwegians, there were a lot of Danes [around Underwood], and there were a lot of Germans, but there were not many Swedes here. I don't know just where there was any Swedish community. They got along fine. There was no trouble. But there was one Irish family, and the Norwegians started a petition to get rid of the Irish, a large family, anyhow. But they stayed. I see their name in the paper now. And they did very well and they married nice girls. It was like the white people who didn't like the Negroes, the black people. And you know it's funny. They did well. They were clannish. The Finnish people were awful clannish. The Norwegians are too and I suppose the Swedes are too." — Clara Johnson (Underwood, ND)

"The Norwegians and the Swedes got along real well, but there was some friction between some of the English speaking people and the

Scandinavians. My dad used to tell of a little fracas that they had over in [school] District Three [Clay County, Minnesota] once. They used to have debate societies in those years, and things like that. And on this particular occasion, the old log schoolhouse was packed full of people and a bunch of these Norwegian young guys and a Swede were standing in back and a bunch of English speaking boys thought they'd have a little fun and they started tramping on the floor. The moderator blamed it on the Norwegians, of course, and told them to quit. Well, they didn't say anything and after a while they started tramping on the floor again. And the third time the moderator told the Norwegians to get out. Of course, they decided they had to do something about it so they used their fists the best they could, and after a while they cleaned out the whole schoolhouse. Just the Norwegians and this here Swede, a fellow by the name of Bernhard Hellgren, and he had been in many fights back in Sweden, I guess. He was a little older, and he had no fear, and I guess they could probably give credit to him. After that they got along much better." — William Nelson (Rollag, MN)

"In our area [north of Hawley, Minnesota] I'd say most of them, seventy-five percent, were Norwegian. There were some Germans, Swedes, Danes, and a couple of families of Bohemians. They seemed to get along pretty good. They had their different churches. The Swedish people, though, came to our Norwegian church. We got along OK." — Johanna Aune (Hawley, MN)

"There weren't very many Scandinavians who could speak English. In this area [Hawley, Minnesota], it was all Scandinavians, just about, and a few 'Yermans,' too. I never learned a word of English before 1912. There were no problems. We were all the same in those days. 'Yermans,' and Englishmen, and Norwegians, and Swedes—they were all the same." — John Norman (Hawley, MN)

"The whole community was Norwegian [in Morken Township, Clay County, Minnesota], but at those parties we young people would mostly talk English, but I guess when my parents were growing up [in the 1890s] it was all Norwegian. I'd say [the Norwegians] were a bit cliquey, but as they got acquainted [with the Germans] they got along all right." — Minnie Tiedeman (Moorhead, MN)

"We seemed to have a lot of Irish to begin with in this country, but they seemed to sort of fade way. North of Lake Park was a lot of Norwegians and south of Lake Park was a lot of Swedes and amongst the Swedes was some Irish, too. My first schoolteacher was Irish and she could not speak Swedish so, of course, I had to learn English a little bit. They all seemed to get along pretty good. They all had to lean on each other." — Amy Erickson (Moorhead, MN)

"In Becker County [Minnesota], there it was about ninety percent Scandinavian. The other ten percent was German. I suppose among the Scandinavians it was about fifty-fifty, Norwegians and Swedes. And the older folks, they got along good talking, but among us kids, when somebody would say something in dialect in Norwegian, he was kind of hard to understand, so among the kids we talked English, we didn't talk Swede or Norwegian unless we talked to our parents. The Germans didn't associate with the Scandinavians, unless they wanted to borrow something, or had some business deal. Other than that, they stuck to themselves." — Charles Westerholm (Moorhead, MN)

"To begin with, I don't think there was anybody but Swedes until 1928 or somewhere and then two German bachelors moved in. They came from Iowa and farmed just a mile from us. I don't know of any other nationality moving in. There weren't any Norwegians near Malmo." — Amy Margaret Erickson (Wheatland, ND)

"Well, I think there was some [ethnic bias in Kittson County, Minnesota]. I think the Swedish people considered themselves to be a little better than the Polish people. This [was evident] in conversation, perhaps, when people would refer to a certain family or something." — Myrtle Rundquist (Moorhead, MN)

"Where they were [near Fertile, Minnesota] there were only two families, who moved in later, who weren't Scandinavians. They were German. They didn't associate with us too much until much later, then it was different. They didn't speak [to each other] either, because one was high

German and one was low, so they didn't understand each other. We always felt sorry for them." — Anna Melberg (Moorhead, MN)

"They were all [Norwegians] in [Ulen, Minnesota] at that time [1880s]. I didn't hear of any other nationality at the time, although later on there were two German families, a Swedish family, and an Irish family."— Clara Hanson (Moorhead, MN)

"The Finns on the Iron Range were very clannish. They stuck to themselves. The old timers, you know, you couldn't get them to speak English. In the stores we had to get Finnish speaking girls to wait on them." — Borghild Overby (Moorhead, MN)

"Lots of foreigners in Ironton [Minnesota] in 1912–1913. Mostly foreigners! Austrians, Montenegrans, Italians, and there were a lot of Swedes. The Norwegian part was very small. And there were different kinds of Swedes. The Finn-Swede and the Swede-Finn. They were hard labor people—saw men and ax men and shovel men—hard labor people. The Swedes were, as a rule, pretty clever, mechanically minded it seemed. The bosses were mostly Swede." — Obert Gregorson (Ulen, MN)

"Oh no, there was only Norwegian and Swede around there [Abercrombie, North Dakota] and there was scattered, like German, when you got further south along the river, and farther southwest there were a lot of Bohemians. But, they were all good people. There was no friction whatever. The Norwegian people they settled with, they were the nicest folks you could wish to have." — Frank Alm (Christine, ND)

"When I was a boy the [Hallson, North Dakota] area was sixty-five to seventy percent Icelandic. There were Germans in Cavalier and some Russians, but very few Norwegians or Swedes." — Wayne E. Dinusson (Fargo, ND)

"It was about ninety-five percent Icelandic [in the Akra, North Dakota area]. There was one family of Germans. They were very nice and we never had any problems with them. As far as church, I don't know where they went to Church. I think ... they got together in their homes because there wasn't a German church there. We didn't have any Norwegians or Swedes in the area. They were all Icelandic." — Diane Volrath (Hitterdal, MN)

"There was a German minister and his family that moved in [to the Turtle Lake, North Dakota area], and the Russians, and there was some English people who came. And we went to school with all these people, you know, and we got along just fine. Of course, they kind of laughed at us because we couldn't talk English. But the Germans couldn't talk English either." — Mabel Fynskov (Osakis, MN)

"The only time we saw those German parents was when we had our annual picnic in school. Then they would sit by themselves and we would sit by ourselves. But it was nice, just the same." — Mabel Enger (Oakes, ND)

"The community [Bowman, North Dakota] was about fifty percent [Norwegian]. There were Germans, Danes, Poles, Bohemians, I don't know a single Swede. We got along very good. Everyone was the same. Neighbors, real friends. They didn't care what nationality you were. If you needed help, you got it. The doors were always open. If you came there and they weren't home, you went in and made yourself a meal and washed the dishes and maybe you left a note and maybe you didn't. You were welcome." — Eloise Kromarek (Boman, ND)

"Maddock [North Dakota] was about seventy-five percent Scandinavian. There was some English and Irish and a few Germans. They got along well together, they just had their own churches. I can't say there was any [rivalry]. Most of the rivalry was between the ministers. They were set in their ways." — Edwin Markestad (Maddock, ND)

"Wolford [North Dakota] was practically all Norwegian. I would say seventy percent, anyway. We had an Irish man who ran the newspaper, *The Wolford Mirror*. Of course that was in later years, and we had Greeks that worked on the railroad, section men we called them. And we had Germans. We had a barber who was a black man. I don't know what their religion was, it was only the Scandinavians who had churches. If they attended church it must have been out of town. There were two Lutheran churches, but eventually they came together. There was always [a rivalry] between the

Swedes and Norwegians, more or less of a fun thing, you know, I don't remember anything serious." — Alpha Bowersox (Wolford, ND)

"There was no telephone and no newspapers. We never had any communication at all unless we went into town. I went to school. I was one of the smartest Norwegians out there because the rest of the kids were all Germans or Russians or Irish [around Turtle lake, North Dakota]. We had scraps in school because of the nationalities. We were five families of Norwegians. And there were some Swedes. The Swedes and the Norwegians were together. We stuck together and we had our own church. … We were in the minority, but we seemed to handle ourselves better than any of them. They seemed to think we were more foreign. I think they got that from home. The Irish and the Germans seemed to have it against the Scandinavians. They were nice kids, but they were not very smart compared to the Scandinavians." — Lloyd Westrum (Moorhead, MN)

"But the Swedes never got strong in North Dakota. You had to go across the river to find bunches of them. They were in Minnesota. But out there were mostly Norwegians and Germans. Oh, I got along good with them." — Oscar Lindgren (Fargo, ND)

"We had some Polish out there [near Westby, Montana], but they kept pretty much to themselves and a couple of Scotch families living not too far from us and then there was an area of Norwegians and a few Swedes. But out there the Norwegians were the Norwegians and the Danes were the

Danes, and the transportation was so slow I think we pretty much just stayed by ourselves, except we did have a few Norwegians in our school when I grew up a little bit." — Philip Andersen (Fargo, ND)

The Scandinavian immigrants to America cooperated with other ethnic groups out of necessity or out of a determination to adjust to an America that called upon them to be part of a melting pot. Perhaps it was easier to tolerate someone of a totally different nationality, however, than it was to tolerate one's Scandinavian cousins. The Norwegians had not liked the Swedes very much back in Scandinavia, and many saw no reason why they should like them in America. The Finns, on the other hand, were often not even considered to be Scandinavian. They did not have their own nation until the Russian Revolution, their language was totally unlike that of the other Scandinavians, and it was suspected that they were of a "Mongolian race." In Norway and Sweden they were viewed as a clannish people who carried knives and drank too much. Just as Old World customs and languages were retained, so too were Old World animosities.

"I think practically the whole community [of Lake Park, Minnesota] was Scandinavian. The Swedes went to the Swedish church in the country and the Norwegians went to the Norwegian church in town. And there were two Norwegian churches, all I can remember about that is that the ministers didn't speak to each other. They were from different synods. They have now joined. There were no Catholics when we were children, if there were, I don't know where they went to church. I think there were about equal Swedes and Norwegians, and they were dispersed through the community, it wasn't all Swedish in one section and all Norwegian in another. They got along, but I wonder if there wasn't sometimes a little enmity between the two sometimes. But two of my uncles married Norwegian girls—the rest married Swedes." — Amy Erickson (Moorhead, MN)

"The Swedes and Norwegians, well, there wasn't any dissension, but when you come to look back, they didn't mingle too much. The Swedes stayed by themselves and the Norwegians stayed by themselves. They were scattered around. I delivered groceries to a place called 'Swedetown' on the north side of Moorhead. They all talked Swede out there. I took the orders in Swede and I would write it up in English." — Vic Anderson (Moorhead, MN)

"I never saw any friction at all between them [in Moorhead]. We got along. We had Norwegian members of our church. Not many, but some. The social life was mostly among the relatives. As far as getting together socially, each one stuck to themselves. ... Well, there's always been some rivalry. I've felt that I was discriminated against sometimes because I wasn't the right nationality. I had seniority once, but I was a Swede and the job went to a

Norwegian. ... But the Swedes have never been as patriotic to their old country as the Norwegians have. But I think most of my friends, when I went to school, were Norwegians." — Robert Carlander (Moorhead, MN)

"I can't really say I ever witnessed any [animosity] between us except just jokingly between the Swedes and Norwegians, except maybe they'd take a shot at each other whenever they could and make a dirty crack. But I think it was mostly in fun, although I heard later they all didn't feel that way. I know in our family we just made fun of the Norwegians, well, maybe we thought they were a little dumber than we were. But I don't know if we really thought that, it was really all in fun. But I do remember that some of the kids made it real tough for some of the Catholics in the neighborhood [in Moorhead] and during the war [World War I] some of the Germans that lived in the neighborhood—no vandalism or anything—but when someone got mad at them they said some pretty mean things." — Gladys Westrum (Moorhead, MN)

"In Moorhead, the Swedes were not the dominant people. They were sort of in the minority, and the Norwegians were the larger group. But, of course, their habits were very much like the Swedes. Most of our playmates were Norwegians and there wasn't much difference. I would say the Scandinavian population of Moorhead was about half, maybe about fifteen percent Swedish and the rest Norwegian and a few Danes. My father liked the Irish. They got along fine and there was a little, I suppose you could call it rivalry, between the Swedes and Norwegians. There were so many more Norwegians, you know, and they sort of felt that they were, I don't know, the upper crust? But they had it over the Swedes. But we got along just fine with them. We'd go to Trinity for their Christmas programs and things." — Hazel Monson Barker (Moorhead, MN)

"When my folks came here in 1871, there was only one family here, and that was a Swedish family down in the Grove [southeast of Hitterdal, Minnesota], and that was Sten Hanson, and we always had a lot to do with them. I think [the Swedes and Norwegians] always got along. That didn't make any difference. We had some of the best friends in the world who were Swedes. Yes, I always liked them. I always liked to go down there [to Swede Grove] when they served something [in Highland Grove Church]. And I tell her, 'We gotta go down to those Swedish women and get some good eats!' They'd come to our place one Sunday and we'd eat and play ball and the next Sunday we'd go to their place and we'd eat and play ball and we'd go hunting and rowing in the boat and swimming and everything together."
— Clifford Hitterdal (Hitterdal, MN)

"It was very common when they first started school [in Hitterdal] that a lot of the pupils didn't know English, and there was friction between the Norwegians and the Swedes. Although I was half Norwegian and half Swede, they called me a Swede. … There were some subtle differences. … Some thought the Swedes were superior. The Norwegians didn't think so, but the Swedes thought they were a little better." — Wilferd Anderson (Hitterdal, MN)

"There was some division between the Danes and the Norwegians. The Norwegians had their Sons of Norway lodge located two miles east of Underwood [Minnesota] and the Danes had their Danish Brotherhood south and east of Underwood, and there was rivalry between the two groups. And then the Modern Woodmen Lodge was located near the village of Underwood and there was more rivalry between these lodge groups than there was between the ethnic groups. There were Danes and Norwegians, and Swedes—all joined the Woodmen Lodge. Sometimes they got into fights. At some of the picnics, well, the evening part of the picnic, there got to be a little too much drinking. And that's when some of these things took place." — John Gronner (Underwood, MN)

"Oh, Finns never liked Swedes. The Danes and the Norwegians and the Finns get along beautifully because they all hate the Swedes for a variety of reasons." — Karen Kivi (Moorhead, MN)

"In 1906 I went to Duluth. I think I paid six dollars for an excursion ticket. There I met my husband. He was a logger. He was a Swede. He wasn't very good at English, to tell you the truth. He was thirty-six years old when he came here. But, you know, the Swedes seem 'superior' in many ways, they figure they're, uh, nothing wrong with them, so if they didn't speak English so well it didn't matter. He had come from a wealthier family.

… My husband, he thought Sweden was much better than America, you know." — Clara Johnson (Underwood, ND)

"Oakport Township [Clay County, Minnesota] was, I would say, about ninety percent Norwegian. There were some Swedes and some English, too, I guess. They got along quite well. The Norwegians would go to the Swedish church and they would have barn dances together." — Lela Hegland (Moorhead, MN)

"In Morken Township [Clay County, Minnesota] there was a sprinkling of Danish and maybe two or three that were Swedish. The rest were all Norwegians. They didn't tend to mix too much. The Norwegians stuck to themselves." — Cora Kragnes (Felton, MN)

"Everybody got along. Well, the Norwegians thought they were Norwegian, you know. I don't think they thought they were more special than anybody else, but you know how it is. But the Norwegians stuck together, they did." — Marie Tverdahl (Abercrombie, ND)

"My dad was Swedish and he was kind of aloof from [the Norwegians] because he just wanted to get away from the Norwegian-Swedish element. We had a hired man from Norway, but Dad didn't let him talk Norwegian. He had to talk English because Dad wanted him to build that up. And my dad wasn't too popular among the other people in that community [Doran, Minnesota]. One is that he wasn't religious, you see, and the other was that he was Swedish and they were Norwegian. And he never did think the Norwegians were so terrific." — Allan Erickson (Moorhead, MN)

"Crookston was a very Scandinavian community. I would say half of Crookston was Norwegian and the other half was French-Canadian Catholic. And there was a Swedish Covenant church in our neighborhood. And there was a definite rivalry between the Swedes and the Norwegians, absolutely! I could just sense it in my home because my mother was very anti-Swedish, and I suppose that was because of her background. Norway had been under the Swedes for a long time." — Ruth Erickson (Moorhead, MN)

"I think they got along very well [in the Clearbrook, Minnesota, area]. There wasn't really too big of a problem between the two of them because most of them were mixed, half-Swede and half-Norwegian. Of course, the Swedes thought they were a little better than the Norwegians and the Norwegian said, 'Well, I'm a little bit better than the Swede.' They'd just more or less say 'I belong to the Swedish church' or 'I belong to the Norwegian church.' Sure, they would have feuds, but it was nothing that polarized people. The Swedish minister would preach in Swedish and the Norwegian minister would preach in Norwegian." — Elsie Gale (Clearbrook, MN)

"We were all Swedish around there [Braham, Minnesota]. We had one Norwegian family that lived right close to us and we got along famously.

We thought a lot of those people. ... There was never any bickering because they were Norwegians and we were Swedes." — Nina Oien (Moorhead, MN)

"In the beginning, I think the Icelanders outnumbered the others for a while, but that didn't last too long, because the other people came in, more Norwegians and people from the east. They were all good people. Now they have their riff-raff." — Anna Bjornson (Fargo, ND)

"It was one hundred percent Swedish and Norwegian mixed [around Abercrombie, North Dakota], because we got moved in by those Norwegians. ..." — Frank Alm (Christine, ND)

"Some was really stubborn about [a Swedish son marrying a Norwegian daughter], yah, some was. And if he had a farm to sell, he wouldn't sell it to me [a Swede] if he was a Norwegian owner, no, he had to sell it to a Norwegian. But I had so many Norwegian neighbors that I learned to speak Norwegian before I learned to speak English." — Oscar Lindgren (Fargo, ND)

"It was very Scandinavian in the country out there by Valley City [North Dakota]. Mostly Norwegian. In the community we lived in they come from Stavanger and everybody was related and come from Stavanger. There was some Danes, but not too much Swedish, and there weren't any other churches but the Lutherans in our area." — Dagne Faust (Colfax, ND)

"We did have the rivalry between the Lutheran and the Catholic church, and there was rivalry between the Norwegians and the Swedes, too.

Because the Norwegians always resented the Swedes coming in and taking over the country and we always thought that we were more intelligent than the Swedes. And the Swedes would stick together, like in the ladies aid, and they, in turn, thought they were far superior to what we were. But we got along." — Flora Fritz (Detroit Lakes, MN)

"There was a concentration of Danes north of Kenmare [North Dakota], but most of that land was taken when Lars came, so the Danes south of Kenmare, well, it's just these three families who acquired adjoining homesteads. And the rest of the people in the immediate vicinity are mostly Norwegians and Swedes. They never spoke Scandinavian in the home when I was a child; it was always English. There was a little friendly rivalry between the Danes and the Norwegians, but nothing that was serious. My mother could speak Norwegian and my father could speak Dane but they could understand each other when they spoke it to keep something from us children." — Walter Christiansen (Kenmare, ND)

"They were crowded with Norwegians up there in Starkweather [North Dakota]. And there was Danes and Swedes, all Scandinavians. They had big families, all of them, and they had Christmas parties together, so I had no problem with my language when we all got together. … The Swedes thought they were better, you know, because they had their own king living in Sweden and the Norwegians got sick of it and pulled away and wanted their own king. So they went to Denmark and asked for a prince and he was willing to come to Norway, and he changed his name and everything. [He] took the name of the old kings of Norway, Haakon." — Kristine Svidal (Starkweather, ND)

"About half of the community [around Larimore, North Dakota] was Norwegian, Swedish, and Danish. And they all got along fairly well. There was some rivalry between the Swedes and the Norwegians, but it was more or less friendly rivalry. And in my home, if we had any criticism of any nationalities we were told to keep that private. You didn't say anything to hurt anyone's feelings. The Norwegians stuck together, but they did welcome other nationalities." — Solveig Johnson (Niagara, MN)

"Around Souris, [North Dakota] well, I would say seventy-five percent was Scandinavian. There was a lot of Swedes out there, too, you know, Norwegian and Swede about half and half. I can't think of any other nationalities around there. Mostly Scandinavian. Unless some peddler came around and had a funny name, they were different. The Swedes and Norwegians got along pretty good. They had their own Swedish church there, too, and we'd go there if they had sales or something, and they'd come to ours. A friendly community! There were a lot of Norwegian jokes, Swedish jokes too, I suppose. We called them 'Big Swedes' and I suppose they called us Norwegians something, too." — Alma Olson (Souris, ND)

"I grew up here in Cass County, near Kindred [North Dakota]. They were all Norwegians. I can think of two Swedish families. They were sort of curiosities. We were conscious of the fact that we were Norwegians. There were not enough Swedes to constitute a rivalry. They were just kind of different. We liked them and got along fine and accepted the differences. But it was very, absolutely, completely a Norwegian community." — Clarence Glasrud (Moorhead, MN)

"There was a good deal of Norwegian spoken [in Christine, North Dakota]. The services were held in Norsk ... and many a time a youngster came to school and he couldn't speak English. On Saturdays, when farmers came into town and bought their groceries, they invariably spoke Norwegian. There were two Germans, and I remember an Irish family. But that's about it. ... There were a few other Swedish families, but you didn't say too much about being Swedish when you lived in a town full of Norwegians. You were quiet about that. ... I think if you live among Norwegians, your language gets to be Norwegian, too." — Anna Hanson (Moorhead, MN)

"As we spread out, everyone moved here and there and soon the whole neighborhood was just American [around Oakes, North Dakota]. They Americanized fast in those days, and it didn't take long until you were the same as your neighbor. We were not clannish. The biggest rivalry was between the Norwegians and the Swedes." — Mabel Enger (Oakes, ND)

"Our community was just a few miles west of the North Dakota border and thirteen miles from the Canadian border. Our community was one hundred percent Danish the first fifteen years I lived there, I'm sure. I knew of no one else but Danes. This was ten miles south of Westby [Montana]. But there were Norwegians just north of us. We had Norwegians only half a mile away. There was a hill between us so we couldn't see their house. But their living habits were so different from ours that there was no way that we would have associated with them anyway. But still, I know when she had her babies over there my mother would go there and act as midwife. And he and my father were friends, too, on a very reserved level, because both realized that they had a way-different living style, and therefore we didn't have that much in common. Well, they were heavy drinkers. They drank every day I suppose. We weren't encouraged to have anything to do with them. However, we walked with them to school; we were friends, but we did not associate with them. They were English speaking by that time. I don't ever remember them speaking Norwegian. ... [Other than that] the first Norwegians came into our community when two brothers married Norwegian girls. This was, I suppose, in the early 1940s. Before this, it was "ethnically pure." My sisters all married Danes. I married a Dane. ... I don't remember if I spoke English when I started school, but I don't think so. Everyone in our school was Danish except that one family that was Norwegian. My parents did not stress it. In fact, they thought the sooner we could learn English, the better. My father had a lot of English books and he read all the time. When he passed away we sent all his Danish books to a younger Danish settlement up in Canada. ... We had one family that came over later than the rest of us, and they were determined to keep their Danish ways. I don't remember them wearing anything but those long black woolen skirts." — Louise Anderson (Fargo, ND)

"There was Carlson, and Swanson, and Johnson, and Anderson, and Lindquist, and a lot of Scandinavians out there [in Glendive, Montana]. We had a ball all winter long. I never had such a good time in my life as I had in my first winter [in America]. Well, it was quite a few Norwegians there too, and Danish people. When they came from Denmark they had good educations, they had money. Some of them started businesses, one had a furniture store and one was a banker, another had a hardware store. They were all pretty well fixed. And you know, this ballplayer, Knut Rockne, he was a cousin to the man that I worked for, and they were Norwegian, too. We all got along pretty good. The Norwegians had a group by themselves, and we said, 'Oh, well, let them alone, let the Norwegians be by themselves,' and some of the Swedes was by themselves, too. They didn't mingle too much, the Swedes and the Norwegians." — Anna Lindgren (Fargo, ND)

The solitary Scandinavian living in the midst of a German community may have had to struggle to retain his cultural identity. In like manner, the lone Swede in a Norwegian community or the isolated Dane among other Scandinavians may have found it difficult to assert his nationality. Even in a community that consisted entirely of one ethnic

group, however, there was sometimes room for disagreement as the immigrants tended to hold on to their Old Country traditions and attitudes, and those Old Country traditions and attitudes often included a strong sense of regional bias and sentiment.

"Whenever you met you'd talk Scandinavian. If he was a Swede he talked Swede, up until the 'thirties,' then it's like it kind of tapered off. But at anything Scandinavian, it was Scandinavian spoken—on the streets, get-togethers, whatever! [The Swedes and the Norwegians] might tell a joke on each other behind their back, but it seemed like they got along pretty good here. Northwest of Hawley [Minnesota] there used to be a lot of Hallings. They sure could tell stories. And of course the way they told them, you know, they could get them on anybody." — Nilmer Bjorndal (Hawley, MN)

"I think that more than anything there was more friction between the Swedish ethnic groups from the various provinces—the Smalanders, the Skanengers, the Vestergotlanders, etc. And there was one family [in the Parker's Prairie, Minnesota area] that was Mission Covenant, and they kind of kept to themselves." — Lillian Strandness (Fargo, ND)

"I think there was a little division between the Hallings and some of the others, like those that came from Trondhiem, and our own ancestors. It always seemed that the Hallings liked to have the upper hand. They came from Hallingdal." — Gertie Holm (Hawley, MN)

"I know there was quite bit of division in the parochial school. The children would bring things up and they were kind of rude and nasty to us. But later on they seemed to accept people better, you know, as they got older. Some of [the Hallings] may have been prone to fighting, especially if they got into some home brew or something. They got pretty lively. There wasn't so much of that, but it would happen once in a while that they would get a hold of it. I think we kind of thought that [the Hallings were more apt to drink and fight] although I can't remember any instance of any fight or anything. It was just more or less talk. They'd get pretty rude sometimes. I actually remember I was hit on the head with a book once in school, came up behind me and hit me with a book! It was that we should stay our distance from them because they were a little superior. You could just sense that, you know." — Joanna Aune (Hawley, MN)

"I don't think the various immigrant groups were as friendly as they could have been. I think they kind of ridiculed each other, from the different provinces, because they had a different dialect. There was a little friction there, because the people who lived up in the northeast section of town [Moorhead], most of them were from Skane, that's the southern tip of Sweden, you know, and their accent was different. They had kind of a sing-song. There was more or less rivalry between the Swedes and the Norwegians too, I guess, but my folks made it a point to get along." — Roy Carlander (Moorhead, MN)

"I would say it was ninety percent Norwegian about where we were, and as you got closer to Ulen [Minnesota] then it must have been one hundred percent. In town there was some who weren't Norwegian. A lot of them who weren't Norwegian learned to speak it. There might have been some Swedes here and there, but there were more south-east of Hitterdal. There were mostly Trondheimers and Hallings around Ulen at that time. 'Kniv-Hallings,' [knife-Hallings], that's what they called some of them. I don't know why, I never saw any of them use a knife." — Henry Jacobson (Ulen, MN)

"I would say [in Hendrum, Minnesota], while we were growing up, it was one hundred percent Norwegian. We did have a Danish doctor, but he lived in Ada, Minnesota. I don't think there was ever any real rivalry [among Norwegians from different areas of Norway], but one thing I could say is that everybody couldn't understand everybody else. We all went to the same church, so I don't believe that there ever was divisions like that. Around Hendrum there were four churches, but they were all served by the same pastor." — Alva Hest (Perley, MN)

"Fertile was a good town. … I ran the Robertson Lumber Yard there in 1912. A little before Christmas a man came to me. He had short whiskers … and he talked Norwegian to me, well I was glad not to use English. 'I'm going to build a house,' he said, 'so I'd like to have you figure on it, but,' he says, 'I have to buy from Jim Hanson because I know him.' 'Well,' I said, 'I don't know anybody here. If you have to buy from him because you know him, I might just as well call on Robertson's and tell them to take out the yard because they can't do business here if you have to know them, because I don't know anybody.' 'Well,' he says, 'you figure it out anyways.' So I got to figure it out. 'By the way,' he says, 'where do you come from?' Well I told him that I was born in Valdres, Norway. 'Well,' he says, 'I'm a Halling!' That's the next valley, you see. 'Yah, well,' he says, 'we had lots of scraps about fishing.' I suppose he meant fishing waters. And then he says, 'And then we used to butcher a goat and sell it for mutton when we'd go to Valdres.' So we had a good laugh on that, you know. So I said, 'Well, do you know some people over there in Hallingdal by the name of Hoppten?' 'Oh, I should say so. I know Hopptens.' 'Well,' I says, 'my great grandfather's mother was a Hoppten. She was buried in 1740.' 'Oh, are you from the Hoppten people?' he says. So we got to know each other pretty good, you know. And I sold him a house, and I sold to his brothers and sons. So you can tell it helps sometimes to know who your people are, don't it!" — Louis Haugen (Crookston, MN)

Chapter VI
"It Was Wheat, Oats, and Barley"

WORKING IN THE NEW WORLD

As the immigrants passed from being Scandinavians in America to being Scandinavian-Americans, they had to face the challenge of earning a living. Most of the immigrants turned to those skills that they had learned in Scandinavia. They were probably not surprised to discover that the axe that they had brought with them from Sweden could chop American trees as well as it could chop Swedish trees. The soil was better in America, but the cows tended to eat hay and give milk in exactly the same manner as in the old country. For the most part, it was only natural that the immigrants would do the jobs that they knew best. A Scandinavian lumberjack became an American lumberjack and a Scandinavian blacksmith became an American blacksmith. But for the most part, the Scandinavian farmer became an American farmer, and one can still travel in the Upper Midwest and see farms that closely resemble farms in Scandinavia. The barns and sheds of Ottertail County in Minnesota or Winneshiek County in Iowa are sometimes exact replicas of those found in Norway.

While many Scandinavian immigrants remained in cities such as Chicago and Minneapolis, a majority of them turned to farming. They

had been able to bring with them from Scandinavia only a meager collection of tools and other possessions, so to be successful on the first farm it was necessary to be as self-sufficient as possible. Self-sufficiency allowed for the accumulation of the capital needed to purchase the large machines necessary for the American farm.

"Our farm was about one hundred percent [self-sufficient]. We had our cows where we ended up getting our milk and our butter and our cream. And then with our chickens we got our eggs and our meat from them. And then we had pigs that we butchered and we shipped the rest of them and that was where we got the money that we needed for flour and clothing and other things that we needed. We made our own butter, but not our own cheese. We didn't [spin our own wool], but a lot of the other families around here [Pembina County, North Dakota] did. ... When they'd butcher in the summer time, the one family would butcher and then all the neighbors would get a certain part of the meat. And then, when everybody got low on meat, the next neighbor would butcher a cow or a pig and then everybody would get some meat. And it was never a case where someone would measure that somebody got the same amount of poundage as somebody else." — Diane Volrath (Hitterdal, MN)

"Dad never helped with the milking. Mother did help with the milking, but it was pretty much left up to us children to do the milking.

Grandma had one cow that she milked by herself. We churned our own butter and made cheese. [Mother] used to spin and weave and knit wool for our stockings and mittens. I still have woolen mittens that she knit for me."
— William Nelson (Rollag, MN)

"Neighbors helped neighbors with labor and what farm implements they had. A neighbor gave a hen to start a flock of chickens and a cow was loaned to supply the family with milk for the winter. Eggs and homemade butter were taken to the store to exchange for coffee, sugar, and other supplies. The yarn for the stockings came from the wool of their own sheep. This was washed, carded, and spun on a spinning wheel they had brought from Iceland." — Rosa Campbell (Moorhead, MN)

Although many immigrants wished to start farming, taking up free land under the provisions of the Homestead Act still required some capital. If one were courageous enough to leave one's homeland for an uncertain future in America, however, that person was not likely to avoid hard work. To gain a stake, many Scandinavian immigrants, especially Swedes and Finns, found jobs in the Minnesota forests. Others got jobs "working on the railroads" and viewed the prairies one railroad tie at a time.

"During the fall of 1880 and the spring of 1881 [Dad] heard about railroad building in Minnesota and so he struck out for Saint Cloud. He arrived in Saint Cloud too early to do any work because of the frozen ground, so he moved on again after hearing about the Black Hills branch of the Northern Pacific that was to be built from Wadena, Minnesota, to Wahpeton, North Dakota, and he headed for Battle Lake, and he took a homestead on some sand hills that were similar to the land around where he came from in Norway. As soon as the frost was out of the ground in 1881 they began to build the Black Hills branch of the N.P., which reached Underwood and Fergus Falls in 1882. I do have a newspaper clipping about my father stating when the shovel and the pick-ax and the wheelbarrow that he had purchased for the contract … was worn out, especially the shovel was worn out, he was appointed section foreman for Underwood." — John Gronner (Underwood, MN)

"In the wintertime I cut and hauled cordwood. I hauled it to Detroit Lakes. I got two and a half dollars a cord. A cord is about four by eight. You could cut about two cords a day. You'd cut it one winter and haul it the next winter. It was mostly popple and birch. There was no coal at that time, they all burned wood in town, so there was a good demand for wood. And we used to cut ties too, for the railroad, that was oak or tamarack. You'd have to cut that down to seven or six inches. Nah, we didn't have anything like [a circular saw] in them days. We did it all by hand." — Charles Westerholm (Moorhead, MN)

"My dad worked up in the logging camps in the wintertime, too, just as they did in Sweden, over in Minnesota. And he did a little farming. He did that for, uh, twenty-five years or something." — Amy Margaret Erickson (Wheatland, ND)

"My father cut wood, different kinds of timbers—railroad ties, and barrel staves, and telephone poles, and cordwood for fires. He did that all winter. He couldn't do anything else." — Mabel Enger (Oakes, ND)

"There was lots of Swedes in the logging camps. But the lumberjacks all understood each other—there ain't no difference. Especially when we went into a town where we could get something to drink." — Andrew Lindgren (Moorhead, MN)

For many, such jobs were often seen only as a temporary expedient until such time as they could began farming—their dream in Scandinavia and their goal in America. Although the methods of farming were perhaps not overly dissimilar, the size of the farms and the extent of mechanization provided a new experience. This new experience often defined their life in America.

"We were told that we could have a room and board until we were ready to leave or until we got a job. We were hunting for jobs the following day. We heard of one farmer ... that lived on the end of Christine Lake who maybe needed to hire a man for one month. I thought that it would be a good place for me. ... We found another farmer about five miles from Evansville [Minnesota] who was looking for a man the whole season and my partner said it would be [a good job] for him. This particular farmer was a very nice fellow to work for. His wife was Irish, so I couldn't talk to her, but he talked very good Scandinavian. And he got up in the morning and milked a few cows and woke me up about six-thirty and then we had breakfast and then we harnessed the horses and I started to work. I hauled dirt and old manure out the whole first week I worked at this particular farm. Then I plowed with a single walking plow for about a week, and dragged it and then he planted the corn while I done some fence fixing, and the corn come up and I done some corn cultivating. ... At that time I got a dollar a day, which I thought was pretty good. ... [Then] I went into Malvey with my trunk. I borrowed a horse and buggy and went on the train, first to Alexandria and then to Henning. I seen the [owners of the blacksmith shop]. They were German nationality, but they had gone to school with lots of Swedes and Norwegians so they could talk pretty good Norwegian. They said I got the job, but said I should wait until after the Fourth of July, so I went and found a place to stay—Uncle Markeson's Boarding House. And I asked them if I could get a place to sleep and eat with them, and the lady said, 'Sure, we got plenty of room.' And I asked what the price would be and she said 'Twelve dollars and fifty cents a month.' I was real surprised how cheap it was." — Henry Holmgren (Henning, MN)

"I was supposed to come home [to Sweden] in 1919 and get the farm, you know, but I didn't go and the old man sold the farm in 1923." — John Norman (Hawley, MN)

"I went out to Steele County in North Dakota out by Hope and I worked three-four years at a farm there. I didn't get much in wages, but I enjoyed the work, anyway. In the spring we got thirty-five dollars a month, and spring work generally lasted two months, so I came home with about seventy dollars, because I had about fifteen dollars along and that generally took care of me while I was out there because board and room was free on the farm. … We started out before seven o'clock in the morning and continued until about seven o'clock at night. Of course, after that we had about twenty-four horses to take care of too, so it was dark before we finished up the chores. We used triple bottom plows when I went out there, that was in 1908–1909, and on a triple plow some used seven horses and some used eight horses. It was quite a lot of work before you got them all hitched up and get going. And we had to have extra plowshares all the time, of course. There were plenty blacksmiths in those days, in every town. It was wheat, oats, and barley." — David Swedberg (Otter Tail Co., MN)

"I worked out there in the fall of 1913, 1914, and 1915, and then I put in the whole summer of 1916 in North Dakota. In fact, I worked for nine months that year around Hamburg, North Dakota, about one hundred and fifty miles from Fargo on the Great Northern main line. At that time they paid a big sum of thirty-five dollars for working on the farm. By the time I quit working on the farm I was getting fifty dollars a month, but then I quit that and started working for a road contractor and got eighty-five cents an hour. That made a lot of difference in pay!" — Louis Westling (Longville, MN)

"I worked for [my uncle] for twenty dollars a month! Day and night! And a neighbor come and he wanted to hire me. He didn't want to see me work so hard for twenty dollars a month, and he doubled my wages. He lived about half a mile from my uncle, but he couldn't say nothing. ... The people I worked for were the nicest people you can think of. Enderlin, Mayville, Portland, Hatton, and Page, and way up by Parshall [North Dakota]. I worked for several years for each one of them. Swell people! On the Fourth of July, 1917, I took the train from Minneapolis to Enderlin, North Dakota. And I was in Enderlin for an hour and then I got a job on a farm and I worked there for several years." — Arne Arneson (Fargo, ND)

"There was only twenty acres under cultivation when we came to Minnesota, and our farm was one hundred and twenty acres. There was some that was pasture, but I don't know how many acres that he grubbed the stumps—cut the trees, and then grubbed them out. That was lots of work with just horses." — Nina Oien (Moorhead, MN)

"They raised wheat and barley and oats lots of oats because they had stock in them days. And some potatoes. They had a quarter that wasn't broke more than two years when they come here. Virgin soil almost. The man who broke up the soil—his name was Charles Olson. He was Swedish. He left and he went up to Hillsboro and from there he went out to Montana. The neighbor girl that he wanted so bad, she didn't want him, so that hurt him so bad he just gave up and wanted to sell." — Cora Kragnes (Felton, MN)

"My dad had a lot of cattle and horses. We must have had over two hundred horses at one time. We had so many we ran out of names for them. And the steam engine came in then, you see, and we were able to break up one hundred and sixty acres of prairie in one summer. And plant wheat! It was just terrific. A threshing rig would come in the fall of the year and we had thirteen bundle carriers, all done with horses, and there would be a straw stack as big as any five story house or building." — Lloyd Westrum (Moorhead, MN)

On every farm, the highlight of the agricultural year was the threshing season. For many Scandinavian immigrants, farming in America was nothing short of an agricultural revolution. The tiny plots in the Old Country, harvested with scythe and flail, were replaced by

one hundred and sixty acres of flat prairie harvested with a binder, a threshing machine, and a steam engine. Threshing time was the reward, in most cases at least, for the year's labor, and the farmer and his wife looked forward to it with keen anticipation. Neighbor would help neighbor and threshing time became a social as well as a work experience. The children, of course, looked forward to the whistle of the steam engine and dreamed of the day when they, too, could be an engineer.

"And then in 1885—I've got the contract—[they bought] a brand new steam engine and threshing machine. So they got a twelve horse power steam engine and a thirty-six inch separator. My dad had to mortgage his horses and all the crops grown on this land. … They bought the rig January 4th, 1885, for four hundred and thirty dollars and thirty cents. My dad wasn't so up on steam engines, so Ole Sather from Ulen came down here. I think he was a steam engineer. And my dad always ran the threshing machine. They had to catch the grain in buckets, you know, one bushel or half bushel, and when it got full they skimmed off the top to make it even. They hauled all the grain in sacks, they didn't haul any grain loose them years." — Clifford Hitterdal (Hitterdal, MN)

"The first rig right in this area [Rollag, Minnesota] was owned by Tom Gunderson. He had a horse power outfit. But in the early eighties, my uncles threshed with steam engines. They had a little up-right steam engine pulled around with horses." — William Nelson (Rollag, MN)

"I went back [to Enderlin, North Dakota] in the fall to help with the threshing. I hired out as an 'oiler' on a big threshing machine out there. We had a forty-inch cylinder and there had to be two men around the separators. We had a self-feeder, so there were two on each side throwing the bundles into the machine. One year I was out there they had thirty-five or forty bushels [of wheat] to the acre. They had real good crops out there. ... Threshing was quite a thing for the kids, because they had up to twenty-four men with the threshing machine, hauling grain, and hauling bundles, and a few men up in the straw stack. It was hard work for the ladies anyway. They had to work maybe a whole week before the threshing crew came to fix the food. We butchered something for the threshing. Five meals a day—breakfast, forenoon lunch, dinner, afternoon lunch, and then a big supper on top of it. Big diner at noon, too. It took three men around the steam engine, the water tank men, the fireman, the engineer, and three on each side of the separator pitching bundles. They were hired by the owner of the rig and he was paid by the farmer per bushel. Most of the farmers put their grain in a granary because they could get a better price for it in the winter months, and it was easier to haul the grain on a sled. We used a sled for hauling as much as possible." — David Swedberg (Otter Tail Co., MN)

"There was a lot of exchange work done between farmers, especially in threshing. Whoever was closest together, be it Swedish or Norwegian or Irish or what, they got together and had their shock runs and got associated pretty much that way. Some who had stacks had to hire help. The stacks were not affected by weather so that was why they had stack threshing late in the fall and even in the winter sometimes." — Amy Erickson (Moorhead, MN)

"It was probably the most interesting time of the year when you got about twenty-five people coming to the place [near Maddock, North Dakota]. They followed the harvest from the south to the north. The guy that owned the threshing machine had a cook car and one or two women would cook for fifteen or twenty men. And then the grain haulers, well, the farmer had to feed them at his house. They slept wherever they could find a place to lay down, in the barn or some shed. They had their blankets along and they put some hay on the floor of the building and that's where they slept." — Edwin Markestad (Maddock, ND)

"I think they had ten bundle teams, that's ten men, a couple of field pitchers, a couple more, several grain haulers, the fireman, the watermen who hauled water for the steam rig—I bet there was twenty men. And that required a lot of cooking!" — Vern Fugelberg (New Rockford, ND)

"When they did the harvesting, they went from one [Icelandic] farm to the other and all the farmers would help each other. It didn't make any difference if they spent one day at one farm and two days at the next. [All the

Icelanders] just helped each other and then they'd take their own team of horses and haul bundles with that and then they'd do all the threshing at one time." — Diane Volrath (Hitterdal, MN)

The immigrant farm wife had more than her share of work and responsibilities. Her primary responsibility was the family, which in many cases would include eight or ten children. It was her duty to feed, clothe, and sometimes even to educate the children. In the tradition of the Scandinavian farm wife, she was frequently a milk maid, and in the tradition of America she was often a field hand.

For the unmarried or urban Scandinavian immigrant woman, the choices for employment were not abundant. In the Old Country, many of them had gone to work in the homes of others as maids and in America Scandinavian women soon gained a reputation of being excellent house servants. For many young girls it was the opportunity to build a hope chest before marriage, for others it was an opportunity to meet someone in a process that led to marriage.

In virtually every case, however, the opportunity for employment for women in America was greater than it had been in Scandinavia. Some of the jobs may not have been glamorous, such as working in a cook car on a hot August day in North Dakota or working as a maid in a railroad section house, but whether the jobs were temporary or not, they

were usually viewed as such, and eventually Scandinavian Immigrant women were working in professions such as teaching and nursing.

"Yah, [the Barnes farm] on the other side of Glyndon [Minnesota], that was a bonanza farm. My mother was a cook there, I suppose she was about fifteen or sixteen. She got up at four o'clock in the morning ... and made breakfast for all these people." — Clifford Hitterdal (Hitterdal, MN)

"My folks did all our butchering and the men on all the farms would help each other out. They'd cooperate. They'd go to one farm and do all the butchering and then to another farm and do all the butchering. And as I grew older I helped. We would can all the meat in two-quart jars. We'd boil it for four or five hours. We did that with beef and chicken and pork and we had a smoke house on the farm and we would make hams. ... During the threshing season, we girls had to help my mother so we were all up at four o'clock. And then we'd make breakfast for them. And they always had a big breakfast, they were well fed. They always had bacon and pancakes and cereal and everything you can think of. My dad insisted they be fed well because they were going to work hard all day. Then we would make sandwiches and a cake or cookies or doughnuts or something like that in the middle of the morning and take two or three big pots of coffee and take out in the field. Then they would stop and have lunch. Then we'd go back and clean up all those dishes and then we'd take dinner out in the field. A good dinner—potatoes and meat and home-made bread and pies—and they would eat their dinner in the field. Then in the afternoon, about two-thirty or three o'clock, we'd have to take out lunch again. But in the evening, they would eat as they came in. There were several bundle haulers, and as each one emptied his bundle rack in the evening he would come in, take care of his horses, and come in to eat, so they would eat one by one. They were usually all fed and taken care of by nine o'clock, but then we still had all those dishes to do, so the women never got to bed until ten o'clock and then we were up at four again." — Solveig Johnson (Niagara, ND)

"When I was fifteen years old I worked on a threshing crew, on a cook car. The cook car was on wheels. In those days they had so few threshing machines. They had steam, and there was twenty-four men on the threshing crew. At the end of the car was a big wooden cook stove. And of course we had to bake bread every day and take out coffee twice a day. We had to have cake enough for twenty-four men and there was just the two of us. The tables were alongside of the car. They would come in, so many at a time. It got really hot sometimes to cook in the summer. We'd sleep in the car overnight then, and they would move to the next farm overnight. They were mostly big farmers. It would start, it must have been in August, and continue until December, just before Christmas. You get into a regimen. We had to get up at four o'clock in the morning to get the breakfast on in the summertime, because they started as soon as it was daylight." — Freda Bjornson (Moorhead, MN)

"On the greatest part of the Norwegian farms the women did the milking, and the chores during the threshing time. And they would do field work, like shocking." — Palmer Tverdal (Abercrombie, ND)

"Mother kept a few sheep. That went with the cows. Just so that we could have the wool. And mother knit all our stockings and all our mittens." — Nina Oien (Moorhead, MN)

"Mother and I would sell the sweet cream to the creamery in Hazelton [North Dakota]. We had to leave home at seven o'clock in the morning, so we could get there before it got too hot. And we had to wrap wet blankets around the cream cans so as to keep it cool 'til we got to Hazelton. They used this cream for ice cream and it had to have very special care. The creamery in Hazelton was pretty close to the track, and you know the horses in those days were scared green of the train, so we would aim to get in there before the old 'Scrap Iron Bill' came roaring down the track." — Matilda Blumer (Hazelton, ND)

"In the summer I taught Norwegian at parochial school for about six weeks, but otherwise I helped my father on the farm. We had only walking machinery. My dad never owned a tractor. So I had to learn to hitch up the harness and hitch up the horses. Haying was the worst season on the farm in those days, because we had to have a mower, and then rake, and then make it into haycocks, all over the field. And if it rained, then we had to go out again and turn it so that it would dry through. And then it was to haul it home and put it into stacks. My mother was usually there to help stack up the hay until we got a barn with a hay loft and then we would put it up there with slings. I always helped in the field—shocking, making the stacks. I've worked most of the machinery on the farm with horses." — Alma Ramse (McIntosh, MN)

"I worked for three dollars a week. My brother's wife's folks had come to America with the whole family. And they were farming north of Devil's Lake [North Dakota]. And so there was two daughters who was both married, but there was three boys at home and she needed help and I went to work there. Three dollars a week to do housework. I cleaned and did whatever else she asked me to do. I worked for other people too. I wasn't married until I was twenty-two or twenty-three." — Kristine Svidal (Starkweather, ND)

"I used to stay all week with some people and work for two dollars a week." — Ellen Abraham (Villard, MN)

"My mother had relatives here and so when she made her home with relatives, a cousin or somebody, she had someplace to go when she came to Minnesota. And then later she went to Minneapolis and worked and then she married my dad and after they were married they moved up to Malmo and made their home next to the people that my mother had lived with." — Amy Margaret Erickson (Wheatland, ND)

"When I was sixteen I went out working for others, and I kept that up until I got married." — Cora Kragnes (Felton, MN)

"Grandmother was an orphan, and she worked at the hotel in Glyndon [Minnesota], which at that time [the 1870s] seemed to be the stopover point." — Amy Erickson (Moorhead, MN)

"My mother came here [from Norway] in 1894, and she got work in the section house. So she worked there and that's how she happened to meet my father who was boarding and rooming there." — Clara Hanson (Moorhead, MN)

"At the 1896 Minnesota State Fair we took in everything from the horse barns and cattle and everything. And I don't know what it was in the evening. Horse racing, I suppose. But I stayed in Minneapolis after that state fair. I got a job there and stayed for about three years. Then I went back to Princeton [Minnesota] and got a job in a store. I always loved it, working behind the counter. … In 1906 I started to work for Norby's Department Store in Barnesville [Minnesota]. They took me in as one of the family. I took care of yard goods and liveries, and all over. I got thirty-five dollars a month, but my room and board from the Norby's was ten dollars a month. I would generally start work at eight thirty in the morning and work until six some days and other days we'd stay open until nine o'clock. That was a long day!" — Minnie Carlson (Fergus Falls, MN)

"Since I was confirmed in Norwegian, I was able to speak the language and this was really quite beneficial because wherever I worked [as a nurse] why, there were so many Norwegian older people who couldn't speak English. So I was an interpreter many times for the doctors."
— Beatrice Schaefer (Osakis, MN)

"I taught in one room schools. We had to make our own fires, and we'd stay with someone in the district [Becker County, Minnesota] and walk to school and make our fire and do our janitor work. I had all grades, and I thought that was kind of frustrating because I could never give them all the attention they needed." — Bernice Herfindal (Lake Park, MN)

On the farm, a large family was seen as a definite asset. Children had chores to attend to at an early age, any many went out to work for others well before they became adults. A sense of family responsibility was instilled and maintained. In many families, an elder brother or sister would help to educate a younger member of the family until a former Norwegian "bonder" could brag that all of his children had graduated from St. Olaf College. The new American school might teach them the skills to advance in the world, but the work experiences and attitudes they gained in childhood helped them survive in the New World.

"By the time I was ten years old I was driving six horses on the gang plow. I couldn't harness them up or hook 'em up, but I could drive 'em after [my dad] got 'em hooked to the plow." — Ralph Simonson (Bowman, ND)

"At the [Twin Valley, Minnesota Children's] Home, we had a hundred and twenty children and five grown-ups taking care of us. And among the five grown-ups, one was the farm manager. We had a four hundred and eighty acre farm. And I remember the first thing when I came to the Home, the first thing that I learned to do was to milk a cow. I had three cows to milk and to take care of. And then I got promoted and I goes to take care of two horses and I didn't have to milk any cows. All the difference in the world!" — Carl Narveson (Moorhead, MN)

"I always enjoyed school, but I didn't get to go much. It was always 'You gotta stay home today. We have to haul hay,' or something like that. In them days they had kids working who were only seven or eight years old." — Charles Westerholm (Moorhead, MN)

"When I was fifteen I went out to work on the farms in North Dakota. It was a pretty big operation, big threshing machines. I drove a bundle wagon and hauled grain in it and pitched it into the machine, which was plenty hard work for just a teenager. They put in too long a day. We worked there for twelve or thirteen hours a day. The old farmer would come and get us at four o'clock in the morning and holler at us to go feed the horses. 'Get up and take care of the horses, they're kicking the barn down.'" — Louis Westerling (Longville, MN)

"Oh, picking potatoes! That's the hardest work there is. You had to wait until the rows were dug up before you started, then you put a whole lot of sacks on your back. They used a potato digger, it had little shovels on it, horse drawn, you know. And it left the potatoes right in rows, in plain sight, right on the top, so it wasn't hard to pick, but you had to bend over so far and it was hard work because those baskets were heavy. At one time it was three cents a bushel, then it was four and five and I think it went up to seven cents a bushel when I last picked. We usually had one week off from school [at Hitterdal, Minnesota] for potato picking. That was in October or the last part of September. We used that money for school clothes." — Violet Anderson (Hitterdal, MN)

"All of us would be out in that potato field. And I can remember that Dad would haul a whole load of potatoes in the wagon. Maybe forty bushels, and had all of us to buy shoes for and I don't know how they did it. I can still see Mother getting the eggs ready, and we'd put the eggs in the case. It held twelve dozen, I think, but it wasn't always full. And Mother and Dad would take the horse and buggy to town and buy groceries, but they just bought the staples like sugar and coffee, and your oatmeal was in a barrel and they'd put it in bulk. You never bought candy in those days, but when Mother and Dad would exchange the eggs for groceries, then the grocer man would put in a little bag of candy for us children." — Nina Oien (Moorhead, MN)

Not all the Scandinavian immigrants worked on farms. In urban settings and in small towns the Scandinavian immigrants also used the skills that they had brought with them from the Old Country to earn a living in America. The Swedish builder was justly famous in Chicago and Minneapolis, but other Scandinavian groups were also builders, as well as musicians, wagon makers, teachers, and, although each group would deny it, thieves.

"The first frame house to be built in Underwood [Minnesota] was built by my grandfather who was a carpenter and a cabinet maker. … My father worked with the public and learned the American language quite readily. He was forced to learn to write because he had to write reports each week on what they did on the railroad and maintaining the railroad. In 1901 my dad was appointed foreman of the crew that laid the steel from Wahpeton to Oakes, North Dakota. And the town of Gwinner was named after my father, but it was spelled wrong by the man who wrote it out." — John Gronner (Underwood, MN)

"My mother's brother Karl as the first to come here, and he came in about 1898. He was a violin maker, and here in this county he had to do manual labor. And he really wasn't happy here so he went back to Norway." — Ruth Erickson (Moorhead, MN)

"I taught school for two years [in McHenry County, North Dakota], but then the wages went down so far I couldn't afford to teach. They were trying to get us to teach for forty dollars a month. Board and room would cost us twenty-three, so you didn't have much left to spend." — Leo Hillman (Mountain, ND)

"They were all bricklayers. All the brothers on my mother's side, three brothers, and my father and his two brothers were bricklayers. They had got their start in Sweden. They were all young. My father was only eighteen when he came here [to Moorhead, Minnesota]." — Robert Carlander (Moorhead, MN)

"The population of Moorhead was about five thousand then. And the first day I went out I had about one hundred and twenty quarts of milk. That wagon had a horse by the name of Molly who had been on the route since Fairmont started the milk route. After we'd been on the route for a week she know every stop as well as I did." — Vic Anderson (Moorhead, MN)

And then there were those who did just about everything.

"He came directly to Oakport Township in Clay County, where he visited with his cousin, in 1895. He worked on farms in Clay County, and then later on he went to Duluth. And he worked on the ore docks in the summer and he worked in the lumber camps in the winter. And from Duluth he went to Tioga, North Dakota, where he homesteaded a quarter of land. And he proved it up and sold it, and then he moved back to Clay County for a year. From there he moved to Sebeka, Minnesota, where he bought some land from which he cut and sold pulpwood. He sold that property and then moved back to Clay County. He got married in 1910 and they moved to Fargo, where Nels had a water route. He owned his own water wagon and a team of horses, and he did that for two years before he moved back to Morken Township in Clay County and started farming again." — Norman Hanson (Glyndon, MN)

The major difference between those who worked in the Old Country and those who worked in America was one of attitude. Back in Europe, a fisherman's son would become a fisherman and a farmer's daughter would marry a farmer. To a large extent, the social standing of a person was determined by his occupation. America offered the chance to break free of a system whereby what you were determined who you were. All things seemed possible in America, including the dream that the son of a 'husman' could grow up to be a minister of the church. The doors of opportunity were wide open, and the first door was that of the American country school.

Chapter VII
"Talk English Now!"

SCANDINAVIANS AND THE AMERICAN SCHOOL

For all immigrant groups, the American schoolhouse would become, as the educational reformer Horace Mann had insisted, the great leveling factor. For many first and second generation immigrants the schoolhouse was not only the first exposure to formal education, it was the first exposure to the English language. The confrontation with an English speaking teacher was often frightening and traumatic, but the patience demonstrated by both the teacher and student would eventually produce a bilingual child who was much more aware of his own country and culture than that of his parent's native land.

For Swedish-American children, as with all of the Scandinavian ethnic groups, education was the first step on the way to cultural and linguistic assimilation.

"As I grew up, when my grandparents was here, I didn't know any English. All I knew was Swedish. I had to learn English from the grass roots up, starting school, and that was the way that most children of this area [Lake Park, Minnesota] learned it at that time. They would learn English, but as soon as they got outside the school they would speak their own Scandinavian language and that continued for some years." — Oscar Olson (Lake Park, MN)

"We started school right after Christmas vacation. There were five of us and we all had to start in the first grade. The oldest one of us was eleven. My brother and my sister and I had gone to school in Sweden. It was hardest for the oldest one, having to learn everything all over. But we had a very good teacher. After she found out we were doing too much Scandinavian talking among ourselves she said, 'O.K., this week you have to stay fifteen minutes longer and the rest of the children can go home and next week those children will stay longer and you will go home so you won't talk Swedish to each other. Because that is what you are doing and you won't learn English that way.' She would even come over on Saturdays and Sundays sometimes to help us. Yes, she spoke Swedish, or at least she could understand it. In the end, one of my sisters taught her children. She would have us get up in front of the class and tell the other children what we knew about Sweden. We would say it in Swedish, mostly, and she would translate it into English. But the majority of the kids spoke Swedish anyway and those that couldn't spoke Norwegian. I suppose I picked up Norwegian enough so that now I feel like I'm half and half." — Elsie Gale (Clearbrook, MN)

"So I said, I know about American history. I learned about that before I left Sweden. Oh, yah, I knew all about the South and the North and all the states in the country and all them big cities, and we had to know America.

We had to know all about Japan and Russia, too. Japan and Russia had a war in 1905, that's how we came to know all about Japan. … We got married the first year we were here. We'd grown up together in Sweden, and of course we talked Swedish at home. We didn't know anything else. And when our kids started school then, well, they had to learn English. There was this school teacher. She was Norwegian but she could talk English, and she said we just had to speak English at home, too, so it would be easier for the kids. They caught on, you know, then, after a while." — Oscar Lingren (Fargo, ND)

"They had an American teacher [at Christine, North Dakota] and it was all English then, of course, which was the best for us. My teacher that started me out was a full-fledged Norwegian, and she could speak it fluently [and could understand Swedish]. I had the same teacher for the first five grades. … But you know how it was with us boys, there was farm work to do and of course to start with, six months of school was what it was. Then they added it to eight, and boy we thought that was terrible. And then it got to be nine months, but we were held out for a few days in the fall of the year. I lost a lot of school. In the fall I was on the plow for about two months." — Frank Alm (Christine, ND)

"My sister was my first grade teacher, and she kind of taught us boys that the English language, well, you better get it, because that's what you're going to get [from now on]. It worked out fine." — Vic Anderson (Moorhead, MN)

"As a child we spoke Swedish at home. In fact, I didn't even know one word of English when I started school [near Wheatland, North Dakota]. I had to start with the ABCs, one, two, three. I tell you, that was quite a traumatic experience to come to school, all the other kids spoke English and I didn't know what they were talking about. And I had to learn English from scratch. Well, my folks spoke Swedish all the time, and we didn't have any close neighbors who had children that we could play with so we didn't learn anything that way." — Amy Margaret Erickson (Wheatland, ND)

"There were fifty-two kids in the room, one teacher [in the school near Erhard, Minnesota], and that ran from 'chart class' through the eighth grade. Chart class, that was a big chart. 'I see a cat. This is my dog.' and so on, and as you memorized, which we did, memorize the pages, then the next one was turned over. I spent two years trying to learn the first page. I didn't have to turn it too much. I went to Pelican Rapids High School, where I brushed up on the eighth grade, and then I went to Northwestern College in Fergus Falls." — Carl Anderson (Erhart, MN)

"They took it for granted [that we would have more education]. And you know, now that I am an adult, I marvel that my father thought that five of his kids could go through college and saw to it that we did. I went to

Gustavus Adolphus, of course. We all did." — Helene Kaeding (Moorhead, MN)

"I felt like I was a big girl. I had gone to junior high [in Sweden]. I had had German, geometry, and I had done many things these girls hadn't done. And it was a little embarrassing having to go to school [in Christine, North Dakota] because I didn't know what they would do with me. I had a very nice first, second, and third grade teacher who was willing to take me in, and I was always grateful to her for that because she wouldn't have had to. She had a room full of kids. But it was embarrassing to sit down in that first grade desk. I felt cramped all day long sitting in it with my skirt laying on the floor. At the end of the day she would read to me. And that was very nice. And then at Thanksgiving time, they moved me into the sixth grade room, and that was wonderful because I had friends almost my age and I thought that was grand." — Anna Hanson (Moorhead, MN)

Anna Hanson started first grade at the age of 14, graduated from high school at age eighteen, and went on to Mayville State Teacher's College and within six years of coming to America she was a school teacher. As such, she was in charge of teaching the English language and American institutions to others. But in addition to the secular "English" school, the Swedes attempted to keep alive their heritage in the Swedish

language and the Lutheran denomination by establishing Swedish summer schools.

"We would attend parochial school at Eksjo church [Becker County, Minnesota]. And it went for a month, full days, and we had reading and arithmetic and writing, besides our Bible studies, and it was all in Swedish at that time." — Amy Erickson (Moorhead, MN)

"They taught a Swedish school. School let out in April. We just had eight months of English school then. So then they had six weeks of Swedish school. We had reading, Bible study, and spelling, and then we had to memorize the catechism. I knew English when I started school because I had older sisters and I learned from them." — Inez Holt (Chisago City, MN)

In many cases, Norwegian immigrants to the Upper Midwest had a less pressing need to learn English because they often lived in a totally Norwegian environment. Nevertheless, parents were determined that their children would become 'good Americans' and would not be handicapped by a foreign language and foreign customs. For many children of the Norwegian immigrants, the first word of spoken English that they heard was in the schoolroom. From Brooklyn to North Dakota the problems and the challenges were the same.

"There were some who came to school who didn't know the first word of English, and they had quite a time, I remember. For many years they did have a Norwegian school in the summer, in Hitterdal [Minnesota]. In school we only talked about America. We never talked about [Norway] at all." — Wilferd Anderson (Hitterdal, MN)

"I was the youngest of eight children, so by the time I went to school I had learned the English from my sisters and brothers. But I had a neighbor boy [near Underwood, Minnesota] who answered his teachers, in Norsk, 'Speak so I can understand you,' because he couldn't understand a word of American." — John Gronner (Underwood, MN)

"Well, they changed my name. She couldn't pronounce that either, the teacher. My name was spelled T-H-Y-R-A. So they gave me the name of 'Tora.' I guess they named me after the name of the telephone operator. Her name was Theresa and they called her 'Tora' too. But the teachers had only graduated from the eighth grade, and some of them not even that!" — Tora Johnson (Brewster, MN)

"When I started school [in Moorhead, Minnesota], that would be in 1911 or 1912, I couldn't speak English. So then I didn't pass the first grade. I went two years. It held me back." — Inga Moore (Moorhead, MN)

"We could hardly speak English when we started school. ... They started me at five years of age [in 1903], so I remember every morning, for a solid week, I cried because I didn't want to go to school. But after that I got along all right. Eventually we went to the consolidated school in Glyndon [Minnesota]. We were on the shy order, we were country kids, you know, and then getting to town, we thought it a big town, you know, that little village of Glyndon." — Eva Thortvet (Glyndon, MN)

"I didn't know English when I came over here. Not a word! Oh, I knew thank you and yes and no, but that's about it. I had to start from scratch. It was kind of interesting because I did it on my own. I went to the grade school … and they put me in the class with the first graders. And I think that scared the wits out of them when I came in and sat on one of those little chairs, but the teacher spoke fluent Norwegian and he asked me if I wouldn't rather go to evening class. And I did, so he transferred me into the evening class. We were practically all newcomers. The temptation was to speak our mother tongue, but he would get up and say 'No, no, no!' We couldn't use Norwegian words while conversing with one another, so he was very good." — Rev. Sven Thompson (Willmar, MN)

"We talked Norwegian most of the time. Until we started school we didn't know how to talk anything else. … I had a difficult time the first few days. We were lucky enough to have quite a few teachers that could [speak Norwegian], but then we got a teacher who couldn't, and she put a stop to our Norwegian on the playground and everywhere else." — Anna Melberg (Moorhead, MN)

"We only went to school about four months. There were two schools in one district and they divided it out so that there were four months in each. Our neighbors were about a quarter of a mile west of us and they had kids going to school so I got a chance to ride with them. I went there thirty-two days. I couldn't read or write or understand a word of English." — Cora Kragnes (Felton, MN)

"Around Rollag [Minnesota] at our school, it seems like they all talked Norwegian. Most of our teachers were of Scandinavian descent, but they, of course, had to talk English. They were all Scandinavians in our area, except for our neighbor who was Bohemian. But there were no Swedes, not when I went to school, just Norwegians." — William Nelson (Rollag, MN)

"I started school when I was about seven. The school ran as high as the eighth grade. We only had one teacher for forty kids. It usually was a man teacher. We quit at Christmas time and then started again at the first of April—three months in the fall and two in the spring." — Ole Olson (Fargo, ND)

"When I started school [in the Lake Park, Minnesota area], I would say seventy-five to eighty percent of the students were Scandinavian." — Amy Erickson (Moorhead, MN)

"Well, sometimes the boys would get a little bit hot, you know, and they would [divide into Swedes and Norwegians], but it was usually a friendly rivalry. They didn't get into any fist fights or anything." — Hazel Monson Barker (Moorhead, MN)

"I could speak English when I started school, kind of broken like. My three older sisters had been going to school and I learned from some of them. Maybe not so good, but I could follow along. My first teacher [in the Hawley, Minnesota area] was Danish, then we had Norwegian ones."
— Joanna Aune (Hawley, MN)

"My mother, before I learned to read, used to read to me, and she read in Norwegian. She read Norwegian fairy tales and Norwegian history, enormously interesting to me. We'd learn hymns, you know, and psalms, and the stories from the Bible. I heard them over and over again until I knew them by heart. My mother never went to school in this country, and although she learned to read English, she would never write English. She always wrote to us in Norwegian. She would speak to us in English and I would write to her in English and she would answer in Norwegian." — Clarence Glasrud (Moorhead, MN)

"We had to speak English all the time in school. There were so many that sometimes it was hard to get individual help. But we had charts and readers and the older ones would help, you know. Most of the time we had one teacher who didn't speak Norwegian at all. … My dad, who had never had an education, always thought that we should be teachers. So when I was just a little girl, before I went to school, I was told, 'If anybody asks you what you want to be when you get old, you just tell them "teacher."' And that's what I lived for all my life. I taught fourteen terms in rural schools, starting in 1913. I was fortunate when I went out to teach southwest of Winger [Minnesota] and I came into another Norwegian territory. I enjoyed my stay out there because I could visit with all the old people and they thought it was fun when the teacher would talk Norwegian. One year I had fifty-two in a one room school, from the first grade on to the eighth. And I had twelve beginners and most of them couldn't speak English when they came to school either. We had courses of study to follow that were given out by our county superintendent and of course we had to use the English language for that. Oh, they would like to speak Norwegian, but then I'd always answer them in English. But it was fun because they couldn't express themselves, the little ones, but then I understood them because when they talked Norwegian or Swedish I could correct it." — Alma Ramse (McIntosh, MN)

In North Dakota, the distance to the school house could be very far, but the Norwegian parents showed as much determination to get their children educated as the children showed in learning their new language.

"After Christmas when we came back to Hillsboro, we started school there. That's when they sent me to first grade. And here I was a lanky boy, fifteen years old almost, sitting in seats in first grade that I couldn't even get into. They had to give me a chair. And there I got a teacher of Norwegian heritage and she also enjoyed speaking Norwegian to me and I got so I got to be bored because every day it was the same. So I called on the superintendent of the school and fortunately he was of Swedish nationality, so he spoke very good Swedish, so I could speak Norwegian to him, and I told him I wasn't getting anything out of first grade. Here I am, fifteen years old, and the teacher is busy with what she's got. So he said, 'I'll send you to the fifth grade, because the teacher is Irish, Miss Isabelle Casey.' She was tickled pink that she was going to help me and she was a delight to be around because she was so helpful to me and encouraged me a lot. I copied her pronunciation to get the inflection in her voice. She spent hours after school with me. I would also try to be with kids that spoke good English, and I copied them." — Leif Christianson (Moorhead, MN)

"Norwegian was spoken in the home when we were children, and I didn't speak any English until I started school [near Niagara, North Dakota]. And our teacher spoke no Norwegian. What we learned about our ancestors we learned at home. She taught us American culture. ... I went to country school until I was in the sixth grade, and then I started town school. We would drive that buggy, and there was a livery stable in town [Larimore,

North Dakota]. We'd have to put the horse in the barn, take the harness off him, and then go and feed him at noon. And then put the harness back on him at four o'clock when school was over and then drive four miles home."

— Solveig Johnson (Niagara, ND)

"We had a sled with a covered wagon box on it. It was kind of specially made so that fifteen students could get into that. Two horses pulling the sled. We had only two miles to get to school [in Maddock, North Dakota], but some had six or seven miles, which would take an hour and a half to two hours some days when there was a lot of snow." — Edwin Markestad (Maddock, ND)

"We didn't have a school. They didn't build a school until we were there [near Hazelton, North Dakota] for a year. And we had some neighbors that had two boys and two girls that were bigger and the first English words I learned were 'a drink of water.' Those were the only English words I could say when I started school. I think I was nine years old when I started school, in 1907, when they built the school about a mile from our place. My mother hadn't taught me at home, not at all. She couldn't speak English, or read it, neither could Dad. I could read in Norwegian and write Norwegian too. We walked to school. Well, in the dead of winter, when it was awfully cold, I remember Dad hitching up the horses and taking us to school in the sleigh. Our term started in September and went to Christmas time, and then they dismissed school until March, so we only had a six month term. That's why it took so long. We were sixteen or seventeen before we got out [of eighth grade]. It was altogether different in those days. And our teacher, she came up from the river bottoms, and she had to live right in the school house. There was no place for here to stay and nobody had a room for her so she had to live right in the school house. And we had to keep the old stove heated and we had to carry water in a bucket to the school. She wasn't Norwegian. It was strictly American. I went until I was sixteen. I went to school in McKenzie for a while. I didn't go to high school anywhere. But I went to Valley City State Teacher's College. In those days you didn't have to go to high school. You could go from an eighth grade education to Valley City Normal. It was probably bigger then than it is now." — Matilda Blumer (Hazelton, ND)

"In school we spoke English. There were restrictions about it. It was clearly understood that you were to speak English in school. The teachers I had in my country school all [spoke Norwegian]. All my classmates were Norwegian. Then I went to school in Horace [North Dakota] where they were [mostly] Norwegian, but there were two that were French. Then when I went to Detroit Lakes [Minnesota] there was a mixture of everything, of course, and it was there that I became conscious of the fact that I had a Norwegian accent. Having a Norwegian accent and being countrified were about the same thing." — Clarence Glasrud (Moorhead, MN)

"When I started school, at six years old, I couldn't speak much English, but we had to learn. We went to a country school near Turtle Lake, North Dakota." — Mabel Fynskov (Osakis, MN)

"When I started grammar school I couldn't speak English at all. I had to learn. The teachers didn't speak Norwegian, they were Swedish. And I remember when I got into second grade my grandfather teased me that I was in '*sekk*-ond' grade. He said I was 'in the bag.'" — Alma Olson (Souris, ND)

"The first teacher I had [in Oakes, North Dakota] was Norwegian, but of course she didn't speak Norwegian to me in school, but she could have if it had been necessary. I just didn't say anything. I looked at the book. There were so many others in the same position. We could speak Norwegian in school. Nobody stopped us. There were many other Norwegian children there, too. The school was divided into three and in the primary grade it was about half Scandinavian." — Mabel Enger (Oakes, ND)

"We spoke Norwegian at home all the time. I didn't know anything but Norwegian until I started school [near Turtle Lake, North Dakota]. Then we weren't allowed to speak Norwegian. The teacher got a lot of laughs out of it because the Norwegians would talk Norwegian and the teacher would talk English. When they asked us 'What is your name?' I thought we were starting to learn something and I said to her 'What is your name?'" — Lloyd Westrum (Moorhead, MN)

"I should have gone to school. I had what you call an eighth grade [in Norway]. I learned to read and write and arithmetic and especially religion. I learned the commandments, the catechism, explanations, Bible history, and all that stuff, and my parents and everybody else living there were very religious. The first thing I had to learn here was how to talk." — Kristine Svidal (Starkweather, ND)

"As soon as we children went to school we learned to talk English right away and then [my parents] learned from us, more or less." — Dagne Faust (Colfax, ND)

"We had primost, rosettes, krumkake, and probably a lot more. We always had those things for our school picnics." — Eloise Kromarek (Bowman, ND)

"I was always astounded by the fact that someone could come to high school [in Langdon, North Dakota], and have such an accent and be a second or third generation Norwegian, but it's because when they lived in the country and their closed societies they all spoke Norwegian as their first language and English was their second language. It was most noticeable among the Scandinavian cultures, particularly the Norwegians." — Maureen Christiansen (Langdon, ND)

"The first year I taught I was seventeen and I had some students who were fifteen. We spoke English most of the time at home. My parents spoke Norwegian to each other, but they wanted us to speak English. I can't remember that [our school teacher] ever talked about [Norway] and [we didn't either]." — Alpha Jacobson Bowersox (Wolford, ND)

In most country schools with Norwegian-American students, the struggle for the language resembled a showdown between the children who were determined to continue to speak Norwegian and the teachers who were determined that their students be assimilated into the American mainstream culture. The English language was the ticket into that culture, and the teachers would often do everything they could to sell their students that ticket.

"The first teacher I had, she could speak Swedish, and that helped. I went to school three years, maybe four. And, of course, the other kids could speak Norwegian. We weren't supposed to talk Norwegian, but we did it anyway. She was mad, most of the time, because she heard us talking Norwegian. And we had one Swede in the school and I remember one time after she had bawled us out he stood up and said, 'Teacher, we didn't talk Norwegian, we talked Swede.' But she was right. We had come to America to be Americans." — John Klukken (Osakis, MN)

"In one school we went to they made a rule that you could only speak English on the premises. The wanted the kids to learn English, you know.

But in our home Norwegian was spoken all the time, until Mother died, anyhow." — Ole Olson (Fargo, ND)

"When we started school a lot of kids spoke Swedish or Norwegian, but not on the school grounds. Boy, you'd get your ears pulled if you did that. If you did that you would have to stay after school—that was the rule." — Clifford Hitterdal (Hitterdal, MN)

"Of course you run into that problem there when the teachers would try to keep you from using the Norwegian language because all the kids here were using the Norwegian language at home exclusively. We didn't realize it, of course, but it wasn't long before I realized they were right in putting that clamp on us, because we had any number of teachers that told us, when our kids went to school, that she could tell from the kids where they were using the Norwegian language at home, because they [the ones who spoke English at home] were in first place, they could use the English language more clearly and were a lot quicker. Most of the teachers we had were Norwegian or at least Scandinavian, but of course they had instructions to try to talk only English. I can't say that I could speak [English] when I started school, but I understood it, because I had three sisters and a brother that had gone to school, so I had that much of an advantage over some of the others who came to school and didn't understand a word of English. I had one little guy who just started school—he was about six and I was about six years older—and he was a sensitive guy and when the teacher came to talk to him he'd start crying, so I had to translate for him because she didn't understand Norwegian." — Oscar Bratlien (Hawley, MN)

"My second grade teacher was a Norwegian and she could speak Norwegian, but the only time she spoke it was when she visited my home, because it was not spoken on the school grounds." — John Gronner (Underwood, MN)

"I couldn't speak English when I started school, but it didn't take too many days before I started to learn it. I wasn't the only one, there was quite a few. She was Norwegian. She could talk it but she wouldn't let us talk it. She'd come around and say, 'Talk English now!'" — Henry Jacobson (Ulen, MN)

"I couldn't understand any English when I started school, but I was fortunate to have a teacher that could understand Norwegian. But, of course, she insisted that we speak English." — Clara Hanson (Moorhead, MN)

"I could speak [English] to some extent, but I wanted to speak the Norwegian, of course. And as soon as we got out at recess, and there was no teacher around, we would speak the Norwegian. Of course, it was easier. We had just as many [teachers in Kindred, North Dakota] who could speak the Norwegian as couldn't." — Gunhild Laske (Kindred, ND)

"There would be many in that community [near Valley City, North Dakota] who would be out playing [at recess] and they'd only speak Norwegian to each other. It was kind of funny because we had a hard time understanding the [other] Norwegians because they were from Stavanger and we weren't." — Dagne Faust (Colfax, ND)

"The first school I went to was the Oscarson schoolhouse. We had what you call 'Norwegian school' there, the month I was six years old. And I learned to write there, read and write Norwegian, in June of 1923. In September of that year, I started common school in Abercrombie [North Dakota]. It didn't help a bit when it came to learning English. There were several of my classmates who couldn't speak English. The teacher was Swedish. I was humorous. She was a strict disciplinarian. After we had been there for a while, speaking Norwegian was frowned on and we had to cut it out." — Palmer Tverdal (Abercrombie, ND)

What the children called 'Norwegian School' would later be popularly called 'vacation Bible school,' and it still exists as a one week period of religious instruction in most of the Lutheran churches in the Upper Midwest. By the time Palmer Tverdal attended, the 'Norwegian school' was one of the most important elements in preserving 'Norskdom' among the second generation of Norwegian immigrants. All instruction was in Norwegian, and many Norwegian-Americans did learn to read and write in Norwegian before they learned to do it in English. Such a school strengthened the intellectual and cultural heritage of young Norwegians, as is indicated by the fact that one of

many St. Olaf College students who got a summer job teaching in such a school was O. E. Rolvaag. For the most part the curriculum consisted of Bible stories and lessons, but frequently intermingled in this course of instruction were lessons on Norwegian history and Norwegian geography and stories from Norwegian literature and folk tales.

"An important factor in keeping us Norwegian was the religious instruction in the summertime. All of the Norwegian youngsters I know attended such schools. After the regular school was over, late in May, then the different congregations would have religious instruction for up to six weeks. Later on they cut it down to two weeks. Religious instruction in June was a must for all these congregations. They'd hold them in the country schools, or the town schools. And they were all taught in Norwegian. They have been continued on in English now. But religious instruction and Norwegian went hand in hand. We had to learn Norwegian grammar ... and we had to learn to write Norwegian." — Clarence Glasrud (Moorhead, MN)

"We had Norwegian school. That was two months out of the year that we had that and then we had regular school, what we called 'English school' in them days. In summer school, that was Norwegian. Just religion, well, no, we used to have spelling, that was one thing, of course, that was all in Norwegian. It was mostly Bible history and an explanation book. And then we had what was called the *lesebok* and that was stories, it means reading book. There were two teachers that were from Norway, and they went back to Norway to live." — Joanna Aune (Hawley, MN)

"There was only one church, four miles away, and we always had a Norwegian minister, no doubt a Lutheran church. We had our summer school there, that's where we got out Christian education. We'd walk four miles every day, stopping at every home that had children who were going, and by the time we got there, there might be twenty to twenty-five of us walking to church." — Mabel Fynskov (Osakis, MN)

"They had Norwegian school during the summer vacation period for six weeks, which was sponsored by the Norwegian Lutheran Church, and the older members of my family all attended this school." — John Gronner (Underwood, MN)

"And we went to Norwegian school every summer for about three weeks. We learned Norwegian there before we had to start to 'read for the minister.'" — Henry Jacobson (Ulen, MN)

"The Norwegian school ran for about six weeks, mostly religious instruction, and we always had men for instructors. And that led into confirmation instruction." — Eva Thortvet (Glyndon, MN)

"We couldn't use Norwegian in school, at least not in the public school. But every summer we would attend what we called Norwegian school [in rural Perley, Minnesota], which of course was for parochial purposes, but we would also study the Norwegian language and we had

Norwegian history. It was about six weeks that we went to Norwegian school." — Alva Hest (Perley, MN)

For many Scandinavian-Americans, the one room school house was just the beginning of the educational process. Norwegian-Americans in the Midwest established Lutheran academies in Canton, South Dakota and in Fargo, North Dakota. They also established Luther College in Decorah, Iowa; St. Olaf College in Northfield, Minnesota; Augusburg College in Minneapolis; Augustana College in Sioux Falls; and Concordia College in Moorhead. In addition, they established Waldorf College, a two-year college, in Forest City, Iowa. Swedish Lutherans established Gustavus Adolphus College in St. Peter, Minnesota, while Swedish Baptists established Bethel College in St. Paul. Danish Lutherans founded Dana College in Blair, Nebraska, and Grand View College in Des Moines, Iowa. While the majority of those interviewed had not gone on to college, many of them had proudly stated that their children had done so. In any setting, from an orphanage to a seminary, the Scandinavian-Americans valued their education. Beyond the opportunities of the public school, the Scandinavian-Americans attempted to provide for their own.

"When we were pre-school age, we practically never heard English spoken. When I was six, that would be in 1915, we had six weeks of Norwegian school, we called it, all day in the country school [in Norman County, Minnesota]. When September came, then of course I had to learn English. I know that some of the older people had reading circles, where someone who was a particularly good reader would sit and read a book while the other people sat listening. I took two years of Norwegian in high school in Twin Valley [Minnesota], and that included Norwegian grammar, mostly the first year, and translating, and in the second year you branched out into Norwegian history and Norwegian literature and we read a number of outstanding works of Ibsen and Hamsun, and some of the other outstanding Norwegian writers and we read them in Norwegian and discussed them in Norwegian." — Rev. Christian Schulstad (Dawson, MN)

"The four of us went to the children's home [in Twin Valley, Minnesota]. That was in 1911, when I was nine years old. This orphanage was maintained by the Norwegian Lutheran Church, and the school was so arranged that we had an hour of Norwegian every day. It was not a public school, of course, and our teachers were usually much better trained than the teachers who taught in the country schools around Twin Valley. They usually had two years of teacher training, and they usually came from the school in Fergus Falls. There was a Norwegian school there, run by the Norwegians. The college, Park Region is what it was called, and Park Region Hall over at

Concordia is named after the college there. But we also had teachers from the Lutheran seminary. So we usually had teachers that were quite well educated. We could notice it when we read for the minister. The children from the Home were so much better prepared than the children from the farms around there. There were about a hundred and twenty children there, about seventy boys and about fifty girls. And the boys didn't talk to the girls and the girls didn't talk to the boys. I don't think I talked to a girl until I was thirteen years old. We were kept separated, but we did have classes together." — Carl Narveson (Moorhead, MN)

"I went to District Three School [eastern Clay County, Minnesota], and I graduated from eighth grade in 1918. The next year, 1919, I didn't go to school. The two oldest boys were both in the service and I had to stay home and do chores. And then I spent some time at Concordia College in 1920. They had what they called a commercial course there at the time. So a lot of us farm boys we went there, it was a three month course. I stayed at a family home. There was just Old Main at that time, and the dormitory with the cafeteria under it. I ate at the cafeteria. Tuition was a hundred and eleven dollars, and that included the meals but not my room." — William Nelson (Rollag, MN)

"There was three business colleges here [in Crookston, Minnesota] at that time [1908] … but I was going to go down to Forest City [Waldorf College]. But they said, 'What you want to go to Forest City for, there's a college here!' O.K., I agreed, college was college to me. But the college here was only to teach newcomers. … So I didn't have much good out of that. Oh I had some good of that. The teacher was a lawyer, and I got a pretty good education in business law. But there weren't any jobs to be had. So I had two dollars left in my pocket so I could get out of town. Later on I told the girl that I married how low I was on money and she said, 'Why didn't you tell me?' But I said I wasn't going to go and tell my girlfriend that I was that short of money. I met her at the college." — Louis Haugen (Crookston, MN)

As was the case with the Swedes and the Norwegians, the other Scandinavian immigrant groups placed a high value on education. Partly because their arrival was later and their settlements more diffuse, the number of Danish and Finnish educational institutions was far less than that of the Swedes and Norwegians. The Icelanders did not establish any institution of higher learning, but perhaps no other immigrant group sought education and achieved success at a greater per-capita rate than the remarkable Icelanders.

Perhaps because they arrived in their prairie settlements directly from Iceland without having the opportunity to learn English or American ways, the Icelanders became passionate in their pursuit of education. Playford Thorson has suggested that in their educational efforts "they surpassed all of North Dakota's European ethnic groups."

For the Icelanders, especially, education did not stop at the school. Reading and literary societies abounded. In fact, in the early decades of the Pembina County settlement there were six reading societies, each with its own traveling library. The 'cowboy Icelanders' of McHenry County, North Dakota, also had a reading society. In families it was common for one member of the family to be the designated reader, reciting Icelandic and English prose and poetry while the rest of the family carded, spun, or wove the wool.

"We went to a Danish school in the summertime, when we were growing up, but we learned to read and write in English at the other school. I don't think I could speak English when I started school, because the language at home was strictly Danish. When I first started school, we only had school one and a half to two months a year. That's all that we could afford a teacher. That was all the education we could get until we grew up a little bit and then my sister and I were sent into town for a couple of years, in Westby, Montana." — Philip Andersen (Fargo, ND)

"In the school here [New York Mills, Minnesota], I would say that at least fifty percent of them were of Finnish background." — Russell Parta (New York Mills, MN)

"We always had school in the summertime because it was so hard to get around in the winter. We tried to go to school in January one time, but the snow was so bad we recessed until March. Of course, that was just grade school. ... I couldn't understand a word [of English] when I started school, and I didn't speak a word. [My teacher] didn't speak Icelandic. Somehow I learned to talk English. In those days we learned the ABCs you know, and I thought I was pretty smart when I learned the ABCs. How the teachers did it, I don't know! The rest of the kids were in the same boat." — Anna Bjornson (Fargo, ND)

"The schools were very important to them, that's where they learn to speak English. Some of the older [Icelanders] never learned to speak English, but the young ones all had to learn it. Some of them never learned it very well. My parents never made too much of a study of English, but they spoke enough to get along. ... Our school was a little different; we had Norwegians. We were about fifty percent Norwegians and fifty percent Icelanders, so in order to communicate, we had to speak English, so in our school we always spoke English. We couldn't understand each other, and we didn't try to."
— Kathryn Thordarson (Fargo, ND)

"We were permitted to speak Icelandic in school, but we didn't often do it. All the classes were in English and the books were in English, consequently we didn't speak Icelandic very much. In grade school, about three-fourths of the students were Icelandic." — Wayne Dinusson (Fargo, ND)

"They had school in Gardar in the early fall and in the early spring, but not in the winter. It was just too cold, and the children had to go so many miles and they had to walk it." — Rosa Campbell (Moorhead, MN)

"We never had any teachers that just spoke on Icelandic things except for the summer classes that we had. There were kids that didn't speak English too much at home that learned a lot at these classes. We always spoke Icelandic at home when I was a child. We went to a country school and I would say probably half of the teachers there were Icelanders who could speak Icelandic, but they used English in school because there was this German family. They did discuss Icelandic history in the school, but also some German." — Diane Volrath (Hitterdal, MN)

"There were usually between twenty to thirty kids in the school [Elm Grove Township, McHenry County, North Dakota]. There were just one or two who were not Icelandic. I finished eighth grade there and went to Upham High School." — Leo Hillman (Mountain, ND)

"I started school way before I should have. I started at the age of five years. And I didn't know any of the English language, so I had to learn the English language after I went to school. It was a rural school, southwest of Mountain [North Dakota], all eight grades. I'm sure there were between twenty and twenty-five [students] at one time, maybe over thirty. All of them were Icelandic. I think there was one family that was Norwegian." — Esther Hillman (Mountain, ND)

Chapter VIII
"They Were Fussy about Religion"

THE SCANDINAVIAN CHURCH IN AMERICA

In 1517, Martin Luther posted his famous Ninety-Five Theses on the north door of Frederick's Church in Wittenburg in Saxony. Within twenty years much of northern Europe and all of Scandinavia was Protestant. The state churches that emerged would become a vital part of the lives of all Scandinavians, as the Lutheran pastor would take his place beside the magistrate as a part of the ruling order. The religion may have been oppressive at times, but it did provide a certain amount of social cement to a community in which everyone knew their place.

In the nineteenth century, in all of the Scandinavian countries, the Lutheran church was beginning to lose the total control that it had maintained over the people for so long. There were now Baptists and Methodists to be found among the Swedish and Norwegian people. The Mormons began to make many converts, particularly in Denmark. The Unitarian movement gained strength in some of the urban areas, and the Lutheran churches themselves began to divide. In Sweden there were groups such as the Jansarna, followers of Erik Jansson, who were forced out of the country and came to America. In Denmark, the followers of Bishop Grundtvig began to question the formalism of the state church.

And in Norway, Hans Nielsen Hauge had a religious experience while plowing his field that led him to take up the cross and preach a more personal, more evangelical Lutheranism.

In Sweden, the state Lutheran clergy denounced emigration and once a member of the flock decided to emigrate the clergy tended to forget all about him. There were, however, several members of the clergy who themselves emigrated and they would become the leaders of the Lutheran congregations in America. Lars Paul Esbjorn formed a Swedish Lutheran congregation in Andover, Illinois, in 1850, and in 1860 the Augustana Synod was created from the merger of thirty-six Swedish and Norwegian congregations. The Augustana Synod would become entirely Swedish in 1870 when the Norwegians withdrew to form their own synod. Unlike the other Scandinavian groups, the Swedes would have only one Lutheran synod.

The second largest Swedish-American denomination was the Swedish Evangelical Covenant. The "Covenanters," or "Mission Friends," had developed as a pietistic alternative to the conservative Swedish state church and in 1885 an American organization, the Swedish Evangelical Mission Covenant was formed. Swedish Baptists and Swedish Methodists did not share close ties with the old country and eventually each group formed a special Swedish conference under the general organization of American Methodist or American Baptist groups. All three of these denominations would create lasting institutions in the Midwest. The Mission Covenant would create North Park College and Seminary in Chicago, the Swedish Baptists would create Bethel College and Seminary in St. Paul, and the Swedish Methodists would create Evanston Collegiate Institute, which became Kendall College in Illinois.

The Lutheran Church in Denmark was made up of three major trends. The *Centrum*, as it was called, was a "high church" party that followed the teachings of Jacob Peter Mynster. A second group was affected by the work of Nikolai Frederik Severin Grundtvig. A gifted hymnist, legislator, and educational reformer, Grundtvig brought a rationalist interpretation to Danish Lutheranism that was in conflict with the orthodox Lutheran position. A third development within the Danish church was the Inner Mission movement, begun in 1850 by Jens Larsen, a blacksmith and a lay preacher. This latter group would have an effect on the Danish immigrants who formed the United Evangelical Lutheran Church, a group often called the "Holy Danes." The Grundtvig group eventually became known as the Danish Church, or the "Happy Danes."

While other Scandinavian groups often had to contend with schism within the Lutheran Church, the Icelanders faced a different situation. Indeed, the Icelandic Lutheran Church remained intact until it merged with the Lutheran Church in America in 1962. Unlike the other Scandinavian Lutheran churches, the Icelandic church had never been split by pietistic movements, and was thus more tolerant and liberal. The major threat to religious unity of the Icelanders came from the outside, in the form of Unitarianism. The Unitarian Church rejected the doctrine of the trinity and emphasized the unity of God. Although there was only one short-lived Unitarian Church established among the North Dakota Icelanders, there were a number of Unitarian churches established among the Icelanders in Canada.

There were three main branches of the Finnish Lutheran Church. The Suomi Synod, which would also merge with the Lutheran Church in America in 1962, most closely resembled the old state church in Finland. Many Finns, with less than warm memories of the Old Country, wished to form their own American "National" church. The split began in Michigan and spread throughout the Finnish communities. This Finnish Evangelical Lutheran National Church of America merged with the Lutheran Church, Missouri Synod in 1963. The Apostolic Lutheran Church, which is still in existence, originated from a revival movement led by a Swedish pastor, Lars Levi Laestadius. His followers brought their fundamental ideas with them as they settled first in the mining areas of northern Norway and then finally in America. One group, called the "Old Laestadians," founded a seminary in Hancock, Michigan. As Playford Thorson has noted, they "emphasized the simplicity of the Christian life," and so forbade "neckties, pictures on walls, taking photographs, hats on women, Christmas trees, life insurance, and flowers at funerals."

In Norway, as in Sweden, the Lutheran Church had been ardently opposed to the exodus of its people. Bishop Jacob Neuman of Bergen exhorted his countrymen to stay home: "Here in Norway rest the ashes of your forefathers; here you first saw the light of day; here you enjoyed your childhood pleasures; here you received your first impressions of God and His love; here you are still surrounded by relatives and friends who share your joy and your sorrow, while there, when you are far away from all that has been dear to you, who shall close your eyes in the last hour of life? A stranger's hand! And who shall weep at your grave? Perhaps—no one!"

There must have been something intoxicating about the air of freedom in America, as the Norwegians seemed to interpret their new liberties as meaning the freedom for everyone to establish their own Lutheran synod. In fact, the Norwegians started fourteen Lutheran synods in America. They ranged from the "high church" ideal of the Norwegian state church as represented in America by the Norwegian Synod, called the *Synoda* Church, to the "low church" ideal of the Hauge Synod. In between and on either side were the United Church, Lutheran

Brethren, and the Lutheran Free Church, not to mention the independent Norwegian Synod, the Eielsen Synod, and the Wisconsin Synod. The issues that divided the synods were, to our modern eyes at least, often quite minor, but that did not make them any less vigorously disputed. The divisions would sometimes separate husband from wife or children from parents as each was sure that there could be only one true way to salvation, and that way led from the Garden of Eden, which was almost certainly located in Norway. The "high church" tradition included an established order of service with university trained ministers wearing a gown and a ruff collar, presiding in ornate buildings and chanting rather than speaking the words. The "low church" movement, associated with Haugianism, stressed much more spontaneity in a modest church in which a minister wore no gowns, was less educated, did not chant, and often served grape juice instead of wine. They both agreed that Jesus Christ was the savior of the world, but it seemed the Norwegians had differing views as to how He wanted them to behave.

As immigrants, the Scandinavians could not pack their rosemaled chests with very many of their possessions. They could, however, take their religion, together with all of their traditions, institutions, and feuds. In spite of the differences that would later be so apparent, however, one of the first things the immigrants did was to establish their church.

"In my childhood it was Norwegian all the time, reading, and writing, and talking. We were [our parent's] teachers. They never went to school to learn the English language. And almost the whole settlement there was Norwegian. There was another community that was Swedish, so you see we were all Scandinavian, and they got along so well with their language. There were very good friends. They worked together and they said they had to have a place to worship their Lord because they had been taught that in their home country and they had brought their Bibles with them. So the Norwegians and the Swedes worked together and they built the church, out in the country near Winger [Minnesota]." — Alma Ramse (McIntosh, MN)

"Around here, they all came from the state church in Norway, and that was Lutheran. And that was very strict. You had to learn religion in Norway if you expected to become 'full.' And if you didn't know enough to get confirmed, you couldn't get a license to get married. It was that strict! I think it was a very good start for people." — John Klukken (Osakis, MN)

"In the 1870s, the first church was built. That was a Norwegian one on the North Dakota side of the river, about three miles north of Hickson. They used to have a circuit rider come around." — Lynn Anderson (Moorhead, MN)

"We had what you might call a traveling minister. It was a Lutheran minister that came from Hazelton [North Dakota]. He would drive out on a Sunday and we'd have services at the schoolhouse, and sometimes in the homes. We had services at our place at different times. And one of the neighbors had a team of oxen and one day—him and his wife were real old—he asked us if we kids would like a ride. And that was a real treat to get a ride [to church] in a wagon drawn by oxen." — Matilda Blumer (Hazelton, ND)

"Grong church was organized in 1872 and at first they held their services in homes around and then in 1874 a large school house was built over in District Three [eastern Clay County, Minnesota] and then they had their services there. The Union Church that the English speaking people had organized also had their services there. About 1878 they built the Grong church. Then there were synodical differences and one thing and another led to strife, I guess, in the community, and in 1898 there was a splinter group that left Grong and formed a separate congregation. They built their first church in 1904. The Rollag congregation quickly grew to be the larger congregation. Grong continued to remain what we called the Lutheran Free Church and the Rollag congregation was the United Lutheran Church. Of course, it's gone through several changes, now it's the American Lutheran Church. Grong is also ALC now. Well, there may have been talk [about merging], but as far as I know, there has been no serious intention of merging. I would say, and to their everlasting credit, the group that has continued to belong to Grong Church has a loyalty that they certainly can be proud of. Probably it is stronger at the present time [1976] than it's ever been." — William Nelson (Rollag, MN)

"They had organized the congregation earlier and that was mostly taken care of by a traveling missionary. And they would meet then, usually in the homes [in the Ulen, Minnesota, area]. That was the Norwegian Church; translating, it would be 'the United Lutheran Church.'" — Clara Hanson (Moorhead, MN)

"The first church that they had, they [Norwegians and Swedes] were together for some years, and then when that blew down, and other settlers moved in here, they started the church in Hitterdal [Minnesota]. [The Norwegians] joined that and then the Swedes organized the Swede Grove Church. One [Norwegian church] was on the east side of the road, and [another Norwegian church] was on the west side. But, there was only one to start with. The one on the west side was the first church, well, they didn't build a church, but it was an organized church and they held their meetings in various farm homes. And then, due to some misunderstanding, not locally but in the higher echelons of the church, they divided and the people on the east side, called the United Lutheran, built a church first and then later on, those on the west side, called the Synod church, built their church a number of years later. And later on, when the older generation died off, the younger generation came in and resolved their differences and they merged."
— Wilferd Anderson (Hitterdal, MN)

"They built the first Lutheran church north of Bagley [Minnesota]. Before this, the minister would come and stay at each home for a short time and then they would baptize the babies and give some instruction to the children. My grandmother Christofferson was so responsible for keeping the Wild Rice Lutheran Church going. That's near Zerkel, Minnesota, and very lovely. One time she told my mother, in Norwegian, 'You can come along and help build on the church, you can't get out of it. It is a big shame how many there are who are against doing anything for the church.'" — Florence Fritz (Detroit Lakes, MN)

"Most of the time, when I was a boy, we only had church services once every three weeks, because the pastor served so many congregations. I can remember him standing there saying, in Norwegian, 'There shall be service three weeks from today.' People felt strongly about their churches, once they got established and once they got a few relatives buried in the churchyard. There are now five generations of our family buried in that churchyard." — Christian Schulstad (Dawson, MN)

"The second or third year we were on this farm [near Bertha, Minnesota], there were some Norwegians around and the first thing they wanted to do was build a church. And they called a minister who was a school mate of my father's from back in Norway, from Gudbrandsdalen." — Art Waldon (Detroit Lakes, MN)

"They established a church and my mother was in the Ladies Auxiliary when they started it from the ground, you might say. And then they built the church, and had an old building for a while and then built a beautiful mission church. My dad helped build it. They had religion, and they had church, and things were pretty good. I got confirmed and married in that church and my husband was a member of that church. They had their Turtle Mountain Church [near Souris, North Dakota] but then some of the old timers figured that they weren't quite good enough in Turtle Mountain so they formed a smaller church. They were fussy about religion." — Alma Olson (Souris, ND)

"My parents were instrumental in organizing the [Norwegian Lutheran] church in Wolford [North Dakota]. Soon after the immigrants came here the missionaries followed after and they would have church services in their homes. They actually had their preliminary organization in our home on the farm, and that was in 1903. [My father] was one of the first deacons. This was called the Engers Norwegian Church and later there was another, the Highland Church, so there was a difference. I don't know if you'd call it friction, but there were two different synods. The pastor came from Knox [North Dakota]. I think it was in 1908 when they started to build the church at Wolford." — Alpha Bowersox (Wolford, ND)

In Lutheran diversity, there was usually a spirit of toleration and Christian charity. But not always. For many Norwegian Lutherans, there was something distrustful about a congregation that tried to curry favor with God by concluding the Lord's Prayer with "forever and ever,

amen," rather than the terse but effective "forever, amen." But such an issue, of course, could divide a community.

"There was some animosity. ... I remember my folks telling when we first came to Hitterdal [Minnesota] that both churches vied for my folks to choose which church they should belong to, and we ended up going to the east side church. Why I don't know. We lived on the east side of town, maybe that's why. We continued to go there even after we moved out to the farm. I was a Norwegian at that time, but then when I got married I got to be all Swede so I had to go to the Swede Grove church." — Wilferd Anderson (Hitterdal, MN)

"I don't know why [there were two Norwegian Lutheran churches in Hitterdal, Minnesota]. It was the same thing. It was just wasting time and money, that's all. They could have gotten along with one pastor and have services more often than to have two pastors come here. Yah, it was only foolishness!" — Clifford Hitterdal (Hitterdal, MN)

"I was confirmed in Norwegian in the Synoda church in Hitterdal, that was the west side one. The east side one was United. I don't think there were any differences between them. They were each served by a different minister. [Some people] would jump back and forth, too. They'd get mad at the minister and go to the other church. They were pretty stiff necked in those days." — William Melby (Hitterdal, MN)

"At first, when we moved to Hitterdal, they had that old-fashioned Norwegian custom of men sitting on one side of the church and the ladies on the other. The young boys sat with their dads and the girls with their mothers. I remember the first time we went to church in Hitterdal. My dad sat with the family and the whole family sat together. He felt so out of place because he was the only man on that side of the church. He didn't continue that. He moved over. I was confirmed in 1912, my brother Russell and I, and we were the only ones confirmed in English. All the rest of the class was confirmed in Norwegian. Pastor Dahlager, the minister, would turn around and take our books and ask a few questions, and then he'd turn around and ask the Norwegians questions and for explanations. The sermons were always in Norwegian." — Gale Iverson (Hitterdal, MN)

"I think there was some degree [of rivalry between the two Norwegian churches], but it wasn't anything bad. It was kind of pride. If one church got some new lamps, the other church would get them too, because they didn't want to be outdone. They were very simple and crude, but both of these churches have been replaced by modern ones. There wasn't any organization for the youth, except the Ladies Aid and 'reading for the minister,' and funerals. There wasn't much to do. They just had the minimum amount of religion, I'd say, to get by with." — Allen Erickson (Moorhead, MN)

"At certain times there had been local strife [between the Rollag churches], so there was a little, uh, they were outsiders to each other. But that quickly dissipated. We now hold Lenten services and things in conjunction with each other. But we had Reverend Hauge here as a minister for over fifty years and he certainly wasn't the kind of person who would look for any strife or friction." — William Nelson (Rollag, MN)

"We had a church right on the corner of our land. Dad donated an acre of ground for it and that was built, in think, about in 1903. That was Parke Lutheran. Reverend Hauge had four churches—Hawley, Gran, Rollag, and Parke, and we had services every three weeks. The [church in Rollag] split into two congregations, but as far as I heard, there was never any real fight among the neighbors. The Rollag, they wound up the United Lutheran and Grong still remained what they called the Free Church. And they stayed that way. Reverend Helgeson took care of Grong and Hegland and Reverend Hauge couldn't hardly even speak to him. They were sure worse than the members in that respect. I can remember that they tried to. One time we had an Old Settler's Picnic over there in Viking Park and they tried to get the two choirs to sing together, but even that didn't work. I lay that to either one or both of the two preachers. I wouldn't lay it to the community, I'd lay it to the preacher." — Oscar Bratlien (Hawley, MN)

"In Lake Park [Minnesota] there was two churches, Synod and United. They did not get along too well. It seemed like the preachers especially had their own ideas and their own ways so sometimes they wouldn't greet each other when they met on the street, so there was some difference there, all right." — Oscar Olson (Lake Park, MN)

"One church, Lysne, was a United church. The Synoda church must have been eleven, twelve miles away [in Hitterdal] and that was a long ways to go with horses, you know, so [our neighbors] didn't get to church so much. They lived about four miles from Lysne church. I think they felt they should be loyal to their home church. They finally did join Lysne." — Joanna Aune (Hawley, MN)

Some of the churches among the Norwegian Lutherans, especially the Haugians, were far more pietistic than others. This in itself would sometimes cause problems, especially among the young people who must have wondered why it was sinful for them to play cards but not, apparently, for their schoolmates who went to a different church. The adults might say otherwise, but every child knew that another church smelled different and felt different than their own. It was always assumed that God preferred the church their parents had chosen.

"What I remember most vividly was when we moved to a little town where the only Lutheran church was the Haugean Church, and at first, [my father] was very doubtful that that was a good idea. It was *not* the same kind of service. The minister had *not* gone to a seminary. He happened to be a fellow they liked very much, and I was in high school and didn't want to go to that church. Eventually I did, and came to enjoy it a good deal. But it was a little bit strange at first, different types of hymns, different kinds of church services. Still in Norwegian, of course. I used to think the squabbling between the different types of Lutherans must have been a disgraceful business and must have been very hard on the church and weakened it. Actually, evidence seems to be to the contrary. It probably strengthened it. Some of these Norwegians were very feisty and may not have had any interest in the church at all. But here's a good fight going on, and the struggles were very hard fought. And actually such a fight appealed to some people, because they wanted to be partisan to one side or the other. Too good a fight to stay out! … Our services always were in Norwegian. We never had English sermons, not in Cass County [North Dakota]! I never heard an English sermon until I got to Detroit Lakes, in 1922. The preacher wore a black gown and one of those ruff collars around his neck. Fine fellow! The [church] we went to was the old Norwegian Synod, the one in Horace [North Dakota]. Four miles away was the Haugean church, and they had joined together five years before, in 1917. But my father was not at all convinced that it was safe. The doctrine was not quite the same and he was very dubious about this other church. There were very great rivalries between the different branches of Lutherans. They didn't accept the other. Oh yah, we associated with them, but they were not quite the right kind of people." — Clarence Glasrud (Moorhead, MN)

"Grandmother's uncle traveled with Hans Nielson Hauge, preaching together. But over here I can't say there was ever a connection between those that felt the influence of it and those who didn't. I think maybe there was in other places, but I can't see that it made too much difference around here. There was a Congregational church in Abercrombie [North Dakota] before there was a Lutheran church, and there was a Congregational church in Colfax before there was a Lutheran church. Well, they've been gone for years and I think it's partly because the Yankees moved out. ... In the Norwegian Synod they had a high respect for the pastor and God's word in the church. No one was supposed to argue or quibble or question God's word in the church. And they had this here 'high church' deal, quite a bit of ritual, and the pastor would cross himself after services. And he wore this ruff collar and it would be dignified. But outside the church, then it seemed like it was forgotten. Confirmation was graduation, and after that you were free to go out and sew your wild oats. You were almost encouraged to do it, partying and dancing and drinking was the rule and it wasn't frowned on. Laziness was the unforgivable sin and hard work would cover a multitude of sins. That was common among the pioneers. If you could make things go, then you had it made. In the other churches, there was no dancing and no drinking and no card playing and none of those things. And yet, there again the people who would practice that to extreme were the most unforgiving Christians you could find. The people who practiced that tended to have a 'low church' type of service. ... I think the Norwegians, in their pioneer days, were fatalists. I remember how even the worst drunkards would talk religion when they were stacking grain, and even the worst drunkards would be talking about this free will business." — Palmer Tverdal (Abercrombie, ND)

"Of course there were certain activities that were not considered proper for a good church member to go to. Such as lodge meetings. Lodges were considered to be really terrible in those days. They thought you were just a devil if joined a lodge. ... Dancing was frowned upon by certain people, and my father preached against it [from the pulpit]. And any kind of drinking was looked down on, any kind of liquor was unacceptable. And then there was card playing, of course, that was looked down on. In our home we could have Rook or those little home card games, but not cards with faces on them. We figured that the face cards were tools of the devil. We figured the devil was in the pictures on the face cards." — Odin Strandness (Fargo, ND)

"That's the way churches were in those days. They were against dancing and card playing and things like that, but I don't ever remember it ever being mentioned from the pulpit. Drinking, that I think he would mention, and Sunday work!" — Joanna Aune (Hawley, MN)

The focal point of the Norwegian Lutheran churches was the pastor. He was respected, loved, and feared by his parishioners, whether he wore a plain black suit or a long gown with a huge ruff collar. The traveling pastor portrayed in Rolvaag's *Giants in the Earth* is a composite stereotype of all Norwegian-American pastors, but it is an accurate description of how the immigrants viewed their spiritual advisors. As Rolvaag viewed him, "the vestments which he wore seemed only to emphasize the strength of his features, whose youthful vigor, in spite of the grey-streaked beard, appeared at this solemn moment to have taken on a new glow of life." They saw him as representing the word of God, and therefore expected him to be stern, strict, serious, and sober.

"The ministers there [around Bertha, Minnesota] had about five congregations that they looked after. And they were run ragged and got very little for their pains. Whenever there was ministers brought in from the outside they were brought to our place because my mother was a good cook and knew how to take care of people. The minister made his headquarters there because he knew if ever he was broke there were a few dollars there. And we furnished wood for him, hay and oats for his horse, and whenever he came to the farm he got eggs and cream and butter and a chicken or two."
— Art Waldon (Detroit Lakes, MN)

"They called it the Scandia Church [near Morris, Minnesota], but that wasn't the real name for it. The real name was the First Evangelical Lutheran Church. It was called a free church, the same thing as the Haugean group back in Norway—kind of against the state church. There were two Norwegian churches there, only a mile apart. We went to church every two weeks, because the preacher had several charges. He had to have several charges in order to make a living. He had to go to four or five churches. He had a horse and buggy and stayed with the families. He had his favorites to stay with. He stayed with us lots of times. … The Ladies Aid would collect money to pay the preacher. Once in a while they'd buy him a new buggy. The people were assessed to pay the preacher according to their means. I know my father was assessed four dollars and fifty cents a year for his family. Boys were assessed a dollar and a half and single girls were assessed a dollar. The preacher got about four hundred and fifty dollars a year. It wasn't very much, but somebody would bring him a load of hay once in a while, and some women would bring him butter and cream and some would bring milk and potatoes and eggs. He had a wife and kids. She was home alone a lot of the time." — Ole Olson (Fargo, ND)

"[At the Twin Valley, Minnesota, Children's Home] the children went to bed at nine o'clock, and after nine o'clock pastors from the different communities would come in and they would have sort of a social hour at the Home. And there would be Haugeaners and there would be United pastors and Norwegian Synod pastors. And they would all get together at the home and enjoy themselves, whereas they might preach against each other on Sundays. But I don't really think there was much of that, because a few years later [1917] they all united into one church, the Evangelical Lutheran Church." — Carl Narveson (Moorhead, MN)

"My father went directly from the seminary out to North Dakota, and he started a small church near Devil's Lake. He originated a missionary church there. I think he had four or five congregations out there; served them by horses, of course. We had a barn to keep the horses in, and the members of the congregation would bring us feed for the horses and they'd bring food for us too, lots of food, probably half a hog or something like that. We always had plenty to eat out there. With five congregations to serve, my father seemed to run all the time. I never saw him walk. He was very excitable too, and he had a lot of close calls, especially in the winter. When I got older I went around the country with him quite a bit. Especially during the flu epidemic, I'd drive for him a lot. I was only about twelve years old, but in those days boys could drive. I remember going to this one house where this young woman said she had gone to a dance the night before and she said, 'I know I brought this all on to my folks.' Two or three members of that family died of the flu and she blamed herself for going to the dance. In just a couple days they passed away, it went that quick. But my dad and I went through that whole territory, seeing sick people every day, and we never got a fever from it. … My mother took care of all the music in church. Of course, in those days a pastor's wife was considered a part of the congregation. She had to do everything. It got so they really wore her out. She had a nervous breakdown from all those demands. She also gave music lessons. She'd play songs by Ole Bull and Grieg all the time. … Oh yah, the pastor's kids—the minister's kids were considered to be perfect, you know. If they did something, you know, that would be terrible. In a small community everybody knew what you did, you know, not like a big city. Whatever you did people watched you. I think that's really what kept me from ever even considering the ministry, because of the experience of being a minister's son." — Odin Strandness (Fargo, ND)

"When I was just a little kid, the church services were all in Norwegian, and I could never understand a word of it. Not a word! They had a preacher that came by a horse and buggy from Rothsay, Minnesota, and he had about three or four churches. We didn't have it every week then. It was the turn of each of the Ladies to entertain the minister. Once a year he'd come and stay at our house. It was quite a deal when the minister was our guest. We were all on our good behavior, and we always said grace. My mother had taught us a Norwegian prayer and we'd rattle that off not knowing what we were saying. But my dad was so impatient, he couldn't wait for that grace and he'd start eating and my mother would scold him."
— Allan Erickson (Moorhead, MN)

The church was much more than just a place of worship, it was also usually the center of social activity. The Sunday service was a constant factor in their lives, the one opportunity of the week when the farmers would see their neighbors to talk about the weather, where the women could see an adult other than their husbands, and where the children could find a welcome playmate to relieve the tedium of summer school vacation. The Ladies Aid societies or the 'circles' provided a much needed social outlet for immigrant women, and the young people's societies, later often called 'Luther Leagues,' were very important to teenagers, especially in a day when many left school after the eighth grade. In the process, the church became part of their lives, and a part that is often one of the most recalled parts of the Scandinavian heritage.

"This Swedish family was our close neighbors. And he was the janitor for quite a few years at Lysne Church. That was an honor then. Those that had any office at all felt it was quite an honor. He was paid about fifteen dollars a year for being janitor. I was the organist. I got fifty cents for each Sunday I played and that was every three weeks. Finally they raised it to seventy-five cents a Sunday. That's the most I ever got." — Joanna Aune (Hawley, MN)

"We belonged to the Norwegian Lutheran church, and all the sermons were in Norwegian. Sunday School was taught in English, but the services were in Norwegian. I always went with my mother to these Ladies Aid organizations, and they just fascinated me, because there were any number of different brogues or accents. You see every little division had its certain speech style; they all had this cadence, so I could mimic most of those people, which I thought was hilarious." — Ruth Erickson (Moorhead, MN)

"All the ladies would serve Ladies Aid. I think it was once a month. They would serve lunch in the afternoon and then a big supper in the evening and everybody went to that. That was fun, because everybody was there. Everybody in town [Niagara, North Dakota] came. And then we'd have choir practice, we had to sing in the choir, so we'd have choir practice once a week. And Luther League once a week, and we 'read for the minister' as we called it, so we could be confirmed. And then there was the annual lutefisk supper. That was a big gathering, because they were noted for being good cooks so everybody came. They were real successful. And whenever there was a wedding in the church, everybody came, whether they had been invited or not. The church was always full because that was a chance to get together, so everybody went to the weddings. Funerals too!" — Solveig Johnson (Niagara, ND)

"Ladies Aid! My mother was the first president of Ladies Aid. They used to serve chow mein. Now I know that sounds funny now, but we always served chow mein, besides the lutefisk and lefse." — Alpha Bowersox (Wolford, ND)

"We had Ladies Aid. We had Young People's Societies. And all the old people came to the Young People's Societies, so there's people there. That was all musical." — Ellen Abraham (Villard, MN)

"We had the Norwegian Free Church, the United Church, and the Synoda, and there was only one absolute English speaking church in town [Hillsboro, North Dakota] until 1920, and that was the Congregational church. The social life, naturally for a young fellow, would revolve around Young People's Societies in their different churches. In those days you would look almost out of place if you went to a church social function that you weren't a member of." — Leif Christianson (Moorhead, MN)

"For confirmation [in 1909] we were twelve girls and four boys. It was in the fall of the year, but still the minister wanted us to be all dressed in white. So we were. But it was a cold drizzly day. Boy was we cold! You know, we didn't have no heat in the church them days, just one small stove in the center of it. My mother made my dress, but we got shoes from this store. We shopped in Moorhead and that was about twelve miles from here. L. S. Moe and Moody's. Those were the two leading ones in Moorhead. Each family had someone come to their homes for dinner then." — Cora Kragnes (Felton, MN)

For most Norwegian immigrants, the religion was Lutheran and the language was Norwegian and the two were practically synonymous. More than any other institution, the church kept alive the 'Norskdom' that was being threatened by the American experience. In the period from 1890 to 1920 more than three thousand congregations in America were using Norwegian as the sole language of worship. This would fade, but it would do so only gradually, and usually only after the First World War. When the Norwegian language passed from usage in the church, its passing was mourned by the old and usually welcomed by the young. By the time the various synods merged to form the American Lutheran Church in 1960, it was an appropriate name.

"Norwegian was the language they spoke. They had Norwegian services for years. I was confirmed in Norwegian. They organized it with their friends and relatives—the Gol Church in Kindred. The hymns and everything were in Norwegian." — Gunhild Laske (Kindred, ND)

"As time went on, the Norwegians married the Germans and there was just the old people left. And the congregation got so small they couldn't keep it going so they all joined Lysne Church [west of Hitterdal, Minnesota]. And that became an English congregation then. Before that it had all been Norwegian. That must have been in the early thirties. They started having English one Sunday and Norwegian the next, and after a while it got to be all

English, because there were too many that couldn't understand the Norwegian language by that time. Even some of the Norwegian children that had Norwegian parents grew up just to talk English and didn't understand Norwegian. ... Reverend Hauge was our minister for fifty-three years. He had five churches, and we had services every third Sunday. Hawley, Lysne, Rollag, Gran, and Parke—that kept him pretty busy. He was born in Norway, but he spoke English very well." — Joanna Aune (Hawley, MN)

"We had a minister [Reverend Hauge] who was to blame for all that stuff, because he was always emphasizing that the children should learn Norwegian first. He put such emphasis in church on learning Norwegian because if they didn't learn that first they could never learn it. He also put it this way, that was showing your elders a little bit respect. I never believed that because I had a dog that had every bit of respect for me and he couldn't speak a word of Norwegian." — Oscar Bratlien (Hawley, MN)

"Grandma dragged me along to that church, and [the minister] had a certain dialect from the southern part of Norway. And as a little kid I had to sit and listen to that tiresome speech in a dialect that I couldn't understand. You know, I think I hated church for the rest of my life. You get so you don't want to go to church." — Clara Johnson (Underwood, ND)

"A lot of churches required my father to speak Norwegian, at least for some services. It got so finally the main services were in English and the special services were in Norwegian. That was kept on for a long time. For some of them, I think, they thought it wasn't Christianity unless it was in the Norwegian language. It tapered down, little by little. There were still services in the 1930s." — Odin Strandness (Fargo, ND)

"Everything done by the church was in Norwegian. The minister wouldn't preach in English. He maybe could speak it, but the two ministers I remember as a child, Reverend Anderson and Reverend Johnson, both fine gentlemen, but neither of them would even think about preaching in English. [When I moved] to Detroit lakes there were plenty of Norwegians there, but there were others there, too. For instance, I was studying for my confirmation at the time and I was studying using Norwegian books, the explanations, and I had to start all over again in English because I had memorized all these answers that I would give while being catechized in Norwegian. I thought that was double jeopardy." — Clarence Glasrud (Moorhead, MN)

"I was confirmed in Norwegian, and so was my wife. I think [Norwegian services] continued until the early thirties [in the Rollag, Minnesota, area]. Oh, there was a little bit of [resistance to English services] by some of the older ones. At first they would divide and have English and Norwegian services and gradually it was all in English." — William Nelson (Rollag, MN)

"I don't know how long they kept up with the Norwegian services [in Hitterdal, Minnesota], but I know my grandfather died in 1939 and his funeral was in Norwegian." — William Melby (Hitterdal, MN)

"I suppose the last time Norwegian services were used regularly was about 1940 [around Abercrombie, North Dakota], or maybe 1945."
— Palmer Tverdal (Abercrombie, ND)

"Norwegian was used in the church [by Perley, Minnesota] definitely until 1916 or 1917. I know the minister that confirmed our class couldn't speak hardly any English. Hagen was the one who confirmed us." — Alva Hest (Perley, MN)

"It was, I believe, in the last part of the twenties that they quit having Norwegian or Swedish services in the local churches [of Hitterdal, Minnesota]. Towards the end they alternated, one Sunday in English and one Sunday in Norwegian, but it was in the last part of the twenties that they cut it out altogether. The younger generation came in and the older people had lost interest." — Wilferd Anderson (Hitterdal, MN)

"This would be in the twenties. They had an English sermon once a month. Then eventually twice a month, and pretty soon they had the English service three times a month and the Norwegian service once a month. And as the years went by they finally had only English services except for special occasions." — Beatrice Schaefer (Osakis, MN)

"In eastern Norman County [Minnesota] … I can't think of a single church that wasn't a Norwegian Lutheran church. The Norwegian language was always used, but in the period between the two wars, there got to be more and more pressure to use English so that the young people could understand it. And that got to be a little difficult, because many of the older pastors couldn't handle English very well. Up to World War Two there were many churches in the Red River Valley that still had Norwegian services every other Sunday or something like that." — Christian Schulstad (Dawson, MN)

"Church services were in Norwegian for a long time, until Pastor Carlson came and he changed it. He wanted English so the young people could understand it. It was hard for some of the older Norwegians. They still wanted to hang on to their language. They didn't like the change. They were stubborn there [near Souris, North Dakota]. — Alma Olson (Souris, ND)

"In fact, we newcomers, we took up the battle against the use of nothing but Norwegian because all the young people went to the Presbyterian church across the river. That's where our young people were and we got sick and tired of being just grandpas and grandmas, so we finally got them to switch. Then they wanted just one English service a month, the rest in Norwegian. But we didn't like that. We said why not have English all the time and go in the evening for [Norwegian service]. And that's what it came to be after a couple years campaigning. ... When I got out to my first parish there they wanted a Norwegian service one Sunday a month. But I told them if they wanted that I would return the call. Because, I said, 'You're eliminating the young people.' And in that big church in town, if they had seventeen [at the Norwegian service], they had a crowd. So we started with

English services every Sunday and within seven months we had two hundred and ninety people there on Sunday. There was English every Sunday and they could plan on it. In order to satisfy those old Norwegians, I said let's have a Norwegian service once a month, at two thirty in the afternoon, which was a lot of extra work for me. I had no assistant, no secretary. That turned out to be one of the best attended services because they came from all over … up to a hundred miles away for those services, because it was a novelty for them. They could go to their own services in the morning and come to Norwegian services in the afternoon." — Rev. Sven Thompson (Willmar, MN)

"I was confirmed in Norwegian. That was about the last class that they had in Trinity [in Moorhead] in 1921, the last confirmation in Norwegian. And I was the only one in the whole class of thirty-five. My mother wouldn't let me change. But the other kids were confirmed in English." — Inga Moore (Moorhead, MN)

"They had Norwegian language services until 1919 or 1920 [at the church in Wolford, North Dakota], because I was confirmed in Norwegian. [At home], we had Norwegian hymns and we always had Norwegian prayers at meals and at night." — Alpha Bowersox (Wolford, ND)

The Swedish-American Lutherans had but one synod, and this tended to limit their opportunity for squabbling among themselves,

although if they put their mind to it they, too, could find something to argue about. For the most part, though, the Swedish Lutherans, like their Norwegian cousins, found the church to be the most important link with the mother country and the mother tongue.

"All of these Swedish Lutheran people got together and donated the work for the church [near Erhart, Minnesota]. They worked for months and got it finished and got a bell, which was a very fine sounding bell, and still is. The wonder of it was that they had a sexton who had been trained in Sweden and he could make that bell talk. It always rang on sunset on Saturday. Today it doesn't sing, because there is nobody who can handle it correctly. It's a far cry from the beautiful tones that floated over the landscape on Saturday evenings at sunset. People felt that it was their duty to go to church on a Sunday morning. If you didn't go to church on a Sunday morning there was something radically wrong with the family, and it was quite universal. I can't think of anyone now who said, 'Well, we don't go to church.'" — Carl Axel Anderson (Erhart, MN)

"Shortly after [my parents] were married, they formed a rural church [in Kittson County, Minnesota], Sicar Church, and that was a Swedish Augustana Church. "Sicar" is a name from the Bible. My father helped build it. It was old Swedish traditional services, the men all sat on one side and the women all sat on the other side." — Myrtle Rundquist (Moorhead, MN)

"I heard that the Swedes stuck together, but my parents were different. They weren't the old dyed in the wool Swedes, you know. They liked to see the community entangled. With the old line Swedes, everything revolved around the church. My parents were different. My dad loved to dance and my mother loved to play cards, which was taboo, you know, years ago. And I know I used to dance as a youngster when my dad would get me out on the floor. In Confirmation class I was in the first English class. And there was some criticism of my parents for letting me learn religion in English. Some of those taking religious instruction didn't know what they were getting out of it. At Bethesda [in Moorhead] gradually they would have one Sunday a month in English and then sometimes they would have the service part English and part Swedish, just like our confirmation class. But it worked out. By the beginning of the twenties, it was all English." — Hazel Monson Barker (Moorhead, MN)

"There was a group of eight people that started the Swedish Evangelical Lutheran Church [in Moorhead in 1875]. When my folks came here they joined the church. There was a Swedish Covenant church on the North side. I was confirmed in Swede, but I was getting to know the English language better all the time. I know it took quite a conversion to get our folks to go to the English language. Around 1922, the Swedish language went out of our church. I think [World War One] had an effect on that because when a lot these—like my brother and a lot of guys that got drafted into the First

World War—well then, that was the English language. Folks had to learn how to interpret and I think that's about the time of the changeover. I used to have to take my father out to Eksjo [near Lake Park, Minnesota] in my brother's 1913 Model T Ford, because he still wanted to hear the Swedish language." — Vic Anderson (Moorhead, MN)

"Church services were in Swedish [in Moorhead] until about World War One, I believe. I was confirmed in Swedish." — Roy Carlander (Moorhead, MN)

"[The Swedes] were all Lutheran [in Scandia, Minnesota]. Beautiful church! The ladies had their ladies aid and the young people had their organization." — Carl Elmquist (Moorhead, MN)

"We had a lot of Swedish books. I was confirmed by Reverend Liehardt in Eksjo n 1912. I was treasurer for Eksjo Church for many years, and in going over the records for our centennial, why, it was very interesting to note that the Swedish language kept on a long time, and finally there got to be an English word mixed in with the secretary's records. The first one I noticed was 'insurance,' when they were going to renew their insurance with the Lake Park and Cuba Company." — Oscar Olson (Lake Park, MN)

"Well, first, you see, it was one church [north of Detroit Lakes, Minnesota] with Norwegians coming to the Swedish church and the minister always spoke Swedish. Well, then the Norwegians wanted their minister in and the Swedes wouldn't stand for that because it was their church so the

Norwegians build a church of their own ... about two miles apart. I'd say this was 'bout 1915 or maybe before that." — Charles Westerholm (Moorhead, MN)

"Well they would have English services three Sundays out of the month and then one Swedish service or he would speak Swedish one half of the hour and English the other half. But it was because there were a lot of older people [in Clearbrook, Minnesota in the 1930s] that really couldn't understand English too well. And of course if there was something special going on, like a wedding or funeral, they would sometimes ask the minister to do it in Swedish." — Elsie Gale (Clearbrook, MN)

"Most of the [Swedish] books we got in Sunday School as gifts, under the tree, and mother and father would read them. And of course we had a Swedish Bible and catechism. We children all took our confirmation in Swedish. And that was a good thing because Mother and Father could teach us or help us because they had studied the Bible in the Old Country. And you couldn't stump them much on the Bible. I don't think we got any English in our church [in Isanti County, Minnesota] until maybe 1915 or 1916."
— Nina Oien (Moorhead, MN)

"They got into a dispute with the pastor there. They were kind of narrow minded, and they didn't believe in insurance. My father was a Woodsman. There were quite a few who dropped out at that time. There was a lot of people, and at that time there was a group at Lindstrom [Minnesota] that had the same problem, and they started a new church there. And they called it the Lindstrom Trinity Church. [My father] was the only farmer there so he dug the basement there." — Inez Holt (Chisago City, MN)

"The Swedes along the river started the Swedish Evangelical church and they had their church right south on the corner here [near Christine, North Dakota]. Now it's been moved over to my sister-in-law's. They use it for a granary. ... We had our youth fellowship and the ladies had their fellowship. The Ladies Aid—our ladies called it WMS—Women's Missionary Society. They got together and made things, had auction sales and it all went to the church. That's been taken out entirely now. In our churches they usually served big suppers and so on but that's taken out too, now. ... We'd have one Swedish meeting a month, and then in the Sunday School session they had a class, so they kind of gradually dwindled out."
— Frank Alm (Christine, ND)

"We had a pastor, Pastor Liehardt, and he could speak English but with difficulty. He could speak English but he preferred not to. And so it was mostly Swedish until he quit. Then afterwards the next minister spoke more American. This was in the 1920s. ... In those days it seemed like you visited more with the people in your church, and I suppose they did the same thing [among the Norwegians] in Hitterdal [Minnesota]. But we went away to consolidated school. That's where the union started." — Violet Anderson (Hitterdal, MN)

"It seemed that our social life revolved around the church. I don't think I was one of those terrible nagging pastor's wives. We were so committed to the pastor's work although the youngsters didn't get to see Daddy very often, because usually he'd come home after they had gone to bed at night and he was often gone before they got up in the morning. But we didn't question it. It was the Lord's work, and the youngsters realized that their daddy had a job to fulfill. I think that, when my husband served three parishes [in Polk County, Minnesota], I think I felt that I had to be a pastor's wife to all three." — Svea Lundgren (Fosston, MN)

The Danes, the Icelanders, and the Finns all, to a greater or lesser degree, focused their existence in the New World on the church. There were divisions, of course, that would reflect a differing degree of pietism and ethnic loyalty. For each of these groups, especially in a rural setting, the church became a defining element in their lives.

"The Danes had their own church, but we were pretty much Lutheran out there [near Westby, Montana]. The Poles were Catholic, of course. Social activity and religious activity went together. The homesteaders that came out there, whether they had any church bringing up or not, they pretty much went to church because that was their only way. I mean, practically the only cultural doings were at the church. The social events were centered around the church more or less." — Philip Andersen (Fargo, ND)

"The church services were in Danish until 1928, I believe, then they were half and half for a little while and then they went to all English."
— Louisa Andersen (Fargo, ND)

"There were several [Icelandic] Lutheran Churches in the area [western Pembina County, North Dakota]. In fact, my father helped build one and my grandfather helped build another one. There were several country churches, less than four or five miles apart, all served by the same minister."
— Wayne Dinusson (Fargo, ND)

"My people were very religious. They had the old Icelandic religion, strict Lutherans. You couldn't work on Sundays, you always dressed up. We couldn't play cards, stuff like that. After we got older we got away from that." — Freda Bjornson (Moorhead, MN)

"Social activity and religious activity went together. The homesteaders that came out there, whether they had any church bringing up or not, went to church. Mountain, Edinburgh, Gardar—they're all Icelandic churches. And they didn't just have churches in town, they'd have churches in the country. Probably one minister had four or five churches." — Diane Volrath (Hitterdal, MN)

"The Icelandic Lutheran Church was the only church in that community. Icelandic was the only language in the home and in the church.

My mother didn't learn to speak English until she went to Winnipeg when she was eighteen." — Rosa Campbell (Moorhead, MN)

"There was the Evangelical Lutheran Church and there was the Norwegian Lutheran Church, but we never did belong to that. There was just one in the beginning but then the Norwegians had their own church. Most of the Icelanders went to the Evangelical Lutheran. We didn't have a real church [in the Souris River Loop area of North Dakota]. We just met in the community hall. We had an Icelandic minister. I thought he was a wonderful minister." — Anna Bjornson (Fargo, ND)

"The schools were built first and they used them for religious purposes until they got their own churches built. They were quite religious people, many of them, and the church meant a lot to them. ... We had a little summer school in the church, mostly for religious instruction, but there we also learned a little Icelandic history. But we heard a lot of it in the family. But my mother's mother, she talked all the time about Iceland. She'd go on from morning to night. She was spinning or knitting or carding wool but she talked all the time. So that when I went to Iceland I felt like I had been there before because I had heard all about it. ... My uncle was the first white child born in that area [of Pembina County]. My grandmother's father had been a minister back in Iceland and she was determined that he should become a minister. And he became one, and he was president of the Icelandic Synod for twenty years." — Kathryn Thordarson (Fargo, ND)

"Very, very strict, yes. The [Finnish] Apostolic Lutheran Church group was a very strict one. It is still somewhat of a pietistic group. But the old Apostolic Lutheran Church was strict as to the clothing they wore and they wore a shawl over their head, the women did, when they went to church. My grandmother did that in Calumet [Michigan]. She had a special apron that she would put on when she went to church, and the women always, on top of their old-fashioned curls, they had this apron and the shawl that they wore when they went to church. The men were not restricted in this way, although there was a small offshoot of the Apostolic Church and they had a congregation in New York Mills, which had about, I suppose, ten family members. They'd meet only once in a while. But that group usually wore neckties, and this set them apart from the others. And of course, when movies came into being, the more strict groups didn't attend movies. ... Of course, there was also in this area a temperance movement. Now the temperance group also had plays and dances and things like this, and they were more church oriented, and people would go to the temperance hall, and they would also go to church. So in this way, the church wasn't completely without some social activity, because you had the temperance group that supplied some of this." — Russell Parta (New York Mills, MN)

Although many Scandinavian immigrants may not have accepted the following statement to be true, there were denominations other than

Lutheran among them. Methodists, Baptists, Congregational, Mission Covenant, and even Unitarians were to be found among the Scandinavian immigrants. They would all, in their own way, ease the transition to a new land while acting to preserve the culture of the old.

"There was a little town [Stanchfield] about two miles from us [in Braham, Minnesota], and they were Swedish people, but they were what they called the 'Dalarna,' from Dalarna, Sweden. And we couldn't understand a word they said, they would speak so fast. And they thought they were a little better than some of the other Swedish people around them, I think, at times. They had a Swedish Baptist Church there. We used to go to the Baptist Church every once in a while because they used to have the Salvation Army come there and we kind of thought that music was pretty peppy, and we liked to go there sometimes. But I think the Baptists actually felt that we people weren't saved who were Lutherans." — Nina Oien (Moorhead, MN)

"We called it a Free Mission Church at that time, it was independent entirely. It was more of a community church. We had ministers of different denominations come here and it seemed to work out real good. There were lots of traveling ministers in those days. We would meet them in Battle Lake [Minnesota] at the train and bring them out and bring them back again. The church holds about one hundred people, and it was really full. And once in a while we would have a mission meeting and then we would only get about half the crowd in, but it was summertime so they could be outside. We supported foreign missions with those meetings, most of them in Africa." — David Swedberg (Ottertail Co., MN)

"There was a [Swedish] Mission church, but that was up in the north side of Moorhead and that was very small. I've never been in it even. I don't know much about it because it was such a small congregation. I knew very few mission people when I got older, and when I was a youngster I never did hear of them." — Helen Monson Barker (Moorhead, MN)

"There was the Lutheran Church and the Free Mission Church, just those two. The free Mission had their congregation and the Lutherans ad theirs and I don't think that they ever went back and forth or anything." — Amy Margaret Erickson (Wheatland, ND)

"In Wolverton [Minnesota] there was a Swedish church. My mother's relatives lived there, and often they would insist that they would come and get us. And that was a little livelier church. It was an evangelical church and we would often hear a 'Hallelujah' or a 'Praise God' while someone was preaching, and my mother rather liked going to church there." — Anna Hanson (Moorhead, MN)

"They called it a Scandinavian Church, but they only had Norwegian pastors there. Norwegian language every other Sunday. But when I first came out [to Glendive, Montana], they used to have those evangelists that used to come from Minneapolis, Swedish ministers, and they used to come to houses

to preach, like Swansons or Andersons, and they'd stay overnight and then get Swedish people to come to their house and have a service there."
— Anna Lindgren (Fargo, ND)

"There weren't too many activities that we were allowed to go to because of our [Swedish Covenant] religion. We didn't get to go much to parties and such because our parents forbid us to do those things. I think I was in the seventh or eighth grade before I got to go to a school party because that wasn't done in our place. As far as outside activities, I don't know what went on at all." — Phoebe Westerholm (Moorhead, MN)

"My family was Baptist. That is, a Swedish Baptist Church. And they used only the Swedish language in church." — Catherine Fossay (Moorhead, MN)

"The people who went to my father's church [Churches' Ferry, near Minot, North Dakota] and the people who went to the Free Church never associated. And there was very little contrast between my father and the pastor of the Free Church. The Lutherans looked down a little on the Free Church perhaps, but it was even more so the other way around. The Free Church looked down more on the Norwegian Lutheran Church. They wouldn't even go through the door of the Lutheran church. They were very strict on their doctrine, the Free Church." — Odin Strandness (Fargo, ND)

"I was born Lutheran, and was baptized as a Norwegian Lutheran, but when we moved up to Virginia [Minnesota] my dad had affiliated himself with the Norwegian Methodist Church there. So from then until I was an adult, I grew up in the Norwegian Methodist Church. And my dad was the choir leader of that church. There was a Norwegian Lutheran Church there, but we were quite separate. All of us, well, we went into each other's homes and everybody spoke a different language, so we were all acclimated, I mean, no one could feel they were a minority group [on the Iron Range]. ... You never grew up in a Norwegian Methodist Church! If you laughed in church there was only one place you were going! I lived in church until I was eighteen. But I think it made me a better person." — Borghild Overby (Moorhead, MN)

"The Lutherans went to the Lutheran Church [in Oakes, North Dakota], of course, but the Swedes had many that went to the Methodist Church. And, there were no Catholics. Oh, yes, there were two families, their name was Branigan, Irish, you know, otherwise there were no Catholics, just the Lutherans and the Methodists. And they were rivals. Instead of working together, they just tried to see which one could outdo the other. But they got along good, friendly. The Methodists had a Ladies Aid and the Lutherans had a Ladies Aid and they each had something going on. Every month the Lutherans would have a sale at their Aid. One lady cut out the garments and then they were passed around for the other women to sew and they'd take them along to the next Aid and there was a man there who was their auctioneer. Everyone went to the Aid meetings except in the busiest season.

My father was secretary for the Aid for many years, and do you know why? He was one of the few who could write. That's a fact! The Methodists had a real good YPS, they called it, Young People's Society. And we had one too, but it wasn't as strong as theirs, so they bested us there. They'd have programs. The minister would lead, he'd say a prayer and talk a little and then somebody that could would sing and somebody that couldn't would play and they'd have a good lunch, you know, and go home. It was not an all-night affair. I went to many of those. It was fun. Fifteen cents we used to pay. The Methodists changed [from Swedish] to English before we did. I was confirmed in Norwegian in 1908." — Mabel Enger (Oakes, ND)

"My mother and father became members of the Lutheran Church when they first came to America. My grandfather built the Lutheran Church which is now in the village of Underwood [Minnesota]. But father and mother joined the Unitarian Church in 1891, that was two years after the church was organized and he became treasurer in 1893 and remained treasurer for the next forty years. The church services were conducted in Norwegian and all the church records were kept in Norwegian until 1923. Then they alternated and this is one of the reasons why the church did not particularly grow. Because the old timers felt that they had to have a Norwegian speaking minister, and they were difficult to find in the liberal state of Unitarianism. We alternated until 1940, English and Norwegian from 1922 to 1940. For [the Lutheran churches around Underwood] I think their timing was similar to ours. There was no animosity between us and the Lutherans. Most of our family and friends were Lutheran. But we were thought of by some Lutherans as non-Christian because of our not subscribing to the divinity of Christ, but that's a matter of interpretation of words." — John Gronner (Underwood, MN)

For the grandchildren and great-grandchildren of the Scandinavian immigrants, the rural ethnic church became an anchor for their heritage. In some areas of the Upper Midwest the church building is now gone and the cemetery is all that remains on the church grounds. But in these simple but beautiful white wooden churches one can feel the aura of a people with deep faith in their God and in their future in America.

Chapter IX

"Everybody Had *Decorah Posten*"

NEWS FOR SCANDINAVIANS

The Scandinavian immigrants to America came from all classes and from all educational backgrounds. There were those who had been trained at a university and those who could not read in any language. Among the more educated, there arose a desire for the creation of their own literary traditions as Scandinavian Americans. In this they were all to a degree successful, in that each Scandinavian ethnic group did develop their own individual American writers. Writing in the Norwegian-language literary journal *Symra*, Peer Stromme, who was a remarkable minister, teacher, politician, and novelist, noted: "It has been an article of faith among us that the art of literary creation … can thrive in Norwegian America. We can assuredly cultivate wheat and tobacco, but not flowers. And for the time being we will have to accept this fact and be comforted by the idea that if no one among us has been given the divine gift of poetry by the gods, then someone must have it coming. It cannot fail that some time among the sons of the saga land in the New World there will appear men who can see great visions and dream beautiful dreams." The Norwegian-Americans were perhaps the most successful in this effort, if for no other reason than the existence of a real "son of the saga land," O. E. Rolvaag, who wrote *Giants in the Earth*. Yet, on a per capita basis even the Norwegians might have been outdone by the Icelanders.

All of the interview subjects were asked what reading materials were present in their homes and about their familiarity with Scandinavian language books, periodicals, and newspapers. Perhaps the most revealing aspect of this portion of the oral histories was the lack of specificity regarding Scandinavian language books in their homes. Those interviewed could recall few, if any, authors. The books remembered were not, as the Scandinavian-American cultural elite would have wished, examples of Scandinavian-American literature, but were instead a collection of religious works, popular fiction, and almanacs. Perhaps most significant, while many of those interviewed were aware of *Giants in the Earth*, few had read it, and those who had read it had done so only in the English translation. Perhaps this should not be so surprising. Most of the interview subjects were in their twenties when the Norwegian version of the book appeared, and had been in public schools during the assimilationist pressures of World War I. Besides, there was always a dichotomy between what Scandinavian-American authors advocated and what Scandinavian-American readers preferred. In her study of Scandinavian immigrant literature, *The Divided Heart*, Dorothy Burton

Skardal claimed that the evidence of such literature indicated that "the majority of Scandinavian immigrants accepted abandonment of their European roots as rapidly as possible," but that "the majority of the Scandinavian language authors, on the contrary, advocated preservation of Old-World culture."

There existed, especially among the Norwegians, a number of cultural periodicals and Norwegian-language literary journals. Among those interviewed, however, there were few who could recall the most significant organs designed to encourage Norwegian literature in America. Neither *Symra*, published from 1905 to 1914 in Decorah, Iowa, by the reading and discussion club of the same name, nor Waldemar Ager's *Kvartalskrift*, published in Eau Claire, Wisconsin, were ever mentioned. Ironically, the one periodical that was most frequently remembered was *Kvinnan och Hemmet* (Woman and the Home), a Swedish language magazine, or *Kvinden og Hjemmet*, the Norwegian name of the same periodical.

By the turn of the century, it had become obvious that the Scandinavian-Americans read their newspapers rather than the works of Bjornson, Ibsen, or Hamsun. Virtually all of those interviewed recalled a Scandinavian-language newspaper in their homes. The newspaper seemed to be a literature for the common man. Many of the Scandinavian-language newspapers made no pretense at neutrality and were dedicated to forming or reinforcing a political viewpoint. But they also carried the news of the community in a way that focused on the common concerns and problems of the transplanted Scandinavians. They were often filled with news of the Old Country, such as the great attention paid in the Scandinavian-American press on the issue of Norwegian independence from Sweden in 1905. Finally, the Scandinavian-American press included news of American markets, government, fashions, and products that aided the immigrant in his assimilation into American society.

At one time or another there were as many as four hundred Norwegian-language newspapers published in the United States. By 1910, the combined readership of the Norwegian-American press was over one million, and six-hundred thousand homes were receiving at least one Norwegian-language newspaper or periodical. They ranged from the huge, consistently Republican Chicago newspaper, *Scandinaven*, to Laurets Stavnheim's voice of the Norwegians in the Non-Partisan League, *Fran*. The Norwegian press of the Upper Midwest reflected the times and the tempo of the new nation. *Normanden* of Grand Forks, edited by the remarkable Hans A. Foss, energetically supported the Farmer's Alliance before returning once again to the Republican Party while the *Statstidende* of Hillsboro, North Dakota, steadfastly remained conservatively Republican. The *Minneapolis*

Tidende generally supported that candidate who was the "most Norwegian."

The overwhelming choice of reading material for the Norwegians interviewed, however, was the neutral *Decorah Posten*, of Decorah, Iowa. There are still many homes in Minnesota and North Dakota that have a framed illustrated copy of The Lord's Prayer written in Norwegian that came as a premium to subscribers of the *Decorah Posten*. It included most of what the Norwegian-American reader wanted out of a newspaper including news of America, news of other Norwegian-Americans, news of other Scandinavian-Americans, and news of Scandinavia itself. It also included a literary supplement, *Ved Arnen: et Tidsskrift for Skjonliteratur* ("By the Hearth: A Magazine of Belles Lettres"). *Ved Arnen* published a rather eclectic array of literature from the writings of Ager, Foss, and Rolvaag to Norwegian translations of Dickens, Anatole France, and Zane Grey. Throughout its long history of publication, from 1874 until 1972, the *Decorah Posten* retained a reputation of being almost a literary journal in itself.

"They kept one Norwegian newspaper all the time, and that was *Decorah Posten*." — Alva Hest (Perley, MN)

"Well, [North Dakota] seemed like home. Yah, we had *Decorah Posten* for years and years, as long as we could get it. I didn't bring anything with me [but that]." — Marie Tverdal (Abercrombie, ND)

"Well, the *Decorah Posten*, everybody read that. The Swedes had their own paper too. I don't remember what that was called." — Louis Haugen (Crookston, MN)

"My dad couldn't read, but my mother used to read the *Decorah Posten* to him." — Oscar Askegaard (Comstock, MN)

"They received Scandinavian newspapers. *Scandinaven*. And of course they had a lot of Scandinavian books that they read. And then there was another Christian paper. And *Decorah Posten*, yes!" — Gunhild Laske (Kindred, ND)

"They had the *Decorah Posten* printed in Norwegian, and there was always a story printed in that." — Kristine Svidal (Starkweather, ND)

"We always had the Norwegian Bible. Whenever Dad read from the Bible it was always in Norwegian, and we had Norwegian newspapers as long as I remember. They kept that up until they died. The *Decorah Posten*." — Dagne Faust (Colfax, ND)

"There was always a Scandinavian newspaper. There was the *Decorah Posten*, from Decorah, Iowa. … We read the English language papers too, like the *Fargo Forum*, but there always was a Norwegian paper." — Clarence Glasrud (Moorhead, MN)

"They used to get a newspaper by the name of *Decorah Posten*. They didn't get it a lot of the time, but we got it. We also got the *Hazelton Independent*. That wasn't in Norwegian, but Dad and Mother learn to read from it." — Matilda Blumer (Hazelton, ND)

"I remember we got what they called the *Decorah Posten*. I used to read it a little bit, but my folks didn't encourage that kind of thing. They wanted us to be Americans. But we did know the Norwegian language. I think they did want to preserve it, but they also wanted to speak English." — Alpha Bowersox (Wolford, ND)

"We had the *Decorah Posten*, printed in Decorah, Iowa. I suppose Father had that for forty years. And we had one from Chicago called *Scandinaven*. And we got one from Minneapolis called *Folkebladet*. That means "People's Paper." And we had the local paper. I read them all. There were stories about politics and stories about religion and news items and they had a paper called *Ved Arnen*, that was a supplement to the *Decorah Posten*, and that had novels in it, a chapter in it each week. They always had a column about Norway and Sweden. 'Pert-near' all of the neighbors took that direct." — Ole Olson (Fargo, ND)

"Oh, we had lots of papers. Chicago had a daily newspaper in Norwegian at that time. Minneapolis had the *Minneapolis Tidende*, we called it. That was weekly. And Fergus Falls even had the *Norlander*. And Eau Claire had *Reform*, that was Norwegian but the word means the same as in

English. And the *Decorah Posten*, all the people had that! And we had a few books. We read the Norwegian Bible and Norwegian history and all kinds of books. Just like now, only all the books were in Norwegian. I even had a Norwegian history of America. I got that book in 1904, I think." — John Klokken (Osakis, MN)

"Occasionally there would come out, generally in paperback, pieces of Norwegian fiction. Generally they were written by American writers in Norwegian, and we had a Norwegian newspaper, the *Decorah Posten*, and one of those issues would have a magazine section that contained mostly fiction. Good stories! And my parents read most of those. I read some, but by that time I was able to check out books from the school library in English and I read some of those." — Christian Schulstad (Dawson, MN)

"From as far back as I can remember, until the paper was out of circulation, we had the *Decorah Posten*. For a while, during the First World War, we had the daily *Scandinaven*. And we had the *Kvinden og Hjemmet*, or 'The Woman and the Home,' and I think we got that as long as it was published." — Palmer Tverdal (Abercrombie, ND)

"I read some of the Scandinavian newspapers when I was able to read. We had the *Normanden*, which meant 'Northern Men,' then we had the *Scandinaven*. They were both Norwegian papers. And then we had *Lutheranaren*, the '*Lutheran Herald*,' you know, and my dad had a mission paper that came from La Crosse. He was great on missions, you know, so we had some of those. And the first paper I had for Sunday School ... was a Norwegian paper. And then we had to read from the Bible, that was Norwegian, and I had to read for my grandparents, you know." — Alma Olson (Souris, ND)

"I remember they took *Decorah Posten* and I don't remember any other. Oh, I remember reading Ola and Per, and I remember there was always a continued story in *Ved Arnen*, that was kind of a supplement to *Decorah Posten* My aunt liked to read those novels. That came once a week. That was an awaited day. We had some Norwegian books around; I don't know where we got them." — Joanna Aune (Hawley, MN)

"[My mother] kept the Norwegian language newspaper from Decorah, Iowa, and the [newspaper] which was published in Fergus Falls and also the women's magazine, the *Kvinden og Hjemmet*, that's 'the Woman and her Home.' And she bound these together to become here encyclopedia, because she had a great memory and when questions came up, she knew just where she could find things in this encyclopedia of hers. That was her reference. She continued to read Norwegian and didn't make the effort in English." — John Gronner (Underwood, MN)

"My dad had several Norwegian papers, four or five I think. It was the *Decorah Posten* and I forget the name of the others. My dad was great for what was going on in the old country. That's why he kept up all those papers. The old timers, the ones that got *Scandinaven* out of Chicago, boy, they were the strict Republicans. As far as *Decorah Posten*, that was neutral, and that's what most people around here [eastern Clay County, Minnesota] read. And I don't know about the Swedes. I think most of them read *Svenska Posten*, and that was Republican." — Nilmer Bjorndahl (Hawley, MN)

"My husband was a Swede, so he had the *Svenska Posten* when we got married. We had the *Decorah Posten*." — Clara Johnson (Underwood, ND)

"My parents had Scandinavian newspapers all right. They were *Decorah Posten*, of course, everybody had *Decorah Posten*, and *Reform*, and *Normanden*, and I think there was another one, but I don't remember what it was. Along with *Decorah Posten* there was a little magazine, *Ved Arnen*, with stories, and everybody seemed to get interested in those stories. ... [We had] *Fram*, and *Reform*, from Eau Claire, Wisconsin, and *Norbund*, published in Fargo. Mother had *Kvinden og Hjemmet* and for us children we had *Ungdoms Vännen*, Youth Friend. But there were other newspapers that other people had." — William Nelson (Rollag, MN)

"[My father] had relatives in Norway that would send him Norwegian papers and we always had the *Decorah Posten*. And of course growing up in a home where everybody spoke Norwegian, it wasn't long before I was reading them too." — Beatrice Schaefer (Osakis, MN)

"It seemed like it was all Norwegian papers until we got our local paper. It was *Decorah Posten*, that was the main one. And *Skandinaven* was another one and *Gamle Orgud* was another one. These were the common ones that the people had. I had the *Decorah Posten* until they stopped publishing it." — Alma Ramse (McIntosh, MN)

"The *Fargo Courier News*, from Fargo, and my father got a daily Norwegian newspaper called the *Skandinaven*, it was published in Chicago. My father subscribed to that especially because they had columns about different parts of Norway so he could get a glimpse of what was happening at home all the time. The Norwegian atmosphere was all the time projected through these newspapers, but they were always very loyal Americans. We used to say in Norway that if you want to become an American you have to be a good Norwegian." — Leif Christianson (Moorhead, MN)

For most of the readers of *Decorah Posten* who were born after 1910, the paper was especially and universally remembered for one thing, *Han Ola og Han Per*. This was a Scandinavian-American phenomenon. The cartoon strip created by Peter J. Rosendahl of Spring Grove, Minnesota, would sometimes contain humor of a universal nature that is still amusing today. At other times, however, it was esoterically Norwegian-American.

"The most important paper we had was the *Decorah Posten*. We got that once a week and we looked forward to it because it was Norwegian and it even had a comic about Ola and Per, which was very funny to us kids. We'd run to the mail box, half a mile, and then hurry home so we could read about Ola and Per. And then Mother and Dad would read the articles that were concerned with government and about people coming from Norway and Sweden." — Lloyd Westrum (Moorhead, MN)

"It had Ola and Per and Lars—lot of jokes about them guys! It was all Norwegian and there was a story. And when Dad got done with it he would send it down to Mother's folks." — Ellen Abraham Villard, MN)

"The only one I remember was the *Decorah Posten*. I remember that as a child. There used to be a comic strip … and I remember my mother reading it to us. Whenever it come we all gathered around and just had to have her read it to us. It was about Ola and Per. She used to read it in Norwegian and then she would tell us." — Vern Fugelberg (New Rockford, ND)

"I remember one where Ola and Per had gone out pheasant hunting in South Dakota. And, of course, that was quite a trip years ago. And they got there and got their hotel room and they went out all day and came back to their hotel room. They were all tired out and they had poor luck. They'd only got two pheasants. So they got down and started to reminisce about their experiences and Ola started to figure out the costs of the trip, transportation, the hotel room, and food and shells and stuff, so they figured out that the two pheasants had come to over thirty dollars per pheasant. And so Per says to

Ola, 'Lucky we didn't shoot any more pheasants!'" — Oscar Olson (Lake Park, MN)

It has been estimated that at one time or another more than fifteen hundred Swedish language publications have been produced in the United States. The first significant Swedish newspaper to be published in America was *Det Gamla och Det Nya Hemlandet* **("The Old and New Homeland"), which was first published in 1855 in Galesburg, Illinois, and later in Chicago. This paper, was exclusively Republican and served as the voice of the Swedish Lutheran Augustana Synod. As** *Hemlandet* **grew more secular, the Augustana Synod began publishing their own organ in 1868 called** *Augustana***. This paper would be found in the homes of great numbers of Swedish-Americans from then until 1930, when it became the English language** *Lutheran Companion* **and would go on to become the paper of the Lutheran Church in America. The Mission Covenant Swedish church meanwhile produced** *Missionsvännen* **("The Mission Friend") and** *Forbundets Veckotidning* **("The Covenant Weekly").**

The largest Swedish Newspaper in America emerged after several mergers as the *Svenska Amerikanaren***, first published in Chicago in 1866. In spite of the great distance from Chicago, many Swedish-Americans living in the Upper Midwest continued to subscribe to this**

paper. Perhaps of more immediate importance to the Upper Midwest Swedish Americans, however, was the *Minnesota Stats Tidning*, founded by Col. Hans Mattson in 1877, which became an important voice for the Minnesota conference of the Augustana Synod. Somewhat later, the *Svenska Amerikanska Posten* was founded and was turned into one of America's leading foreign language newspapers by Swan Turnblad. Turnblad would help create the American Swedish Institute in Minneapolis and his mansion is now the headquarters of this organization. There were also a number of publications of a literary and cultural nature, among which *Ungdoms-Vännen* ("The Friend of Youth") and *Valkyrian* ("The Valkyrie") were most prominent. At one time there was a Swedish publication to be found in thirty different states, and in Minnesota alone some thirty different towns published Swedish newspapers. In virtually all of the interviews with Swedish Americans, there was a mention of at least one of the above named publications. Because the Norwegian language newspapers were often more accessible, a significant number of Swedish-Americans also reported that they received Norwegian-language newspapers in their homes.

"My dad used to get a Swedish newspaper, and I think it came out of Minneapolis. And he would really look forward to that because it was all written in Swedish. That was his recreation. I peddled the *Moorhead News*." — Vic Anderson (Moorhead, MN)

"My dad had a Swedish newspaper that came every week and then they had a Swedish magazine that came. *Svenska Posten*! And the magazine was *Skoleskrift*." — Amy Margaret Erickson (Wheatland, ND)

"Newspapers were kind of slow. I remember one of them, *Minnesota Stats Tidning*." — Carl Elmquist (Moorhead, MN)

"Because they didn't read the English language, they had to resort to something like this. I recall that there was a newspaper that came from Chicago, I believe, and it was called *Dagens Nyheter*, which means "the Day's news." This was a weekly paper, which means that it had to hold them for a whole week, as far as reading was concerned." — Katherine Fossay (Moorhead, MN)

"We got the *Svenska Amerikanaren*. It came from Chicago." — Anna Lindgren (Fargo, ND)

"We got the *Swedish Tribune*, and then *Skandinaven* was another paper, and Woman in the Home, *Kvinnan och Hemmet*. She read those with care and saved them, and reread them. And we had quite a few Swedish books that she treasured." — Anna Hanson (Moorhead, MN)

"I remember we received the *Minnesota Stats Tidning*. It had a very archaic headline banner across the top, looking very Swedish. I think it was published in Minneapolis. And we received Swedish books at Christmas time from the Sunday School." — Lillie Strandness (Fargo, ND)

"One was the *Forbundets Veckotidning*, or something like that, and the other was the *Missionsvännen*, and they read those very avidly. My father had a Swedish Bible, and he read that every morning and my mother, too. It was a really very Swedish oriented household." — Alice Oliver (Moorhead, MN)

"My father took the *Svenska Amerikanaren*. And he read that religiously. I'm sure he read every page of it, because there was a lack of reading material in the Swedish community. As a teen-ager, I was very hungry for reading material. And I can remember in Langdon [North Dakota] that the newspaper contained novels, and I started reading those continuous novels and I couldn't wait for them one week to the next. And that's one place where I really learned to read [Swedish] a little more fluently than I would have with just our knowledge of Swedish from Sunday School and confirmation class." — Myrtle Rundquist (Moorhead, MN)

"I had three Scandinavian papers, four sometimes. I got two that were printed in Minneapolis and I got two that were sent all the way from Sweden." — John Norman (Hawley, MN)

"We got the *Svenska Folks Tidning*, that was the 'Swedish People's Newspaper.' And then we had different ones, the *Svenska Amerikanaren*, of course. And the Norwegian ones, of course. The *Decorah Posten* was the common one here [Lake Park, Minnesota]. It was noted for its cartoon of Ola and Per." — Oscar Olson (Lake Park, MN)

"We had a Swedish newspaper up until about 1925 or 1930. They had the church paper, of course, the Augustana church paper. My dad also had some Swedish books on theology." — Roy Carlander (Moorhead, MN)

"My uncle had something called *Minneapolis Tidning*, the 'Minneapolis Times,' and Uncle Ole had *Skandinaven*. That was quite a large paper. And then there was the church paper, *The Lutheran*." — Clara Hanson (Moorhead, MN)

"We had two Swedish newspapers. We had the *Minnesota Stats Tidning*, it was called in Swedish, and the *Augustana*, which was a magazine that came out from the Augustana church synod. They also read the Fargo paper, *The Morning Fall*, and the *Moorhead Daily News*. We had Swedish books around the house, but we never looked at them, except maybe the folks did. My father had a geometry book in Swedish, but most of them were religious books." — Robert Carlander (Moorhead, MN)

"He took the *Svenska Posten*, but my mother had a magazine called *Kvinnan och Hemmet*, 'Woman and the Home.' And they would always have the *Minneapolis Tribune*. That Minneapolis paper was really a boon to our family. And we took a weekly from Breckenridge and a weekly from Fergus Falls. Later on, the *Fergus Falls Journal* started publishing a daily and we got that." — Allen Erickson (Moorhead, MN)

"My dad's father lived with us for fifteen years, and we had to scour the town to find Swedish books for him to read. But I also know he read the newspapers from beginning to end, because at the dinner table he would mention little articles in the middle of the page that he had spotted. He got the Swedish newspaper and the daily English paper." — Amy Erickson (Moorhead, MN)

"We got a Swedish newspaper, *Missionsvännen*, 'Mission Friend.' And I can see my mother taking a little lamp and sitting by the table at night when she was through with her work, putting her glasses on and reading that [paper] and she would read it from top to bottom, and Dad the same thing. It was quite a big paper. But that's where they got all their information. I remember when the *Titanic* went down, Mother and Dad had to read all about it in that paper. I think we had that paper until she died. Oh, my, they sure looked forward to that paper!" — Nina Oien (Moorhead, MN)

"They got their Scandinavian newspapers here. He subscribed for the *Minneapolis Tidning* they would call it, that would be the 'Minneapolis Times.' It was just a small daily paper. He had that as far back as I can remember. It was just two sheets, four sides. And then there was [another] Swedish paper, but that was twice a week, and that as printed in Chicago. He got all the local papers, too. Dad could read English and he spoke, well it got broken but it was understandable. They loved the Scandinavian [language)] the best, of course. It was the easiest." — Frank Alm (Christine, ND)

The Danes, the Icelanders, and the Finns also had periodicals published in their own language, but because their numbers were fewer, there were fewer publications in these languages. In the case of the Danes, furthermore, their diffusion tended to hinder the growth of Danish language publications. The most important and longest lasting Danish newspaper was *Den Danske Pioneer*, founded in Omaha, Nebraska, in 1872. Unlike most of the Norwegian and Swedish newspapers, *Den Danske Pioneer* was Democratic in politics and decidedly anti-clerical. It was also essentially rural in outlook, unlike *Nordlyset* ("The Northern Light"), which was published in New York, or *Bien* ("The Bee"), which was founded in San Francisco. Many of the Danes in the Upper Midwest also received a Danish Lutheran publication called *Kirke og Folk* ("Church and People").

The small number of Icelanders in the Upper Midwest produced a rich and varied literature. Icelandic-American poetry was popular not only among the Icelanders in America, but among the citizens of Iceland as well. The Icelandic-Americans generally received either or both of the Icelandic newspapers published in Winnipeg, *Heimskringla* and *Logberg*. The foremost Finnish newspapers were *Amerikan Uutiset*, *Raibaaja* ("Pioneer"), and somewhat later many of the Finns in the Upper Midwest read *The Minnesota News*, published in New York Mills.

"We got a Danish church paper, and I believe there was another one, *Kvinden og Hjemmet*. I believe it was Danish, but I wouldn't swear to it. When we started grade school, we also had a month of Danish school in the Danish language. And we also spoke it at home all the time. We got Danish books from the publishing house in Blair, Nebraska." — Louise Andersen (Fargo, ND)

"There was a group of [Danish] papers there. Most of the homes got a lady's magazine I remember so well, *Kvinden og Hjemmet*, 'Woman and the Home.' And then there was a Norwegian newspaper that Dad had for a while, the *Decorah Posten*. But his main paper was the *Skandinaven*, which was strictly a Danish paper that was published in the States here. And, of course, when we children went to Sunday School we had our own paper called the *Barneblad*, which was a Danish Sunday school paper that we all got. That came from Blair, Nebraska. But I remember best the *Decorah Posten* because that had Per and Ola. We had quite a lot of Danish books in the house. My dad did a lot of reading." — Philip Andersen (Fargo, ND)

"About the only newspapers that we had was the Icelandic newspaper, and that was printed in Winnipeg and that was called *Logberg* and *Heimskringla*. We got the news because we used to read that." — Freda Bjornson (Moorhead, MN)

"They had Icelandic books. Anything new that came from Iceland, boy oh boy, they had to be read. And they also had the Icelandic papers. Some got them from Iceland and there were two printed in Winnipeg, *Heimskringla* and *Logberg*. We got *Logberg* and our neighbors got *Heimskringla*. Well then they'd exchange papers and read them. And the same thing with books. They were used." — Kathryn Thordarson (Fargo, ND)

"There were two newspapers printed in Icelandic in Winnipeg, and [my parents] received one or the other until the late 1940s." — Wayne Dinusson (Fargo, ND)

"Most of the newspapermen, editors, and so forth, weren't basically novelists. Some were poets, there was a lot of poetry. Like Mr. Adolf Lundquist, and his partner here [in New York Mills, Minnesota], during his lifetime he was very poetic. He would write poems not only for the Finnish newspaper, but also for the large Finnish summer festival. ... All the Finnish newspapers in the state were general, and some had backings from different groups, of course. Some were socialist backed, some were backed by church groups, some were backed by independents. ... The Finnish Lutheran Church required that in order to be confirmed, one must read and write. So the church took it upon itself to get everyone to read and write, even a hundred years ago, or even more, for them to be confirmed, unless they were so far back in the woods that they couldn't join a church. When they came to this country, those that wanted to find a new place to live, this literacy came with them, and of course the demand for Finnish reading that came with it was because they all knew how to read. Whether you had a newspaper had to do with whether you had political ideas." — Russell Parta (New York Mills, MN)

Whatever the ethnic group, the Scandinavian language newspapers served a number of important functions. They helped teach the immigrants about conditions in the United States. They also helped the immigrants maintain ties with the Old Country by printing news from Europe. Finally, they began to mold together an American ethnic group by reporting on fellow ethnics in America.

Chapter X
"'Democrat' Was a Word for Something We Didn't Like"

THE POLITICS OF THE NEW AMERICANS

Politics, for most of the Scandinavians, probably played a minor role in the decision to emigrate. Nevertheless, with masses of people leaving the homeland it became a vital political issue and on the national level emigration was solidly linked to political dissent. In Sweden, furthermore, there was considerable emigration to escape compulsory military service. A royal decree prohibiting the emigration of Swedish military conscripts was a significant obstacle to emigration. At first, permission to emigrate was rather routinely granted, but by the end of the nineteenth century, permits were generally issued only to those who had completed a period of service. Such political regulations led to a significant degree of illegal emigration, mostly by way of Copenhagen, Christiania, and Trondheim, and a growing market developed for counterfeit emigration certificates.

Although the governments of the Scandinavian countries were evolving into democracies during the nineteenth century, many of the Scandinavian immigrants got their first breath of political democracy when they immigrated to America. It was often an exhilarating breath,

as increasingly they began to make their presence felt in the various state legislatures and congressional delegations in the Upper Midwest.

While Scandinavians could be found at all points along the political spectrum, they often tended to be politically homogenous. A political appeal to the Scandinavian element would often be broad enough to include all Scandinavian ethnic groups. For the most part they were Lutheran and, because of the requirements of the state churches in Scandinavia, they had been taught to read at least well enough to get through Luther's Small Catechism. Furthermore, with the exception of Finnish, their language was at least mutually comprehensible. There also existed a shared political tradition in Scandinavia of written constitutions that guaranteed certain civil liberties and which provided for elected legislatures. By the twentieth century, politically active Scandinavians were expressing themselves in temperance movements, women's suffrage movements, and cooperative movements.

The class structure in Scandinavia was becoming less rigid throughout the nineteenth century, but many of the immigrants did not participate in a political movement until they came to America. They discovered that they did have a political clout, and that, as Playford Thorson has observed, they had a lot in common in that there were Swedish Johnsons, Norwegian Johnsons, Danish Johnsons, and Icelandic Johnsons. The Norwegians would soon become aware of their potential political power. Laurence Larson wrote that "the Norseman is by nature a politician" and Odd Lovoll, in *The Promise of America*, summed up their political participation in writing "familiarity with democratic reforms and local self-government in Norway, a dislike of officialdom, and a heightened assertiveness stimulated them to participate in local government in America."

In places like Trempealeau County, Wisconsin, and Winnebago County, Iowa, the Norwegians would control politics on the local level by uniting to vote for their fellow Norwegians. In some areas, such as in Norman County, Minnesota, where the census of 1900 revealed only one farm that was not owned by a Norwegian, they controlled local government by default. For the most part, however, appeals were not made for votes along strict ethnic lines, but on definite regional, economic, and ideological issues.

The Norwegian-Americans would be most successful in electing political leaders in the Upper Midwest. Perhaps the most notable early political success in Minnesota was Knute Nelson, who was a Civil War veteran who set up a law practice in Alexandria and who would eventually serve as a U.S. congressman, Minnesota governor, and as a U.S. senator for twenty-eight years. Until modern times, the Minnesota congressional delegation has continually had Norwegian-American members, including Andrew Volstead, the author of the Volstead Act, which established national prohibition, and two senators who went on to be vice presidents, Hubert Humphrey and Walter Mondale. In the twentieth century, only one governor of Minnesota has not been of Scandinavian extraction.

In stressing the commonality of their heritage for political purposes, the Norwegians may have been more successful than the Swedes. This may be because the Norwegians left their country at a time of rising national consciousness whereas Swedish nationalism at the time had reached a low point. Yet, Swedes would play an active part in the political life of the Upper Midwest, beginning in 1864, when Lars Johan Stark was elected to the Minnesota legislature and in 1869, when Colonel Hans Mattson was elected as the Minnesota Secretary of State. At least two Swedish-American Minnesotans, John Albert Johnson and Floyd B. Olson, were considered potential Presidential candidates.

Unlike the Swedes and Norwegians, the Danes were not particularly active in American political life, although Danish born politicians have served as governors of Minnesota, South Dakota, Iowa, and Wyoming. Several politicians of Danish ancestry have also been prominent in American politics, including the 1988 vice presidential candidate, Senator Lloyd Bentsen of Texas.

Because of the small number of Icelanders in the United States, they did not make their presence felt in politics on the national level. In

North Dakota, however, their political impact greatly exceeded their numbers. In pursuit of higher education, the Icelanders of Pembina County surpassed all of North Dakota's ethnic groups, and they became especially well known in the field of law. There have been three Icelandic Justices of the North Dakota Supreme Court and four Icelandic Attorney-Generals, and by 1925, there had already been a dozen Icelanders elected to the North Dakota legislature.

The Finns, who came to America somewhat later than did the other Scandinavian groups and often under less favorable conditions, did not make a similar impact in politics on the state level. The Finns would later be attracted to more radical politics and would be very influential on a local level in the formation of cooperative movements and in the Socialist Party.

For most Scandinavian immigrants, however, the first real political decision that they made was to become United States citizens. In many cases this was done as quickly as possible, but there were several cases where the newcomer decided to wait until he became sure that he wanted to stay in America or until he felt confident enough to complete the application. After all, there were some for whom the promise of America would be empty, and after a few years of prairie hardships, the Old Country didn't look so bad after all. The majority stayed, however,

and an affection for the new country began to replace the nostalgia for the old.

"He went to file for his citizenship papers right off the bat. He wasn't in this country more than four, five hours before he [filed for] his citizenship papers." — Louis Westling (Longville, MN)

"Some in the family became citizens before the others. Some had gone to college and wanted to teach so they became citizens right away. And my brother was drafted into the service and went into the service he automatically became a citizen. Others, when time went on and they got a job, they felt that if they had a job, well, they should be citizens. At the time I became a citizen, my father, my mother, and one of my sisters became a citizen. I was about thirty-two years old by that time. [The politicians] would come around naturally, and they'd talk and we were very polite to them and wish them good luck and hope they would win—whoever came—but we'd just tell them that we couldn't vote because we weren't citizens. And then they would say, 'Well, why don't you? After all, a vote might mean something someday.'" — Elsie Gale (Clearbrook, MN)

"It was easy to become a citizen then. They had to take out 'intention papers' to begin with. Then you had to wait for five years until you got the real citizenship paper. But with the intention paper you could vote. Yah, we took out citizenship paper. Most people did that. Once in a while there was somebody who didn't take it out. There was always people like that, you know. At that time, you know, the politicians, in the fall, running for congress or the legislature or something like that, they could help you get citizenship papers so you could vote for them." — John Klukken (Osakis, MN)

"My grandfather was in the Civil War [and he became a citizen]. The crops were so poor, and he needed the money and at that time those drafted could pay someone else three hundred dollars to go in their place. … They all sought citizenship right away because they were all thrilled to be here. They thought this was such a wonderful country and they wanted to be part of it and they got their citizenship papers right away." — Florence Fritz (Detroit Lakes, MN)

"She wanted her citizenship papers, and so these two kids were promised a penny for every word they would teach my mother. But that went rather slowly. She would forget the words. She thought it wasn't that important. … Well, finally, the morning arrived when she was to go down to Wahpeton to have her hearing and get her papers and she had a way about closing doors with a bang, and that morning she did, and as she left she said, 'Well, Moses is governor, that much I know!' And then they proceeded to quiz her in various ways, 'Will you name the thirteen original colonies?' And I think she got about four. And then, the man who was doing this said, 'Mrs. Melin, do you think if we wait until next fall, could you come back and get your papers then?' 'No,' she said, 'I think I would be yust so dumb then as I am now.' And she got her papers." — Anna Hanson (Moorhead, MN)

"This was during the Wilson administration, and things were hard. You were lucky if you could get a dollar a day. I got to be a citizen when I was in the army. They didn't ask me any questions then." — Andrew Lindgren (Moorhead, MN)

"That's how I got to be a citizen. I married one who was born here. In 1907. I got that paper yet!" — Kristine Svidal (Starkweather, ND)

"My father applied for citizenship just about as soon as he got here. He couldn't speak English at all when he arrived. And that is one of the reasons he went out to North Dakota to work for this Irish family because that was one way he could learn English [and get his papers]." — Oscar Olson (Lake Park, MN)

"Dad made application for citizenship before he could file on his homestead. And then he was supposed to live five years on his homestead before he could get his patent, they called it. The government gives you title to the land. I never took out citizenship papers, I got by without it because my father had his citizenship papers before I was twenty-one." — Ole Olson (Fargo, ND)

"I didn't have to get citizenship papers because I was able to become a citizen when my mother and dad did. My brother was too old, though, and he had to take out his own papers. But they waited sixteen or seventeen years before they became citizens. It didn't seem to be such a big thing. Of course, at that time we went through that World War I, and afterwards there was such a turmoil." — Borghild Overby (Moorhead, MN)

"In order to have their homestead land, they had to become citizens, so that was the first thing on the agenda, to become citizens." — Amy Margaret Erickson (Wheatland, ND)

"They didn't become citizens very soon. I can remember when my father took out his second papers. I was small then." — Mabel Enger (Oakes, ND)

"I was here twenty years before I became a citizen. You had to be here five years first to get the first paper. And after I was here for that long, then I was going to Fargo to get the papers. But the day I was going I got sick in bed, and I let it slide and I let it slide and when I did go for it the guy asked me all sorts of things I didn't know nothing about. Who was senator and all that political stuff." — Oscar Lindgren (Fargo, ND)

"I believe they became citizens when the state became a state, in 1889, and of course the children became citizens, too." — Wayne Dinusson (Fargo, ND)

"They became citizens as soon as they could. My father returned to Denmark, my mother never did." — Louise Andersen (Fargo, ND)

The Scandinavian-Americans tended to be solidly Republican. To a large extent, this was traditional, in that the Republican Party had been anti-slavery and pro-tariff, two issues about which the Scandinavians were deeply committed. For the most part, however, the Scandinavian-Americans did tend to support the progressive wing of the party. There were Scandinavian-American Democrats, of course, but one often had to look hard to find them.

"I think everybody was Republican around Osakis [Minnesota]. I really believe that. And I'll tell you why. It was a Norwegian from Voss [Knute Nelson] who came over here quite early and he became a congressman, and I believe he was governor of Minnesota at one time, and he had his home in Alexandria. He was a strict Republican, and I think all the Norwegians were Republican because of him. They didn't know anything else. Democrats, at that time, were looked upon as sort of questionable, they were looked upon as Socialists, or maybe something worse than that. I guess we had one in our neighborhood. He was running for office in Long Prairie and his ticket said he was a Democrat. And he came around and my mother said she would never understand why people would elect a Democrat. There was a few [Progressives] but it helped to develop people to more progressing. I don't think anybody really belonged to it, but we read about and heard about it, and it helped people to progress in their own mind quite a bit. There had to be something more progressive and liberal than old Republicans, because the old Republicans, they were pretty strict in their beliefs." — John Klukken (Osakis, MN)

"My father was a very staunch Republican, so we were Republican, and most of our friends were. In fact, I can't remember any of the groups that my parents were associated with who were not Republicans. ... My mother was so anxious for us to be good Americans that a lot of the Scandinavian things weren't stressed or even talked about." — Ruth Erickson (Moorhead, MN)

"My folks were Republican because they said Cleveland, you know, was President when they started there, and at the time I was born, and they said money was tight then. There was not much money circulating when Cleveland as President so they were Republican. ... It all depended on what papers they read. I don't know which one was for what, but there was a [political] difference. And a lot of mail would come from one political party or another, and whoever read the thing that they thought was right, that's what they'd be." — Mabel Enger (Oakes, ND)

"They were Republican when they came here [Christine, North Dakota], and they stayed Republican until the day they died. They were staunch Republicans. They voted Republican whether the man was a Republican or not. They voted that way, not that they had any hatred for the other party or anything like that." — Frank Alm (Christine, ND)

"Everyone was Republican around there [Morris, Minnesota]. I carried a torch light for McKinley in 1896 [at the age of 18]. And also carried one in 1900 when he was re-elected. I remember the day he was assassinated. I was working in a store that day and we got the day off for the funeral. I put up a big showcase with his picture in it. Teddy Roosevelt was a great man, too. I used to go to Medora [North Dakota], where he held forth. He had a cattle ranch out there." — Ole Olson (Fargo, ND)

"A majority of the people at that time were Republican [around Perley, Minnesota], as I can recall it. I know my family were all Republican." — Alva Hest (Perley, MN)

"Typically your average homesteader, realizing that the Homestead Act was passed under a Republican administration in 1862, typically he would be a Republican. But there were movements, like the Granger movement, and the Populist movement. As far as I can recall, Democrats were never very strong in Waukon Township [Norman County, Minnesota]. There were mostly Republicans. Then you had in North Dakota in the 1920s the Non-Partisan League movement and that spilled over into western Minnesota. They had a lot of excellent ideas. They stood for a lot of reform and things, but at the same time, a lot of people found them to be socialistic." — Christian Schulstad (Dawson, MN)

"I know my parents were Republicans all the time. I can't remember any Swedish Democrats. The one thing I remember, was my dad used to remember with joy how he met Teddy Roosevelt. He was over to Island Park in Fargo and gave a talk and they had a big barbecue. ... And they all had a great big hunk of meat, but it was too raw and most of 'em brought it home, and cooked it at home." — Hazel Monson Barker (Moorhead, MN)

"I shook hands with Teddy Roosevelt when I was a little kid. He was scheduled to stop in Fargo. We went to the Moorhead depot by mistake. All the crowd was in Fargo. The train stopped in Fargo, but it pulled up in Moorhead and stopped again. And my father and I and President Weld of the Teacher's College were there and President Roosevelt came out at the rear of the train and shook hands with the three of us." — Robert Carlander (Moorhead, MN)

"I think it was Republican way back. Everybody voted. We had a good turn out on election day [in Moorhead, Minnesota]." — Anna Melberg (Moorhead, MN)

"The Swedes around here [Moorhead, Minnesota] never went into politics much. I can't ever remember my folks saying anything about being a Democrat or Republican. But I can't remember my dad voting for anyone but a Republican President. I would say it's typical of that era." — Vic Anderson (Moorhead, MN)

"My dad was a good Republican like most of the people in Moorhead, the old timers like the Comstocks. In 1892 or so, they got the contract for the first buildings at Moorhead State, the Normal School they used to call it." — Roy Carlander (Moorhead, MN)

"I thought all there were Republican when I was a kid [in Moorhead]. I guess I didn't even know about Democrats. None of our people were anything but Republicans." — Gladys Westrum (Moorhead, MN)

"Seems to me, as I remember, [Lake Park, Minnesota] was a strong Republican community." — Amy Erickson (Moorhead, MN)

"It was pretty solidly Republican [near Lake Park, Minnesota]." — Oscar Olson (Lake Park, MN)

"I have a feeling that a great many of them were Republicans at the time I grew up [near Ulen, Minnesota]." — Clara Hanson (Moorhead, MN)

"Oh, there were very few Democrats [around Fertile, Minnesota], I know that. 'Democrat' was a word for something we didn't like." — Louis Haugen (Crookston, MN)

"I didn't know any Democrats when I was young. My folks were Republican and I think everybody was around [Hitterdal, Minnesota]. 'Democrat' was a dirty word for a long while. ... The depression was when I changed over. There are more Democrats than Republicans now. [We changed] when we got educated enough to walk and chew gum at the same time." — Wilferd Anderson (Hitterdal, MN)

"Hitterdal was Republican. We used to say there was one Democrat, and his name was Hartse." — Gale Iverson (Hitterdal, MN)

"I think they were pretty solid Republican, but I don't think it was very important. It was taken for granted, I think. In later years, after I left, things changed radically. But at that particular time everything was stable, you know. There was some fuss during the war, I remember that, because Wilson was a Democrat." — Carl Elmquist (Moorhed, MN)

"I don't think we were very politically minded, except we were Democrats from the year one!" — Florence Fritz (Detroit Lakes, MN)

"There were always some Icelanders who were interested in politics. … There was a lot in the Cavalier Courthouse that were Icelanders. They felt that if they knew someone who was in there it was easier to go to them and talk because they felt they knew their problems better." — Diane Volrath (Hitterdal, MN)

"We always used to think that the Norwegians [in Moorhead] had control of both the mayoralty and the council, and if not, they were behind the scene controlling it. Now, maybe that's just the way we saw it." — Elsie Holmquist (Moorhead, MN)

"I think church affiliation was much more important than the political affiliation." — John Gronner (Underwood, MN)

All the Scandinavian immigrant groups contained elements that were drawn to radical politics. Jon Wefald, in *A Voice of Protest: Norwegians in American Politics, 1890–1917*, wrote that the Norwegians

"were unrelentlessly progressive, frequently radical. Their politics were uniformly left of center, varying from progressive and radical Republicanism to Populism to Socialism. In fact, the Norwegian-American stood far enough to the left during the period from the 1890s to World War One to be ranked as one of the consistently reform-bent ethnic groups in American history."

Many of the Scandinavians in the Upper Midwest were drawn to the Populist movement of the 1890s, and continued to sway between the Republican Party and various reform parties. In 1915, the Republican Non-Partisan League was formed in North Dakota, with a program that advocated the state control and operation of grain elevators and the sale of wheat. The movement spread to Minnesota and South Dakota and was fairly successful for a time, gaining several state offices in North Dakota and forcing the Republican governor of South Dakota, a Norwegian-American named Peter Norbeck, to accept much of their program.

Minneapolis and Saint Paul became centers of Swedish and Norwegian Socialist activity, and there was later considerable Socialist and Communist activity among the Finns in the Iron Range area. In addition, the Finns organized cooperatives in several North Dakota counties and in the New York Mills area of central Minnesota.

"They took their politics very seriously. My mother's people were much more radical because they had less money always. They left this area [the Red River Valley] and went out to western North Dakota in 1905 and homestead out there. My mother didn't because she had already married and stayed here. All the rest of her family—mother, father, and brothers—went out to western North Dakota because land was opening up and it was too expensive to buy it here and [they all became involved in radical politics]."
— Clarence Glasrud (Moorhead, MN)

"I don't know. I guess most of them belonged to the Non-Partisan League [around Bowman, North Dakota]. It was important in them days. You don't hear any more about it now." — Eloise Kromarek (Bowman, ND)

"[The most important political party was] the Non-Partisan League, which was affiliated with the Republican Party at the time. Then the Non-Partisan League switched to the Democrats and then the town was about evenly divided." — Edwin Markestad (Maddock, ND)

"The Non-Partisan League was very strong up in that area [near Minot, North Dakota], you know, the party of William Langer and that got to be a hot political potato. I remember Dad having a lot of arguments about that. He was very opposed to the principles of that party. And, oh yes, he mentioned politics in the pulpit. He had a very powerful voice, and he spoke without any loudspeaker, and he made some people turn in their shoes sometimes. Of course, the people who would have taken offense at it weren't there in the church." — Odin Strandness (Fargo, ND)

"Well, one of our uncles used to drive around during the Non-Partisan time, you know. He used to drive around [Clay County, Minnesota] plugging for some of the candidates running for office. He wasn't in our immediate neighborhood. I don't even know how he was received."
— Gertie Holm (Hawley, MN)

"Dad never had anything to do with politics; it didn't appeal to him. But Uncle Matt was all for politics. He started out on the local level. He was one of the founders of the Non-Partisan League and the Farmer's Union in Hazelton and one thing led to another and he finally wound up in Bismarck as a representative and was Speaker of the House for one term and he was elected to the Office of Commissioner of Agriculture and he held that post for about sixteen years, I believe. Uncle Matt was a born dyed-in-the-wool politician if there ever was one. The rest of the family was Republican, as far as I know." — Matilda Blumer (Hazelton, ND)

"I suppose when the people came here they started these cooperative movements. I think the cooperative movement is also a political movement, in a way. It was more than an economic movement. … Well, cooperatives are a phenomenon among Finnish, as well as all Scandinavians, I think. … A fellow got more money, and the consumer got a better product. But then we had the consumer cooperatives, which are strong in New York Mills, and all these communities, and any place where the Finnish people are strong. And this is a combination I would say, of the political philosophy and the economic philosophy. ... But there is a sizeable community here, so sizeable in fact that it was known among Finnish people all over the United States that New York Mills was a radical community, although the community itself wasn't, but a large segment of people here were. And they had the hall, and of course they had the newspaper here which was established in 1884 by the Milan Brothers, and was sold in 1921 to People's Voice Co-op Publishing Company, and this was an arm of the Radical movement. ... And here's another thing about the Communist, Socialist, and IWW movements among the Finns. It doesn't seem as if they were greatly political, the political activities amounted mostly to the polemics they had among themselves. And they would argue about doctrines among themselves, and the doctrines of the other groups, if they differed from theirs, the other one was wrong and theirs was right. And the actual activity in an area like New York Mills that they might have done on a political basis was very little in evidence, as far as I can see, that they never amounted to anything politically, but socially they did. Because even in the hall, they had a small theatre, and you might look for these people to take part in the Finnish plays. And this was the great thing among all the Finnish radical groups. They had their halls, in which they had plays and so forth, doings and basketball teams for the young people. And it seemed there was emphasis, I mean, that it seems that whatever they might have contributed, it seems much greater in this field than in the political field." — Russell Parta (New York Mills, MN)

One Swedish-American poet summed up the romantic idealization of American politics in his poem, "Den fjarde juli" ("The Fourth of July"):

No chains in this land shackle any man's thought

Lest you forge the iron with which they are wrought.

No church council bans your creed or belief

Lest you acquiesce in timid relief.

No rich man's vote counts more at the poll,

Lest you throw yours away or never enroll.

If it's freedom you want, it is yours without flaw,

For you live among free men, where respect is the law.

Chapter XI
"Now Speak Norwegian!"

HOME LIFE IN TOWN AND COUNTRY

The memories of one's childhood are usually not filled with detailed recollections of theological or political disputes. The most remembered things are often the most personal events that shaped one's life. Yet, these memories often reflect quite intimately the extent of the Scandinavian heritage in the home.

Waldemar Ager was editor of *Kvartalskrift*, an organ that provided a forum for the presentation of views and controversies affecting the Norwegian-American community. In an essay that appeared in the January, 1908, issue, Ager vigorously defended the use of the Norwegian language in America and called for the preservation of the mother tongue. In the article, entitled "The Language Is Most Important," Ager charged that "Experience has proved that with the decline of the Norwegian language there also falls interest for the rest of the ancestral heritage." Decrying the trend toward assimilation, he wrote, "If we want to preserve and promote the interest for *Norskdom*, then we must preserve and promote the interest for the language."

In examining the oral histories of the Scandinavian-Americans of the Upper Midwest, it is revealing to probe the gradual disuse of the

Scandinavian languages in light of Ager's assertions. Many of those interviewed said that although they could not speak English when they began school, that language had gradually replaced the use of the Scandinavian language in the home by the time they left school. Furthermore, although Ager maintained that "if there is an area in which the language ought to play the least role, then it would have to be the church," it was that institution, more than any other factor, that kept alive the Scandinavian languages in the homes of Scandinavian-Americans.

"It was all Norwegian. When I started school [in 1921], I talked Norwegian. I read Norwegian. I couldn't even talk English. Mother and I used to talk Norwegian on the telephone all the time, but she died in 1975. But that's fifteen years ago and you forget a lot. ... My grandpa never even talked English to us. He always talked Norwegian and we'd answer him in English. He died in 1945 and he still talked nothing but Norwegian to us."
— Ellen Abraham (Villard, MN)

"But my first job was to learn English. I understood it a long time before I could talk, just how to say it, it was a tongue twister. After I understood it I had to pronounce it, while I was alone, because I didn't want anyone to hear my brogue. So when I hung out clothes on the clothes line and I was all alone I would practice my English. ... My kids don't talk

Norwegian very well. They understand it because there was always newcomers coming over, relatives, who lived with us, and they couldn't talk English so they learned it a little bit." — Kristine Svidal (Starkweather, ND)

"The traditions faded quite fast when they started to speak English. … I suppose Norwegian was probably the first words I used, but then my mother was born in the United States. … I was speaking English when I started school. I never heard my teacher speak Norwegian, but I think she could." — Edwin Markestad (Maddock, ND)

"Norwegian was all my sister could speak when she started school and the other kids made fun of her, of course. They were German. And so then my folks quit. They just wouldn't talk Norwegian. They spoke English to us kids all the time." — Ralph Simonson (Bowman, ND)

"I was told by my parents that I spoke Norwegian fluently until I was about four years old. And then they decided that I only had two years before I started first grade so they would just speak English and just talk Norwegian to each other when we were asleep. They loved to talk Norwegian but they didn't. I could speak English when I started school, in fact, I had forgotten most of my Norwegian." — Vern Fugelberg (New Rockford, ND)

"They became citizens as soon as they could. My father had learned some English from when he was in the Army in Norway and my mother had learned some during her training. They never used Norwegian much at home.

My older brother and I never learned to talk Norwegian until we were about to be confirmed." — Art Waldon (Detroit Lakes, MN)

"They spoke no English when they came, but they were self-taught. They taught themselves by reading children's schoolbooks and they learned right along with their children. They wanted to become citizens so badly that they studied and they did become citizens." — Solveig Johnson (Niagara, ND)

"We spoke Norwegian, you know, because then there were too many old-timers that didn't speak English even if they did know it. My dad talked about Norway, but my mother never talked about it. I don't even have any relatives back there. They all came here." — Clara Johnson (Underwood, ND)

"In our home we spoke Norwegian until my brother started school and he had such trouble because those teachers did not speak Norwegian and he had a hard time at first so then [my parents] decided that we would never speak Norwegian at home and we spoke English all the time. And I think that was true of many homes." — Florence Fritz (Detroit Lakes, MN)

"Practically only Norwegian was spoken in our home. I suppose I knew some English before I started school. I was in the middle of a family of eleven and the others had gone to school, so I suppose I knew some. It wasn't quite as difficult as it was for the others. … But we had to speak only English, especially inside the schoolhouse or even on the school grounds. …

It just kind of came gradually. ... My parents knew English, but they didn't talk it. The changeover in the church services was in the thirties and the changeover was quite gradual." — William Nelson (Rollag, MN)

"Oh, yes, my folks spoke English regularly, with a strong accent, of course, but regularly. But Norwegian is my native language. I learned that long before I learned English. We all did until 1920. After that it all stopped. It was very sudden. When I went to country school I didn't speak English at all. I had an older sister who moved away from us and she came back talking English and I thought that was very queer. It seems odd, but I have no memory of learning English. As soon as we started going to school it seemed much more natural to speak English. For a while I'm sure we spoke both interchangeably and go back and forth without thinking about it."
— Clarence Glasrud (Moorhead, MN)

"Norwegian was spoken in our home. Father and Mother spoke it pretty much. Our two closest neighbors, the Robinson family and the Meyer family didn't use the Scandinavian language. And it so happened that [they] were my playmates and so I learned the English at an early age." — Norman Nelson (Rollag, MN)

"My father never learned the English language. Only rarely did he try to use it and then he spoke broken English." — Beatrice Schaefer (Osakis, MN)

"I could speak Norwegian fluently and well, and correct, correct Norwegian! Most of the farmers and other people around here [Twin Valley, Minnesota], they talked a *lingua franca*, an accommodation between the Norwegian and the English, and they would mix it up pretty well. Most of the farmers didn't speak English very well, but they had to learn some of the words." — Carl Narveson (Moorhead, MN)

"My brother and I were never allowed to speak English even after we had learned to speak English. We'd speak English and Dad would say, 'Now, speak Norwegian!' I continued that at home until I was twenty years old. He wanted us to know the Scandinavian language and know it well." — Clara Hanson (Moorhead, MN)

"[My father] couldn't speak a word of English when he came over, and [he never learned] very much, because there was no reason for them to speak English because everybody [in the Hendrum, Minnesota, area] was Norwegian." — Alva Hest (Perley, MN)

"Father came in 1907. He came to Tamarack, Minnesota, and then he moved to Moorhead. I was born in 1927, and Norwegian was about the only thing we did speak at home. Mostly the neighbors were from Telemark. My father attended Concordia College one winter to learn the English language." — Regina Hanson (Glyndon, MN)

"My folks never learned English very well, but they did get along. There were plenty of Norwegians in the Comstock [Minnesota] area. ... I'd say the English grew up with the family. I'd say that I didn't have much of a vocabulary in English when I was finishing up eighth grade, but I was building up myself. Every new word I'd look up in the dictionary and get the meaning of the word. It didn't mean anything to me otherwise." — Oscar Askegaard (Moorhead, MN)

"My dad went to the Riverside School where he learned to read. Mother never went to school. [When she came over] she went to work for a Mrs. Parkes, near the Red River. And she couldn't understand Norwegian and my mother couldn't understand English. But she was very good. She taught her [English] and taught her how to read. She didn't want to work for a Norwegian because she wanted to learn English." — Cora Kragnes (Felton, MN)

"My mother was deaf, and they sent her to the deaf school in Devil's Lake because it was one of the few schools at that time that taught lip reading as well as sign language. And they were a family that always believed in education. My mother's uncle was a regent at the University of Minnesota. They all decided that the best thing was to go to Devil's Lake, and that's where she met my father. At my mother's home everything was Norwegian, everything that was spoken at the table and everywhere I went it was Norwegian. But I really wasn't upset about it because most of the guests that we had at our house didn't speak at all. They used sign language so I was used to interpreting things by facial actions and movements of that sort. My mother used to do [Norwegian] handwork, embroidering, and that sort of thing, and the cooking, we had all the traditional foods, cookies, lutefisk, and lefse and so on, so I have that as a reminder of the culture." — Maureen Christianson (Kenmare, ND)

"After we started school, and we started to learn English, well then, I suppose we sort of mixed it up for a while. Eventually even Mother and Dad just spoke English all the time. And they learned to read and write English. I suppose we sort of helped them along a little when we were in school. I remember reading out of a book to Dad. He was real interested and he was real quick to pick up things. ... My grandfather tried to talk to the neighbor who came over, and my grandfather tried to talk Norwegian and the neighbor tried to talk English. And it was something about planting seeds in the spring, about making a garden. And he told us about radishes and different things like that. In fact, I think he brought the seeds over. And Grandfather was so frustrated that he couldn't understand what the man was talking about—well, none of us could—and they were just yelling at each other trying to make things out." — Matilda Blumer (Hazelton, ND)

"My grandpa never learned English and my dad spoke mostly Swede. My dad talked mostly Swede, but on occasion when somebody came to visit and he knew they were not Swedish and couldn't speak Swedish he could speak good English. Really surprised me! Mother went to night school to learn to speak English and write. When she worked in Minneapolis she went to night school." — Amy Margaret Erickson (Wheatland, ND)

"My father was nineteen when he came over, and I can't remember him speaking Swedish. It was always in English. If someone spoke Swedish to him he'd come back in English. He didn't know any English before he came to America. He was born in 1868. When he came here he went to his cousin's, about six miles south of Moorhead, and stayed there for a little while and then he went out to Perley and he bought a farm there. But he wasn't happy farming. He missed the bright lights. So he came to Moorhead." — Hazel Monson Barker (Moorhead, MN)

"Grandfather learned to speak English, but Grandmother never did. Never! She died in 1923. It wasn't necessary for her to learn the English language, because at church she could converse with everyone there, and we could always talk Swedish to her at home. I couldn't speak English until I started school." — Amy Ericson (Moorhead, MN)

"My dad [who was Swedish] did real good, but my mother [was Danish], and she kind of had her [English] a little mixed up and couldn't pronounce the words just the way they were supposed to come out, but still she made herself understood. She learned Swedish, my dad didn't learn Danish. The only time she got into Danish was when her sister came. There were mostly Swedes there [near Audubon, Minnesota], the Norwegians were further north." — Phoebe Westerholm (Moorhead, MN)

"My dad learned to speak English, but my mother never did. They spoke Swedish to each other as long as they lived." — Charles Westerholm (Moorhead, MN)

"In Moorhead Township I believe there must have been ten Swedish pioneer families who established themselves. … My very first words, I suppose, were Swedish. But after I started school [in 1898] my parents encouraged us to talk English, and discouraged us from talking Swedish, more or less, because they wanted to learn English themselves. After a while we stopped talking Swedish entirely at home." — Robert Carlander (Moorhead, MN)

"All the people I knew seemed to be Scandinavian and they all talked Swedish. We talked Swedish at home all the time. In fact, before I started school I couldn't talk English." — Helen Furcht (Moorhead, MN)

"My father was Danish and my mother was Swedish. When they talked to each other they talked Swedish." — Henrietta Burgess (Moorhead, MN)

"We talked Swede all the time until I started first grade. I can still quote you the Ten Commandments and the Lord's Prayer in Swede. Everything, the conversation at the table was said in Swede." — Vic Anderson (Moorhead, MN)

"In our home, Swedish was spoken exclusively. I was six years old when I started school. I knew one English word, and I pronounced it 'can-ife': knife. That was the extent of my English knowledge." — Carl Anderson (Erhart, MN)

"[My grandfather] just spoke Swedish when he came here, and it was a gradual thing. ... As I remember him, he spoke a little Swedish and a little English in the same sentence." — Judith Nelson (Hibbing, MN)

"[My grandfather] had a friend that went to [Carrington, North Dakota] and live and he kept on writing and writing to Grandpa to come to the United States, because it was better than living in Sweden and so he thought about that for a while and then he took his family and came over. ... There were mostly Swedes living around here [Clay County, Minnesota], that's why it got its name, 'Swede Grove.' They talked mostly Swedish in the home when we were growing up. [My sister] and I talked Swedish all the time when we were younger. Which seems strange, because I can't imagine talking Swede now. It seems now that I never did that, but I did." — Violet Anderson (Hitterdal, MN)

"My dad wanted to speak Icelandic, but my mother spoke English. She was only five when she came to this country. But my dad never learned it. It was hard for him. So, we spoke mostly Icelandic at home." — Freda Bjornson (Moorhead, MN)

"My father knew some [English], and he did very well. My mother could understand it and speak some when she had to, but she didn't like to.

My grandmother did not. Of course, there was no illiteracy in Iceland, so they could all read and write, of course." — Anna Bjornson (Fargo, ND)

"In Hibbing they had quite a collection of Finnish books in the library, and she learned to read English by going to the public library and she would take Finnish books out for herself and then she would take children's books out for me, and she would read them to me. So this was one of the ways that you learned to read Finnish." — Karin Kivi (Moorhead, MN)

In most cases, the Scandinavians faced the same frontier experiences that other ethnic groups did, but they faced them with the traditional Scandinavian traits of stoicism, modesty, and determination. Out of these conflicts would come a second generation of Scandinavian-Americans more adaptable to the New world social relationships and family relationships were seen in a new setting but through old eyes.

"The father was the head of the household, all right. But my mother always used to say—there was an eighteen years difference between them—she would say, 'It's better to be an old man's darling than a young man's slave.' We had a trunk that my dad brought over—it's about one hundred and sixty-five years old now—and I still have a set of spoons he brought over. We had some rosemaling around the house, and I remember my mother had a pillow with Hardanger on, but I know we didn't appreciate that like they do now. ... Our dad was the one who always put us to bed and always the one who punished us. My mother never did. My dad was gone one time and mother had to dress up in his clothes to get us to bed." — Alpha Bowersox (Wolford, ND)

"My dad had rented a farm pretty close to where Marcus lived, and Marcus and his family had a threshing rig, and they did the threshing for my dad. And that's where I met him. He and his four brothers ran the threshing rig and they came and threshed for us for a week. And during that time, of course, my mother and I did the cooking for them. I was just sixteen years old at the time, but Marcus had already made up his mind that I was the girl he was going to marry." — Dagne Faust (Colfax, ND)

"He finally came to America, but he had already married in Sweden because I married after I was here two-and-a-half years. So I wrote and told him and he said to my mother, 'Anna don't belong to this man. She belongs to me!' But then he married another girl and I understand that they came to Minneapolis but I never did see him." — Anna Lindgren (Fargo, ND)

"It isn't good to live in this world for one woman alone, so I married him. He had no family, and he was from the same part of Norway as I so he was just about made to order." — Kristine Svidal (Starkweather, ND)

"Alvin asked me to marry him, then he went out and homesteaded in Canada for three years. It was almost four years later that we were married. So we went up to Flaten's Photography. And the minister met us there and we were married there and we had out picture taken. And then we went back to his mother's place, then we went to Minneapolis, where we stayed for our honeymoon for a while. It was the World War. He was drafted into the army, but he got out because he had so much land and it was hard to get help in those days. My wedding dress was white pussy-willow taffeta." — Cora Kragnes (Felton, MN)

"My husband taught school at Svold [North Dakota] so we lived at Svold. It was just a general store and a post office and two houses. And we lived upstairs in the post office. We were there for five years. Then he taught one year at Akra. When we were still at Svold we built a little two room house. So then when my husband moved to Akra, the farmers all pitched in and got their horses and moved the house to Akra. There was beautiful people up there, all Icelanders, of course." — Freda Bjornson (Moorhead, MN)

Family relationships may have been strained by the immigration experience, but for the most part it was the family relationship that helped the immigrant to persevere. Unlike the other Scandinavian groups, who often spent some time in older settlements before moving to the prairie, the Icelanders often came directly to Dakota Territory. In many cases, entire family units, consisting of grandparents, brothers, sisters, in-laws, roomers, and hired hands would come at one time. They

would keep these close connections, frequently marrying only other Icelanders. The Finns also tended to marry their own. In the North Dakota Census for 1980, for instance, it was revealed that forty-one percent of the Finns declared only one national ancestry, compared to twenty-eight percent of the Danes and twenty-seven percent of the Swedes.

"Mixed marriages" were very common for the Danes, but mostly out of necessity. One such Danish immigrant tried to convince a Danish woman to come to America and be his bride. The following letter written in 1907 to "Katrine" reflects the desire to establish a traditional family in the New World:

> *If you are unwed, you can find a good home with me. I own my own house in town and I earn more than 10 crowns per day. It's been about 20 years since we saw each other, and you probably wonder who I am. My name is Ejner who worked in Halsted for Adolf Jensen when you were at the Andersen's, and you were my first love. If you cannot come, ask somebody else who is willing to become a good housewife. ... I shall write some words in English: I am loved you of all my Hart; have bin driming af bort uoy y hoppes dat uoy vill be my wife. I am sand uoy one worm kiss. respechtifulli GoodBye.*

"Everyone had big families in those days because I think they felt by having those big families, that they would have help to do the work, and I think all the older Scandinavians also felt that they would have someone to take care of them when they got older. And of course there was no contraception in those days." — Nina Oien (Moorhead, MN)

"I was born in Petersburg, North Dakota. My folks took homestead there. I was six years old when my mother died. And you know, we had a big shed on the north side of the house and she laid there, on the flat, you know, and my dad wrote to Grand Forks, to his brother-in-law, I suppose they telegraphed, and he bought the coffin and sent it to Petersburg and then it was sent to Underwood." — Clara Johnson (Underwood, ND)

"Mr. Morken was kind of a, I don't know what to say, they called him in anyway. And he had some kind of instrument in his hand and he would bleed the patient and that seemed to relieve them some." — Minnie Tiedeman (Moorhead, MN)

"John, the oldest, when he was twelve or fourteen, was taking a gun out of the buggy and nearly shot his arm off. They were twelve miles out here and the father drove the horse into Moorhead to try to get a doctor. He was out on call, and a snowstorm was raging, but he was informed to come out as quickly as he could. In the meantime, my grandfather drove back. The doctor came out in the next morning, and in the meantime, Grandpa had gone down to Fort Abercrombie, some eighteen miles south, to get the government doctor, and he came out. And I don't know if it took two of them or what, but at any rate, it was eighteen to twenty hours later that they operated on the kitchen table, and cut his arm off." — Lynn Anderson (Moorhead, MN)

"All their neighbors were Norwegian. [My father] paid the passage for his nieces and nephews to come over here, and then they would work it out or pay him back and then they went on to get married and work for other people and get into some kind of business or move to some other area. I remember two nephews, one of them was a sailor. He didn't live here at our place so much, but the other one did, and a young cousin, and there were, these would be my cousins, three or four girls that he brought over. Meanwhile, there were ten of us, three boys and seven girls." — Alpha Bowersox (Wolford, ND)

There was a solidarity in the homes, and it was here that some of the most important decisions affecting the retention of Scandinavian customs, connections and customs were made. Some of these decisions were conscious attempts to distance themselves forever from the homeland, but most of these decisions were the result of the erosion of time and distance.

"There were [Norwegian] 'newcomers,' as we called them, who were always appearing on the scene [near Perley, Minnesota]. And many of them would stay with my folks. We had a small home, but there was always room for the newcomers." — Alva Hest (Perley, MN)

"They all changed their names when they came over here. They seemed to want to change it for the locality where they came from."
— Matilda Blumer (Hazelton, ND)

"We didn't learn Norwegian songs, or talk about Norwegian folklore or history." — Allan Erickson (Moorhead, MN)

"My grandmother would get letters from her relatives, but she would read them with a broken heart because it was always written that they were still angry with her for eloping with my grandfather. My great-grandparents had already chosen someone else for her." — Florence Fritz (Detroit Lakes, MN)

"I believe they wrote back to Norway every week. Father had sisters and mother had some sisters and they all wrote letters. They never came to America. ... After the second generation [the Norwegian language] sort of petered out. The first and second generation generally kept it up, but the third generation didn't pay much attention to it. Like my son, he can't talk a word of it. We never spoke anything but English in our home." — Ole Olson (Fargo, ND)

"Well, my dad couldn't write, but my mother wrote and so did my younger sister. She lived in Oslo and she wrote to me once in a while, but the others didn't. I got two sisters back home and I don't even know 'em, and they don't know me either. Well, they were crawling around on the floor when I left." — Arne Arneson (Fargo, ND)

"I had an uncle, married to my dad's sister, he returned to Norway, but he came right back again. He claimed he didn't like it. It wasn't home anymore to him." — Eloise Kromarek (Bowman, ND)

"My father could never afford to go back to Norway, but Uncle Ole returned for good in 1910 [after twenty-eight years in America] and also this cousin of mine who came over to take care of us kids when my mother died. She came and stayed here for six years and then she went back to Norway never to return to America. When she got back to Norway, Uncle Ole helped her and her sister buy a little shop in Oslo which they still had when I visited them in 1950. ... They definitely and very regularly kept contact with relatives back in Norway. My father had three brothers and three sisters back there." — Clara Hanson (Moorhead, MN)

Perhaps it was not a simpler life then, but at least it was a life in which the family worked together to adjust to new surroundings. It was a life in which the members of the family cared about each other and worked together.

"When I think of Icelanders I think of my grandmother, who was never idle. She would be knitting as she walked, like stockings. She would keep the ball of yarn under her armpit and keep on knitting." — Ellen Abraham (Villard, MN)

"I think most about the Icelanders in the early days; in the evenings we'd had one [member of the family] reading a story and the rest of the family listening, and we kids would either card the wool or get it ready for carding and mother would be spinning or if she wasn't spinning she'd be knitting. The whole family sat around the pot-bellied stove." — Leo Hillman (Mountain, ND)

"One person would read out loud and the others would listen. And many times we would be doing hand work of some kind. And then after the reading there would be discussion, which was a very good part of it, because then they really got a hold of what they were reading, could understand it, and could apply it." — Kathryn Thorvaldson (Fargo, ND)

"I lost my mother when I was seven and I was only twelve when I had to take over and do the work. A person had come from Norway and cared for us until I was twelve years old and then she moved into town to work in a store. And from then on I did the bread baking, the clothes washing, going to school, and everything. When my father finally moved into town [Ulen, Minnesota] in 1910, then I helped out first caring for children and helping some of the neighbors and after a while I ended up clerking in a store. All the while I was studying, getting all the schooling that I could with the help of high school teachers and those that were interested in helping me and finally took up parochial teaching so I taught parochial school before I was married for about nine years." — Clara Hanson (Moorhead, MN)

"We had cows and chickens and hogs and Dad never really learned much about farming. He couldn't milk a cow and he couldn't harness a horse, but he was a good boss. He saw to it that the rest of us learned how to do things and do them in time, because that's what he learned on the railroad." — John Gronner (Underwood, MN)

"We helped milk cows and it was up to us to churn the butter. We made our own butter. And then my mother would put the butter into five pound stoneware jars and then we had customers in town [Niagara, North Dakota] that would buy a five pound jar of butter every week. All worked about the same. The kids worked every summer and they had to help with the chores, but during the school year the children didn't have to help, because they wanted them to have an education. And that was the same procedure on every farm. The kids all went to school." — Solveig Johnson (Niagara, ND)

"I very much wanted to be part of the group. My first year in America was a little rough. The girls wore clothes that I didn't have. There were some things I wanted, but my mother was saving money to pay back for the tickets. And they wore their hair a little differently from mine. They had black sateen bloomers that I just didn't get, and I thought that was such a shame I couldn't be American the way they were. There were such little piddly things that I remember." — Anna Hanson (Moorhead, MN)

"Two of my sisters were so small [when they were born] they put them in a shoe box. Around three pounds! It's sort of a miracle that they did live, but they made sort of an incubator and put them on the oven door just to keep them. My godmother was always there when children was born."
— Alpha Bowersox (Wolford, ND)

"The first thing I noticed when we came over here was the difference in the shoes. We figured the people in [Sweden] were old fashioned, but they weren't. We wore slippers there, and here they wore button-up shoes. So my aunt decided, well, we should be like the children here so she went out and bought button-up shoes. Well, that didn't go over too good. We didn't wear them." — Elsie Gale (Clearbrook, MN)

Living conditions were often primitive on the prairie. Anyone who has read Rolvaag's *Giants in the Earth* can appreciate the challenge of living like a human gopher in a sod house. The immigrants to the plains were always sustained, however, by the conviction that the first house was only temporary, and that eventually they would prosper enough to be able to build a white frame house with a broad porch, all trimmed in green. They also had faith that the forlorn willows and box

elder saplings would grow into trees to surround the farmstead and that the pole shed would be replaced with a big red barn.

"I was born in the sod house in 1907. The midwife was an old Russian woman who didn't speak English, and she took care of everything. She took care of my three brothers and sisters. And I was born in the bedroom of the sod house that just had a kitchen and a dining room. I remember that sod house! It had really small windows, you known, so you could just look outside. And when the wind blew it would blow dirt in on the floor. And we didn't have any linoleum or anything on the floor. It was really tough going in those days. It was just a rough lumber floor. Mother would sweep the dust into the cracks. ... Dad built an addition on the back of the house so we had an extra bedroom when I got older. And when it rained, boy did it get muddy with all the kids coming in! We'd be playing outside, in the spring of the year, and we'd track in all that mud. It wasn't too bad, because mother did a pretty good job of cleaning up. The inside walls of the sod house were all wooden, you know, rough lumber. We had a coal stove. There was no wood to burn out there [near Turtle Lake, North Dakota] in those days, you know, not a tree in sight. The coal was all black, and that part of the kitchen was all dirty or black with coal. We got the coal twenty-four miles away at Velva, where there was an open mine." — Lloyd Westrum (Moorhead, MN)

"The first house they built was a sod house on the claim. They found a good slough, a hay slough, and used a good breaker plow and broke up part of the slough and then they would haul the sod in strips to their houses and lay it down, flat on the ground, and start building that way. Some of the walls were three foot thick at the base and they worked up to the top. On the inside some of them put boards on the wall. I don't remember whitewashed walls so much, but I know that some of 'em would use paper whenever they could get hold of it. Some used the local newspaper. But my folks used real wallpaper of the walls." — Philip Andersen (Fargo, ND)

"My mother used to say it was harder to keep the wooden floor clean than the sod floor. I remember when we got the log addition on to [the sod house]. We had so much more room. Up till that time we just had one room and we had some curtains across for partitions on one end of it. And after they built the log addition, Andrea and I, we had a room to ourselves. I remember that first night, I thought 'This is really something.'" — Matilda Blumer (Hazelton, ND)

"There were nine of us children and we had a four room house. And now I don't know how we survived, but we did. There were two bedrooms, and there was a folding cot in the living room. In the summertime, sometimes the boys slept out in the hayloft. ... We had running water. I ran out to the well to get it and I ran back to the house with it." — Ellen Abrahamn (Villard, MN)

"Before my dad dug the well he carried drinking water six miles from the Whiting sheep ranch, with one of them things over his shoulders he carried two milk cans, and that was the drinking water. And right below the sod house was a grass bottom pond—nice clear water—and they used that for washing clothes, watering the livestock, and stuff." — Ralph Simonson (Bowman, ND)

"We had a little better house than a lot of them at that time, a lot of them had sod houses, but we had a frame house." — Clara Johnson (Underwood, ND)

"It was just a two room log house." — Amy Margaret Erickson (Wheatland, ND)

Not all the Scandinavian immigrants moved directly to American farms and homesteads. A significant number of immigrants went directly to America's cities. Although some worked in factories and building trades only long enough to gather enough money to begin farming, the number of Scandinavians who lived in an urban environment grew rapidly. This urban growth was particularly significant after 1890. The Swedes tended to congregate in the cities to a greater extent than did the other Scandinavian groups. By 1910, sixty-one percent of America's Swedish-born population lived in large cities. Only Stockholm, for instance, had more Swedish residents than did

Chicago. There were also sizable numbers of Norwegians and Danes in Chicago where the Scandinavian presence was quite noticeable in business and the building trades. During the later stages of immigration, many Scandinavians also began to remain in New York City.

The Scandinavian urban populations seemed to provide a focal point for many of the Scandinavian-Americans. In Chicago, Minneapolis, Saint Paul, and several smaller cities, they found their own distinct neighborhoods. Minneapolis, more than any other large city, became America's Scandinavian center. Cedar Avenue, often referred to as 'Snoose Boulevard,' was home to tens of thousands of Scandinavian immigrants. Norwegian, Swedish, and Danish was heard on the streets and in the saloons. Musical acts, such as the Norwegian Olson Sisters and comedians such as the famous Swede Olle I Skratthult presented programs of Old Country music and skits. Skratthult, who had come to Minnesota as a bricklayer in 1906 and was supposedly the only Swedish American to make a living as a full-time entertainer, wrote and performed the most famous of all Scandinavian American songs, "Nikolina." With the development of the Scandinavian dialect joke, they had gained the confidence to laugh at themselves during evening hours after gaining the confidence of others through their cooking, building, and sewing during the day.

"I settled for a while in New York. That part of New York was so Norwegian, even the Jews talked Norwegian. If they wanted to stay in business they had to, 'cause in that particular area, what they called Washington Heights, nine out of ten of those who lived there were of Scandinavian background." — Sven Thompson (Willmar, MN)

"When I got off the ship I had eight dollars in my pocket and no job. I got a job in a hotel kitchen in Brooklyn washing pots and pans under two Italian cooks. But I had a job and I stayed with a Filipino family down on Atlantic Avenue, in a room that almost defies description. I had a bed, and a chair, and a chest of drawers, and a light—nothing but a gas pipe that I lit with a match. Then I got a job in a bank in Manhattan, the Twenty-ninth Street and Fourth Avenue branch of the Corn Exchange Bank. I stayed there for two years, first as a bookkeeper and then as an adjuster. But I didn't like to live in New York, and that's why I came out to the Midwest and ended up in Valley City. I had an uncle living there and he urged me to come west. He had a job for me. Then I took a job as a manager of an estate and food store in Cooperstown, North Dakota, and stayed there for about a year and then found a little store to buy in Chafee, North Dakota. I had taken two years of English in high school [in Sweden], so I could read and write and spell it, but I couldn't say I could converse and feel sure about it." — Hartvig Johnard (Hawley, MN)

"My dad and my uncle learned a trade, and that was the cement business ..., which really turned out to be a wonderful thing for the two of them. ... I thought that we were poor, but I realize that in the eyes of the people back in Sweden we were indeed well-to-do." — Helene Kaeding (Moorhead, MN)

"He was not trained in any special field, so when he came to Chicago, he had to get any job available. He was always full of fun and he was delighted to tell how he applied to drive horses for delivering meat for the stockyards and had never known how to drive a horse. The horses were well trained and stopped at the regular markets automatically and the butcher would come out to take their allotment of meat." — Svea Lundgren (Fosston, MN)

"Mother started to sew immediately with a Jewish family who said they would pay her what she was worth. They were so pleased with her they promised to keep her busy, but they paid her only twenty-five cents a day and board and room. The first Sunday after a party they came out with clothes and a brush and indicated she was to brush them. She became furious and declared in Swedish 'I'd never brush clothes for anyone in Sweden and I've never come to America to do it here.' She threw down the brush and began to get dressed for church." — Nina Oien (Moorhead, MN)

While in the large urban areas the Scandinavians could be seen either as an important ethnic block or as a curiosity, in many small towns in the Upper Midwest they dominated. Furthermore, their imprint on many of these small towns seems to have been permanent.

"My dad managed grain elevators. At first he was assigned to Manvel, North Dakota, and not liking hat he asked for a transfer to Hitterdal, Minnesota. Coming there was almost like coming to Norway. Everyone talked Norwegian. We had lived in a non-Scandinavian community, and here everything was in Norwegian. We couldn't understand the kids, at first, that we played with. Before long we caught on to it. My [father was Swedish and my mother Norwegian but they] never spoke Norwegian or Swedish. I think the whole town was Norwegian. And they were so interrelated that we were almost the only outsiders. The signs in the stores were English, but there were lots of kids who came to school who couldn't speak English at all. The teachers must have understood Norwegian because they finally taught the kids to speak English." — Gale Iverson (Hitterdal, MN)

"When we moved to Hitterdal, when I was five years old [1908], most of the kids that I played with couldn't understand English. And I couldn't understand Norwegian, so we had a time there. It was very common, at that time, that a lot of kids, when they started school, didn't know English. There was friction between the Norwegians and the Swedes. Although I was

half Norwegian and half Swede, they called me a Swede. My folks never talked Norwegian or Swedish at home, so we never had an opportunity to learn it. Although I did learn some phrases, I never became fluent. ... Most of the public places you went into they spoke Scandinavian. ... I think they were all either Norwegians or Swedes in Hitterdal at the time I was a kid. I can't recall any family that wasn't. The first Norwegian words that I did learn were cuss words. I got bawled out a lot of times because I'd come home and say something and I didn't have the least idea what it meant."
— Wilferd Anderson (Hitterdal, MN)

"Most of the stores in Ulen were run by a Norwegian. There were four elevators in Ulen at one time, and they were all run by Norwegians, Norwegian managers anyway." — Henry Jacobson (Ulen, MN)

"At that time Ulen was a store down by the river, near the railroad bridge, and the one widow who had three children lived right in what is now the center of town. And then, of course, the blacksmith shop a little further south. So my father helped build it. Whatever went on they took a part in, because they were interested in the progress. After a while, when the town finally grew, after some years then they were interested in getting a church. And that, both my uncle and father had a very active part in building. The dedication was, I think, in 1902." — Clara Hanson (Moorhead, MN)

"My mother's folks were all over here by then, and they all lived in a little group of homes [in Moorhead] where Sharpe School is now standing.

My Uncle John went and parceled out a lot for each—about six or eight lots—a lot for each relative. And that's where I was born. The Swedes were here earlier than the Norwegians. They built the Hope Academy, a three-story building on the north side. My uncle built that. My dad said the Indians used to come to the area around what is now Oak Grove Park. And he said once he went across the river and bought a birch bark canoe from them for a dollar." — Roy Carlander (Moorhead, MN)

"My uncle came from Smaland, near Kalmar, and my mother came from Vestergotland, near the city of Goteborg, in about 1880 or 1881. They came directly to Moorhead. My mother's brother was settled here at that time. He was a contractor. He built the first teacher's college building, he built the first courthouse in Clay County, and he worked for the Northern pacific Railroad from Montana to Wisconsin." — Robert Carlander (Moorhead, MN)

"[My mother] came at the invitation of a girlfriend who had the finest restaurant in Moorhead, Carlson's Restaurant, and she came as a second cook. And that's what she did. In those days [1896] they didn't have too much education. One winter, though, she lived in the home of Senator Knute Nelson, of Alexandria, so she could go to school." — Hazel Monson Barker (Moorhead, MN)

"The north side [of Moorhead] was where the Swedes thought the town was going to grow. So that's why they built their academy out there,

Hope academy, and that's here they started the hospital. That was where the town was going to grow, but it fooled them and went the other way."

— Gladys Westrum (Moorhead, MN)

"[When I came to Christine, North Dakota] I thought the whole thing was lovely. It was a pretty small town then, but there was a lot more business going on then. The wooden sidewalks intrigued us." — Anna Hanson (Moorhead, MN)

"I had a room in Valley City in a private home. Dad would send me a check every month, and you know what I paid for board and room? Sixteen dollars! I went in the spring and stayed until the later part of June, and then I got married." — Matilda Blumer (Hazelton, ND)

"I used to drive down [to Fargo] to get snoose. It was a dirt road from Enderlin and you couldn't get snoose in North Dakota, so I went to Moorhead and Dilworth. I went by motorcycle. That's how I got the booze too! They didn't sell liquor in Fargo, then. But they did in Moorhead."

— Arne Arneson (Fargo, ND)

"Westby, Montana, was fairly Danish. The name is Danish. It means 'West town.' Originally it was in North Dakota, but the railroad wanted a town in Montana and prohibition was a big issue. Saloons couldn't locate in North Dakota, but they could in Montana, and they eventually moved many of the main buildings to the Montana side." — Philip Andersen (Fargo, ND)

"Gardar was a little town, and there was a community store there that belonged to Eric Bergman, who they referred to as 'the kaiser.' He was the merchant. He lent money to people, too, but money had a way of clinging to him, I think." — Kathryn Thordarson (Fargo, ND)

"Well, the cultural life of any Finnish community would center around what's called the Finn hall. And every community in Minnesota or around the country would have a Finn hall. And this is where you would have dances and they would have theatricals, locally produced. I remember as a little girl being just very intrigued because we would have companies come from Finland and they presented plays." — Karen Kivi (Moorhead, MN)

Chapter XII

"They Pert'near Kicked the Ceiling"

SCANDINAVIAN-AMERICAN ENTERTAINMENT

The Scandinavians have a well-deserved reputation for creating and performing beautiful music. While all of the Scandinavian immigrant groups loved music and dancing, it was perhaps the Norwegians who most intensely created and retained their musical heritage. Perhaps the folk tales about the adventures of Askelandin or the travels of Pehr Gynt touched the wandering spirit of the immigrants. In any event, they retained their love of music in the New World, and the compositions of Ole Bull and traditional pieces such as *Hils Fra Mei Der Hjemme* could be heard in many prairie homes. The Hardanger violin, usually called the Hardanger fiddle, was a uniquely Norwegian instrument with four resonating strings that produced a haunting, almost mournful, sound. After being very carefully packed in the immigrant trunk, this fine crafted and beautiful instrument would be unpacked in America and would hang in an honored place on a log or sod wall.

"Once there was a lady who came to visit in my home. And she had a Hardanger fiddle and she was dressed in a Hardanger outfit. And she had a string on the end of her finger and on the other end of the string was a little *Nisse*. And as she played this little *Nisse* would dance with the music."

— Palmer Tverdahl (Abercrombie, ND)

"We'd have parties, and the young folks would sing Norwegian songs that went with certain games, but little by little it got to be all English. We'd sing and play games to that kind of music. The homes were all too small for dancing, you know. We had dances, but they were far from our place. My father was a good singer and he used to rock us to sleep, I remember his Norwegian songs, and he knew a couple of Swedish songs, too. And he could play the accordion. He never had a music lesson but he was a one man orchestra for what dances they had around the neighborhood. But our family grew so fast and he couldn't go anymore so he sold his accordion and gave it up altogether. I never heard him play. And he had a brother in Norway. My uncle in Red Wing said that Uncle Jens was the best violin player in Norway. Of course, he always built things up a little." — Mabel Enger (Oakes, ND)

"My father played violin. He played both classical and Norwegian dance tunes. He would probably have carried on with classical music if he had stayed in Norway, but over here he was just working too hard. And he played the accordion and the piano, and my mother sang." — Solveig Johnson (Niagara, ND)

"Well, in winter we generally had parties in the homes that were large enough so we could really dance in, so that was fun. Generally it was two violins and an organ or a piano, whichever they had in their homes. It was all standard music. Eddie Teal, the Mansager Brothers, and Oliver Kragnes—all Norwegians! In Moland Township somebody played the Hardanger violin. [My father] played the violin, but not the Hardanger violin—ear music! In those days they had wooden cigar boxes, and he cut some hair off a horse's tail and he fastened that to that, and then he made himself a bow from another stick of wood and some more hair, and he played! And this got to be so noisy in the house that Grandma told him he should play for the cows, so he went out to the barn. He got some work and he took that money and he went into a secondhand store and he bought a violin. And he happened to get one that was a genuine Stradivarius. But he didn't know the value of it. He sold it for eight dollars in 1905." — Cora Kragnes (Felton, MN)

"Whatever music there was to start with was from the folks and that was Scandinavian, but after the kids grew up they got hold of an old organ, even my oldest brother would play on that and sing 'Little Black Mustache.' The same with the girls, they played away. Some of them took music lessons." — Frank Alm (Christine, ND)

"My grandfather was a violin player, and two of his sons also played the violin. And they played for barn dances. And one daughter was given a pump organ by a teacher, and that was in the home for a number of years and then they bought a piano, which is still out on the farm today." — Lela Hegland (Moorhead, MN)

"We all played musical instruments. We had the organ, and a guitar, and a cello, and I played the violin. Three-four of us would get together, you know." — George Jacobson (Perley, MN)

"She used to sing, all the time, 'Can You Forget Old Norway?" And that was meaningful then. On many occasions they'd sing that song." — Delsie Holmquist (Moorhead, MN)

"They had some great violin players, you know, the Norwegians. Every house had a violin in them days. My brother played it, and my uncle played it." — William Melby (Hitterdal, MN)

"Olle I Skratthult and them, I can remember their singing those songs. And that was quite a thing. I'll always remember those songs, yah, *Nikolina.*' I remember that!" — Nina Oien (Moorhead, MN)

"As far as the music, it was usually either a violin—my father used to play the violin—and the accordion. These seemed to be the ones that the Scandinavians enjoyed." — Bernice Herfindal (Lake Park, MN)

"Our family, too, was very musical, and we always sang. I had learned to play the organ when I was seven or eight years old, so usually I would play the hymns and the rest of them would sing then. We had an organ at that time. The songs were in Swedish, of course." — Katherine Fossay (Moorhead, MN)

"My grandfather had a beautiful voice. He used to sit there and play the organ every morning before breakfast. That's the first thing he did when he got up." — Clara Furcht (Moorhead, MN)

"One of the first things my parents bought when they came to this country was an old piano for the family. My father had brought his violin, he used to play the violin back in Denmark. So my father would play the violin and my mother would play the piano." — Henrietta Burgess (Moorhead, MN)

"My father was the youngest of twelve, and being he was the youngest, he also had the best education. He also was a very gifted musician. From the time I was a little girl, there was a lot of music in our home. My Dad, besides playing the violin, he gave lessons on that and on the cornet." — Borghild Overby (Moorhead, MN)

"My brother and I picked potatoes to earn enough to buy a piano. We picked potatoes until we had made one hundred dollars and then we bought a piano for two hundred dollars." — Minnie Tiedeman (Moorhead, MN)

"When we had our farm southeast of Bertha, a bunch of young fellows, practically all Scandinavians, started a country band. And that boomed along very well, and they built themselves a clubhouse and they had dances and so on." — Art Waldon (Detroit Lakes, MN)

"My dad used to sing songs about Norway. He remembered the land of Norway and used to sing about the trees and the valleys, landscape songs.

Our piano was a grand piano, a big one that took up about a fourth of our living room. It had been sent to Souris [North Dakota] from France. I had a French piano teacher and she wanted to sell it so Dad bought it for fifty dollars. They finally used it for putting oil barrels on it because the legs were so strong. Great big wooden legs, carved, you know. But Mom was happy to get it out of the house because it took up so much room." — Alma Olson (Souris, ND)

"My dad played the violin. He used to sing Norwegian songs. He also directed the choir out at Zion church and we sang many songs in Norwegian." — Dagne Faust (Colfax, ND)

"Organ and violin and guitar, and they had harps around here then too. And the music was either Swedish or Norwegian. They were both here, of course, so the music got to be both." — Oscar Olson (Lake Park, MN)

"When we had company come over, which happened quite often on Sundays, my uncle had an organ, a guitar, a violin, and a harp, and played them all. And they would sing one song after another. I don't think I heard anything but a Norwegian song in that home." — Clara Hanson (Moorhead, MN)

"We had Swedish church music, but I can't think of any others. Well, I remember the Swedish national anthem, I heard that sung at home. My father would often take a notion to sing a little bit—'Our Land, Our Land, Our Fatherland.'" — Vic Anderson (Moorhead, MN)

"Mama just played the organ and she played old schottisches with Norwegian words to it. And I remember she used to play 'The Dying Cowboy.'" — Eloise Kromarek (Bowman, ND)

In the years after the immigration and well into the lives of the second generation, Scandinavian music, dances, and traditional entertainments provided a tie to the homeland. Most of the traditional folk dances, however, were rather quickly abandoned in favor of the dances being done in the New World. Perhaps the most notable exception was the Norwegian Halling "Spring Dance," which was performed far into the twentieth century.

"I used to dance the Halling 'Spring Dance.' You know, how they jump way up in the air. I think I learned to dance before I learned to walk." — Clara Johnson (Underwood, ND)

"They had a dance that included sort of a kick, and this dance is called a *Halling kust* [custom]. [My grandfather] was not only a good fiddler, but he was an expert in this *Halling kust*. He used to practice in the woods [in Norway]. He used to practice on stones and stumps. The *Halling kust* is a kick when you stand and you suddenly turn and you kick as high as you can and you have to come down in the same spot and stand exactly the same way as you were before you kicked. And the story is told that when my grandfather was eighteen years old he joined the army, and he was up at Frederickstad, which is up near Oslo, and the king came to visit. And the king wanted to find any soldier who could kick his hat off a sword when he was sitting on a horse. That's a pretty high kick! And the only one they knew who might be able to do this was my grandfather. So the king asked about it, and they pushed him forward. He didn't want to do it, but finally he did. So the king sat on his horse, put his cap on his sword, and my grandfather kicked it off. And he broke the hat, so he was kind of scared about that. But the king gave him four dollars in gold, which was a lot of money in those days. He had a lot of sons, the oldest one was my father—his name was Knut. My grandfather's name was Narve Knutson, so when my father came to this country with his brothers—there were seven brothers—they took the name of Narveson." — Carl Narveson (Moorhead, MN)

"Our neighborhood was a dancing neighborhood, … and we really had a good time because there were so many young people at that time that lived lose by. And there was kind of a line between Moland Township and Morken Township, so we didn't associate much with the Molands because they were more churchy than we were. … My dad played the violin and there were always organs or pianos in the homes and there was always someone who could chord on the piano. My father played mostly waltzes and schottisches and old time dances, but by the time I started dancing there were more modern dances. They were mostly in the homes. Those that had larger

homes as a rule had large dining rooms and we would dance there. Everybody would usually bring along something to eat for the midnight lunch, but as I got older we went to Felton [Minnesota] and danced. They had a lovely hall there and they had traveling orchestras there. I suppose I was about eighteen years old then, so that would be about 1914–1915."
— Minnie Tiedeman (Moorhead, MN)

"My mother wasn't really very much in favor of playing cards, but they used to do that in the neighborhood. They used to have house parties, in the homes, and they'd clear out the kitchen and they'd dance till the stove pipes fell down. In Cromwell Township [near Hawley, Minnesota], there were a lot of Hallings around there and I remember them talking about 'Spring Dance.' It's a Norwegian traditional folk dance, and there was something they called the *Halling kust*. Of course, we were small and we didn't get to go to some of those parties." — Joanna Aune (Hawley, MN)

"We had the different Norwegian dances, you know, polkas and square dances, and then there was the Hallings who had their Halling dance. They'd strut around for a while and then all of a sudden they'd kick and they'd see how high they could kick until they pert'near kicked the ceiling. They'd dance around for a while and all of a sudden up they'd kick."
— Henry Jacobson (Ulen, MN)

"We'd have Swedish music for dancing, polkas and schottisches, but nobody in our house was musical." — Amy Margaret Erickson (Wheatland, ND)

"They loved music—violin playing. My dad was a beautiful violin player. They had a choir [in the Turtle Lake, North Dakota, area], a wonderful choir. They had three or four violins and then they sang. And they loved to dance! They just loved music! Dances were held in the homes, some of them had bare floors. We'd go to the homes and we children would lie down on the bed and the rest of them would be dancing and singing and playing." — Mabel Fynskov (Osakis, MN)

"I learned dancing just a little, because my parents frowned on dancing as a recreation. But as an exercise, or as a game, it was OK. And I did learn some of it because our neighbors taught it, but they didn't approve of public dances." — Louise Andersen (Fargo, ND)

"It was waltzes, polkas, schottisches, two steps, sometimes square dancing. And my dad and my three brothers were all fiddlers, especially my one brother. He played at most dances. When I was young I got in on those dances, too. They had a lot of barn dances then. They would have coffee and doughnuts, the men would choose their partners, then ate with their partners, and danced the first dance with them. But they wouldn't necessarily have them for the rest of the evening. The barn dances sometimes wouldn't be over until the break of dawn." — Eva Thortvedt (Glyndon, MN)

Holidays were a special time for all immigrant groups to the United States, and the Scandinavian groups were no exception. In some cases, they were the traditional celebrations as they had been observed in the Old Country, while in others they assumed an American veneer. On December 14th, for instance, many Swedish Americans continued to observe Santa Lucia Day, as the eldest daughter of the family would arise before anyone else to prepare a breakfast of sweet buns and coffee. On the third Sunday of June, many Swedish-Americans celebrated Midtsommarsdag much the same as they had in Sweden, an event now marked by the annual Svenskarnasdag in Minnnehaha Park in Minneapolis. The Danes have their national day, of course, and the Icelanders traditionally celebrate the Second of August.

The traditional Finnish day of celebration (not counting the recently contrived St. Urho's Day, celebrated on March 16th to commemorate when St. Urho chased the grasshoppers out of Finland) was the 24th of June, which is also St. John's Day. The Finns often celebrated their Midsummer's Day picnic on this date. They would often gather at the Finn Hall, a marvelous and uniquely Finnish institution. While in some communities the Finn Hall was used as a place of worship before a church could be erected, in other communities it existed almost as a rival to the church. Although the Finn hall would sometimes be vilified by Finnish temperance organizations, it served as a focal point for Finnish cultural life and regularly featured music, drama, debates, lectures, and athletic organizations. The Finn Halls also served as one of the central points for Finnish political organization.

Of all the Scandinavian immigrant groups, however, the Norwegians, with their observance of Norwegian Constitution Day, *Syttende Mai* [May Seventeenth], remained the most dedicated to an Old World event. Yet for all of them, the Fourth of July equaled or surpassed any ethnic celebration.

"Lucia Day was important in our home. That comes along in December. And we invariably made what my mother would call *yulebrod*. They were shaped like the number eight, and they were good. We had them with coffee." — Anna Hanson (Moorhead, MN)

"Easter time the tradition then was to boil a big kettle of eggs, as many as you could have. We had chickens, you know, and we were allowed to eat just as many eggs as we wanted to Easter morning. That was our Easter." — Amy Margaret Erickson (Wheatland, ND)

"We had *Midtsommar*! The church had a big dinner. There was a park and that's where they had a pavilion, and that's where the ladies cooked and served." — Inez Holt (Chisago City, MN)

"For the Highland Grove Lutheran Church *Midtsommar* picnic we always went to a place that had a big grove and they'd set up tables. It was really nice there then—now it isn't so nice because it's a pasture but it was beautiful at that time and we had it there for many years. And people would bring their food in great big baskets, and oh, everything, salads, and sandwiches. I remember going to those as a kid. We just ate. Oh, the men played horseshoes and there were softball games. No girls, just the men! And the minister would have a little service. In Swedish, of course." — Violet Anderson (Hitterdal, MN)

"One big event was the *Midtsommar* picnic, which was always around mid-summer and which was a tradition carried over from Sweden. They celebrated that." — Bernice Herfindal (Lake Park, MN)

"We had some friends that we got to know, and they were from Sweden and they always had a big bonfire and we'd dance around the fire and they'd have a big wheel, sort of a *Midtsommarfest*." — Elsie Gale (Clearbrook, MN)

"We had our *Midtsommar* day, of course, and maybe we'd have a picnic. But other than that, it didn't seem as important as it was with the Norwegians and their *Syttende Mai*." — Catherine Fossay (Moorhead, MN)

"When we were members of the rural church, we always celebrated Midsummer's Day, like *Midtsommarsdag* in Sweden. There was always a festival and a picnic and a social gathering. And that continued for several years after the use of the church was discontinued." — Myrtle Rundquist (Moorhead, MN)

"Oh, we had *Syttende Mai* celebrations, and we danced like the dickens, you know." — Clara Johnson (Underwood, ND)

"We didn't use to do anything special for *Syttende Mai*." — Matilda Blumer (Hazelton, ND)

"The Seventeenth of May was usually celebrated. We had great big celebrations, and we also had celebrations when school was closed in the spring. We had games. We played ball in those days, too. And 'pom-pom-pullaway,' and 'last couple out,' things like that. 'Drop the handkerchief' was a real good game. And then we had programs and the parents would bring lunch." — Alma Ramse (McIntosh, MN)

"My mother was quite the head of our home and she felt that it was not important [to celebrate May Seventeenth]. She didn't have the ties to Norway." — Flora Fritz (Detroit Lakes, MN)

"On *Syttende Mai* we went to the closest town and watched the ball games and they had parades." — Marlene Lien (Wahpeton, ND)

"*Syttende Mai* was always observed [in the Larimore, North Dakota, area] and they would have a gathering at the church. That was always observed. That was quite a holiday. They'd have a picnic and talk about the homeland." — Solveig Johnson (Niagara, ND)

"The Second of August is the big Icelandic celebration. They used to have like two days in Mountain [North Dakota]. And everybody went to Mountain for August for the Two. It was like the fair for a lot of people." — Diane Volrath (Hitterdal, MN)

"One thing I liked about the Fourth of July was that I could get all the ice cream I wanted. Beautiful fireworks in the early years. We'd go as families to see the fireworks at Bottineau [North Dakota]. We didn't have many celebrations at *Syttende Mai*, but my dad belonged to sons of Norway many, many years ago. But he didn't like it and he dropped out and so then we didn't have it here for years and years." — Alma Olson (Souris, ND)

"We didn't pay any attention to the Seventeenth of May, but the Fourth of July, we made big doings out of that day. We had to go to horse races and dances and have a lot of big explosions, big fireworks and bombs. All day long." — Ole Olson (Fargo, ND)

"They always flew both flags. My parents brought with them from Norway a Norwegian flag. And we had two flagpoles and they would always hoist two flags, but the American flag was always just a little bit higher than the Norwegian one. But that was the way we celebrated both the Fourth of July and *Syttende Mai*." — Solveig Johnson (Niagara, ND)

"[The Norwegians] celebrated the Fourth of July with a picnic in some grove or by a small lake, with a baseball game or a tug-of-war. [My folks] never got into that celebrating. Most of the people that did danced, and they didn't dance too often." — Edwin Markestad (Maddock, ND)

"We had two important celebrations each year. The Seventeenth of May and the Fourth of July were of equal importance to the people of the [Underwood, Minnesota] community until I was grown up. The Seventeenth of May celebration entertainment was pretty much between the 'races.' Even though there was a lesser amount of Swedes and other minority 'races,' they had contests between them. And this probably shouldn't be taped or printed, but one particular time they had wrestling matches. My father was a very, very strong man, six feet-two and all muscle and bone. They offered a drink for each Swede he could pin and he pinned seventeen Swedes and took a drink for each one he pinned, but the eighteenth Swede pinned him. And they had boat races. On the lake right adjacent to town they used to have the boat races and they would have to row across the lake and get out of the boat, touch the ground, and get back in the boat and row back again. And my father won that race for four consecutive years and then they framed him. They tied metal under the boat so he couldn't steer the boat and so he came in second place and it wasn't in his nature to want to be second-best in anything he did. I remember them talking about how Dad got even. … And, of course, they had a band. My family was not particularly musical, but my father was a marching band leader. His height and his spirit made him quite a leader for the marching band. This band led the parades both for the Fourth of July and the Seventeenth of May. The Seventeenth of May thing went out of the picture, you know, as the first generation of the American born Norsemen [grew up]. They were finally washed out because the Fourth of July was the important celebration to all of us Americans." — John Gronner (Underwood, MN)

"Just about every Fourth of July, for many years, we used to have a Fourth of July celebration [in Henning, Minnesota]. And in order to start that right, in the morning, we used to have what we called an 'anvil firecracker.' We took two anvils outside of my blacksmith shop and a sledge hammer without the handle. Then we filled the whole in the sledge hammer with black powder and put the second anvil on top, balanced. Then to ignite the powder, we had a stick, at least twenty feet long, with a rag on the end that we used to put some oil on or kerosene. Then we lit that rag on the end and we put that up on the anvil to ignite the powder. And it made such a terrible noise and it shot the second anvil twenty, twenty-five feet in the air. We used to do that three or four times in the morning. Woke up the whole town!"
— Henry Holmgren (Henning, MN)

"In 1915, our neighbors to the west of us built a new granary. They had a dance there [near Bowman, North Dakota] on the Fourth of July. And it snowed that night. People would come in from the outside and right in front of the door was a big puddle." — Ralph Simonson (Bowman, ND)

Other than the special holidays, the two most important sources for entertainment of the Scandinavian-Americans was the church and the school. In churches, schools, and community halls, Scandinavian-Americans would gather to exchange news, recipes, gossip, views on the weather, and, occasionally, lies. Outdoor sports and indoor games helped relieve the tedium of daily chores and the loneliness of the isolated farmhouse.

"Social events during the year probably centered around the church and the school. The church gatherings, besides the service, were Young People's societies and once in a while some dignitaries would come and then there would be special gatherings. And the school gatherings, usually we'd have a program at Christmas time and then again at the end of the year. Sometimes two school districts would come together. And the Old Settler's Picnic continued for many years and that brought large crowds. … Luther League, the Young People's Society, as we called it then, seemed to be our main entertainment. We had that every third Sunday in Rollag and then we'd go to other places where they had it on the other Sundays, so we'd get to know a lot of people outside our own community. Back in the Twenties, Ole Rolvaag, the author of *Giants in the Earth*, and a fellow, the editor of *Reform*, I think he lived in Eau Claire, Wisconsin [Waldemar Ager], came to Rollag, and they spoke at the Young People's Society one evening. And I was there and I remember Waldemar Ager was kind of a comical fellow and he was telling stories. I remember one especially. He was telling about a farmer in Wisconsin who had a hired man, a newcomer. And this boy looked a little stupid and I guess he wasn't so wise either. One morning the farmer came down to the barn to do chores and the young boy was sitting in the doorway of the barn, and he said, 'What are you sitting here for?' 'Oh,' says the boy, 'I'm waiting for the cow to calf.' 'Have you sat here long then?' the farmer asked. 'Yah, I sat here since seven-thirty last night.' 'Well, then I think you'd better move,' he said, 'because that cow thinks she has calved.' Waldemar Ager would read from his stories quite often from *Reform*. He called it, when he had been out on a trip like that, he called it '*uta med skrippen*.'" — William Nelson (Rollag, MN)

"Our social activities were centered around the church. It would be a Christmas festival, of course, naturally, and we looked forward to the Christmas program because it was the highlight as we were growing up. And I suppose some of the younger folks had their fun, as we called it, but there was nothing very special about it as we know it today." — Alva Hest (Perley, MN)

"And we young girls had what we called *pega forin*. *Pega* means young woman. And we'd pay five cents every time we'd meet. So that was just like a ladies aid, only we were young people. We just had fun and talked, and had a nice lunch. And always at the homes, never at the church." — Eva Thortvedt (Glyndon, MN)

"The main things were through the church. We had our Young People's Societies, they called them, I guess, and of course they served lots of meals to raise money to pay for the church. The ladies did a lot of that." — Alpha Bowersox (Wolford, ND)

"We had Young People's Societies, and we had a choir. Everybody took part, whether we could sing or not, but it turned out pretty well. It was Norwegian all together." — Anna Melberg (Moorhead, MN)

"They had quite a few basket socials in schools, and the boys, a girl that they really liked, they bid that basket up pretty high." — David Swedberg (Otter Tail Co., MN)

"We had our basket socials before Christmas [in Lund church, near Detroit Lakes, Minnesota], so we could get enough money to buy apples and candy. And the Norwegians also had a basket social in their church. And my dad would always say 'Why do you always go to the Norwegians and buy their baskets when they won't buy ours?' And that was true." — Charles Westerholm (Moorhead, MN)

"At a basket social at a school house, the young people would speak the Norwegian amongst themselves." — Gunhild Laske (Kindred, ND)

"Our social events got to be more of a mixture as time went on, American and Scandinavian, and sometimes German and Bohemian. For

example, when we had a gathering at the schoolhouse, we would have basket socials. A girl's basket would be sold and a fellow could bid for it. And after that was over with we'd push the desks aside and play these circle games, like drop the handkerchief and stuff like that. Some of those were in Norwegian or Swedish, possibly, so the Scandinavian influence hung on to that aspect. I think several of the games had come from Scandinavia."
— Christian Schulstad (Dawson, MN)

"In the spring of the year we used to have a basket social and in most of the places they used to have some good looking school marms. And we tried to find out what basket she had and we tried to bid that basket up just as high as we could, so even if one of us got stuck with it we didn't mind it so long as we could have lunch with the school marm." — Henry Holmgren (Henning, MN)

"We had basket socials when I was growing up. We tried to make the most beautiful baskets we could. We would take some of those great baskets, wooden ones, and decorate them up and put a cover on them and put a lot of good food in them, pies—we had pie socials, too, where fellows could buy a pie, they'd buy your pie and you'd eat it with them—and we had these double baskets or triple baskets and there would be guys who would get together and buy them. They didn't know whose they were, see, we had our names in there. They were in the summer and spring, mostly. But in the winter we had literary societies where we would get together and play games.

We had all those Norwegian games, and 'Here we go round the Mulberry Bush,' and 'Drop the Handkerchief,' and all those things. And we had some dances sometimes. We'd sneak away to the dances. We weren't supposed to go but we did. We got caught, too. No, we weren't supposed to play cards either, they didn't think much of that. They were kind of strict." — Alma Olson (Souris, ND)

"We had a little entertainment every Saturday night in the school building. We'd have a debate, and a recitation, sing songs, and have a literary society." — Ole Olson (Fargo, ND)

"Around the turn of the century, for baseball games we went all the way along the line here. We went to Borup and Ada and over in Dakota—Hillsboro, Grandin, Kindred—all around, with us in the middle." — George Jacobson (Perley, MN)

"We played a lot of 'Mumbeley-peg' when we were kids, with a knife, you know, and we played hide and seek, and 'pom-pom-pullaway.'" — Wilferd Anderson (Hitterdal, MN)

"Well, they played Swedish games, I know, during recess and noon hour. No, I didn't have any trouble understanding them. I think I could understand Swede better than I could Norwegian then." — William Melby (Hitterdal, MN)

"Well, anybody got married, we 'chivaried' [charivari] them. Well, they took saws and hammers and shotguns and made all kinds of racket.

They took a hammer and pounded on the saw. They'd go to a couple's home at night. It was a surprise, unless somebody told them. And then they came and asked for five dollars or ten dollars from them. Well, then after they got that money, they made a dance up for that. And then when the dance was over, they took up a collection and the couple that got married, they gave it to them." — Charles Westerholm (Moorhead, MN)

"They were going to 'chivarie' us, you know. The gang gets together with bells and plowshares and anything they can make a lot of noise on, you know. And maybe they'd take the groom out and haul him off or maybe they'd take the bride or something, and we didn't want that. So Alvin had a dance at a farm home on the east edge of town." — Cora Kragnes (Felton, MN)

"In those days the farmers would make this home-made beer. They'd drink it by the tubfull, and they'd serve that at many of the gatherings. My dad used to drink that beer. They didn't consider that an alcoholic beverage. Oh, there would be a few who would drink too much." — Odin Strandness (Fargo, ND)

"There wasn't much [liquor] served indoors, because the women at that time really didn't drink except maybe wine or something like that, but outside it was pretty lively. I think it was mostly beer and of course they would have their mixes." — Minnie Tiedeman (Moorhead, MN)

"No women were influenced by alcohol. Women didn't drink at all. Never! Not in our social gatherings anyway. Of course, they did in Fargo and Moorhead. But not in our community. But we made very good wines, chokecherry, wild grapes, delectable wines. Gooseberry and plum, too!"
— Eva Thortvedt (Glyndon, MN)

"I know that if we went to somebody's house for a meal … they might serve a little wine, but otherwise I always thought Swedes never drank. I thought other people drank, but not the Swedes." — Gladys Westrum (Moorhead, MN)

"We used to have sleigh rides parties and house parties. We finally had to quit those house parties because they just got too big. Once people started driving cars you never knew who was going to be there and it just got so crowded that nobody had any fun. It got so people you didn't even know came up to you and said, 'When do we eat?'" — Gale Iverson (Hitterdal, MN)

"Skiing was the main thing in the winter for us boys. We had a bluff on the south side [of the school house] and we made big jumps there and we could really go on skis. My grandfather made skis and he was very good at it too." — David Swedberg (Otter Tail Co., MN)

"We would all ski across the field, or the river. The easiest way to get [to school] was to ski. Except when it was very cold, then my uncle would take us with the horses or a neighbor would take us or they would take turns, one would take us and the other would pick us up. Oh, yes, the skis were homemade. My uncle made skis for all of us. We skied for many, many years." — Elsie Gale (Clearbrook, MN)

"Skis were very important in them days. We used them for fun, but we also used them for walking when we were working in the woods. We walked in there and cut cord wood. But almost every Sunday we would ski up in the hills north of home. Especially there were newcomers from Norway who got us interested. They were great skiers! My uncles both made skis and they were what we called Numedahl skis, but there were other types that looked a little different. The Trondheimers made a kind of a more clumsy looking ski, but they had carving on them and seemed to be kind of a heavier ski. But the Norlandings made a ski that turned up both in the front and in back. I don't know the reason for that, but I remember some of the skis that the Norlanding boys had that their great uncles had made and they turned up both in front and in back." — William Nelson (Rollag, MN)

"And every Finnish community, there again most of them have gone, but at one time you had public sauna—one or two, I can't remember. For a while our community had two saunas, and a barber, and a pool hall and the Finns, of course, like to drink and we had a couple "blind pigs" before prohibition. There were mostly Finnish songs at the Finn Hall, but [it was] a very, very musical culture. Many of the activities at the Finn hall would be musical and members of choirs, groups would get together and sing. Many of the productions were musical." — Karen Kivi (Moorhead, MN)

"Father was one of the charter members of the Modern Woodmen Lodge, and I remember the Woodmen Lodge had uniforms and [various activities that] kind of took the place for a few years of the early Norwegian folk dancing here in Underwood [Minnesota]. I know in other parts of the county, Fergus Falls, for instance, they kept these folk dances up for many, many years and I think they still do." — John Gonner (Underwood, MN)

"The Woodmen's Lodge—that was one of the most active organizations at that time. They had picnics, they were very active. They used to put on a lot of good plays. … There was a little bit of trouble one time when this fellow, he belonged to the Woodmen, and he died. And when the pallbearers in the funeral procession came to the church—he belonged there—the minister wouldn't let them in. He wouldn't let them take the coffin in! You can imagine there was indeed an uproar, when they refused to take the coffin. The minister, he was awfully strict." — Clara Johnson (Underwood, ND)

Chapter XIII
"It Grows on You"

SCANDINAVIAN FOOD ON AMERICAN PLATES

One tradition that has been preserved through all generations of Scandinavian-Americans is the preparation of Scandinavian food. As any good Scandinavian will attest, the two most important ingredients for Scandinavian cuisine are love and butter, and when any recipe is in doubt, it is recommended that the cook simply add more of these two ingredients. Icelandic prune cake, Danish pastries, and Swedish meatballs are all internationally famous, of course, and the American Scandinavians can readily attest to the savory nature of these delectable items. But the Scandinavians also brought with them some dishes that seem to appeal only to other Scandinavians, such as *grøt*, lefse, and lutefisk.

Lutefisk and lefse have become a rather unfair stereotype of the Scandinavian-American diet. In some respects, they are a typical food in that they were relatively cheap and were eaten by peasants. Lefse, made from potatoes, lard, and flour, is like many other Scandinavian foods in that it is colorless and bland. But although the ingredients are simple, lefse, which is essentially a Norwegian delicacy, is not easy to make. Lutefisk, the butt of so many Norwegian-American jokes, was eaten by

both Norwegians (in drawn butter) and Swedes (in a white sauce). This aromatic dish (critics would unfairly call it a "smelly concoction the preparation of which causes the flowers on the wallpaper to wilt") has become legendary in the Upper Midwest and its consumption is seen as almost a rite of passage among the Norwegian-Americans.

A collection of memories as to the foods consumed in the Scandinavian-American homes is more than a recitation of what people ate. First, it is for many the most significant aspect of their heritage. When asked what they remembered about their homes that was specifically Scandinavian, the majority of the people interviewed immediately volunteered that their food was Scandinavian. Second, when asked what Scandinavian traditions they carried on in their homes at the time of the interview, the most common response was that they still ate their lutefisk and lefse. Finally, the response of the Scandinavian immigrant to American life can be partially measured in the response of the Scandinavian palate to American foods. Perhaps the ultimate assimilation is represented in a Norwegian Lutheran church that serves an annual "chow mein supper" or the current commercial production of a "lefse burrito."

"We had Danish food all the time, I suppose, but we didn't realize it at the time because the people we visited with were practically one hundred per cent Danish. Of course, the Danes had pastries of their own, like *kringle*, and *ebelskiver*, with butter or syrup or sugar. And they'd have what you call sweet soup, with dried fruit, made up and served up as a soup. Most of the dried fruit and vegetables came from an order put into Montgomery Wards. They had a large sale catalog that came out in the fall with practically everything in the line of food. And those orders were generally got together after harvest. ... And they would make a soup out of kale, chopped up kale and would sometimes start out with a ham bone and potatoes. Sort of like a soup. And they would have different kinds of cabbages they'd serve, too. Much of it from a red cabbage." — Philip Andersen (Fargo, ND)

"What I remember best [about Danish food] is the buttermilk soup, fruit soup, and what they call *Alebrød*, beer soup. And then there was homemade heavy dark bread, that you dry in the oven and then it gets poured boiled milk over it. ... And then you ate it like a cream soup. And that was kind of good. And Danish pastries, oh yes, cream puffs and coffee cakes."
— Louise Andersen (Fargo, ND)

"My father liked to make smoked mutton, like they have in Iceland, which is delicious. Just like a ham, only better! At Christmas time we always had *vienerterta*, and of course when company came and nothing was ready, they'd make *pönnukokur* to serve with coffee. Like crepes, only better!"
— Anna Bjornson (Fargo, ND)

"The [Icelandic] food, especially for Christmas, was something. *Dinafesta*, a many-layered cake with prune filling, and most people like it very, very much. And then they had 'shavings'—would be the translation. They call it *Halmama*—when you shave in wood. It was a bread stuff that they would wrap around a broom handle or something and form these little forms. Then there were current cookies, and a half moon that was cookie crust with prunes inside, and *klingas*, they were very good." — Kathy Thordarson (Fargo, ND)

"Foods were very important. We always had *vienarterta*, which is a layered torte with a prune filling; *skyr*, which is similar to yoghurt but which is pretty much the mainstay of summer meals, at least at supper time; and *kleina*, which is a type of doughnut; *hangikjöt*, which is smoked mutton; *rúllupølse*, which is smoked flank; *slåtur* a type of sausage, liver or blood sausage—it doesn't sound too good but it tastes very good." — Esther Hillman (Mountain, ND)

"I suppose the [Icelandic Dessert] that is known the widest here is *vienerterta*, which is several layers of cake with either a prune filling or a jelly filling. And that was always served at Christmas. And then, of course, *saetsupe*, a sweet soup. ... And we'd have *skyr*, which was made from 'klobbered' milk, which looked something like a soft cheese, maybe like cottage cheese except it was much smoother, and we'd eat that with sugar and cream, too." — Wayne Dinusson (Fargo, ND)

"[My mother] used to make smoked meat—smoked mutton—called *hangikjöt* and she always made another Icelandic custom, *saetsupe*, sweet soup, I think they called it. There was nothing wasted when they butchered the beef or sheep, you know. Out of the blood they made blood sausage and out of the liver they made a liverwurst. They used to save the intestines and we had to soak them in lye, you know, we had to scrape them. Oh we used to hate that! That's what they made sausage in, all sewn by hand. We made *vienarkaka*, kind of a crumb cake with layers, and *růllupølse*, that's make out of lamb shanks rolled up and spiced. You have to cure it and stuff." — Freda Bjornson (Moorhead, MN)

"[The Swedes liked] boiled potatoes with their jackets on, and *sild*, that's herring, they'd buy that in a big wooden pail. Of course we children didn't like it, but Mother and Father liked that. And this *knakkebrød* that she used to make, of course that was so delicious. She also make a lot of other bread, sixteen loaves at a time! She'd make eight of white and eight of the dark bread." — Nina Oien (Moorhead, MN)

"[The lutefisk] came into the store in big barrels and just about everyone bought it. It was passed along by word of mouth that the lutefisk had come in. And I remember the price, in years back, seven cents a pound we thought was reasonable. And then there would also be barrels of lingonberries. They came in water, I think, and we bought them by the quart. And they made very good sauce. I remember we had so very little to live on in Sweden. I remember standing in line one time, waiting for hours and having people who were taller than I, and bigger, pull my hair and fighting to get ahead of the line. And I came home with a rutabaga … and I was exhausted and felt like crying and so, well, here was America with all the food you could eat, and if my aunt had roast at noon, she probably had pork chops for supper. … We ate mightily, and I was fat as a tub at the end of that first year. I was ashamed of myself, but the food was so good. … My mother made meatballs, and they were good. And we had pancakes, and they were good. And we had lingonberries more often than we had cranberries. I had never heard of lefse in Sweden, and we thought it was a little strange at first, but it grows on you." — Anna Hanson (Moorhead, MN)

"We'd cook brown beans with vinegar and things like that in it, and sausages, coiled, with barley. We'd get the casings and make our own sausages. And we used to make pickled herring and hard bread. And of course, I make Swedish pancakes. You get bacon and you make it in a big skillet and you call it *'fleske'* pancakes. And then you have whipped cream and cranberries to put on top of it. You make it in the oven." — Anna Lindgren (Fargo, ND)

"I remember *surtost*, a flour concoction. But they sure thought a lot of it, it actually looked like Crackerjack. They did something to the milk, curdled it or something, then boiled it and it was kind of sweet. Oh, that was a tremendous delicacy amongst the Swedes. I never cared for any of that stuff. And then they'd have their different *gröts* and stuff." — Carl Elmquist (Moorhead, MN)

"[My mother] fixed traditional [Swedish] puddings, sort of a plum pudding that we would have at Christmas time, and then she made her own dried lutefisk, and people just raved about that because it seemed to have something that others didn't have. And then the big deal was *fleske pankake*, pork pancakes. It was the most delicious meal. It was the high-water mark of all our meals. It's made from ground-up salt pork. And then we'd grind up raw potatoes. And then they'd mix the ground pork and potatoes and flour to make a cream, and salt and pepper were put in that and then it was put on a griddle and fried on a pan cake griddle. And then we'd eat this with a fruit, something like cranberries." — Allan Erickson (Moorhead, MN)

"Potato sausage. It's a mixture of potatoes, pork, and beef. I love it! But then it got mixed up with the Norwegian dishes, so it got to be lutefisk and lefse and whatnot, you know. The other night, you know, the Seventeenth of May, they had the doings in Christine, and there they had torsk, and then the Norwegian dishes that goes with it." — Frank Alm (Christine, ND)

"Many of the kids that I grew up with remember coming over to my mother's and getting the things that she had learned how to make in Sweden. And, of course, for Christmas we always had lutefisk and lingonberries, and prune pudding, flatbread … and many of the other things that they had in

Sweden, like headcheese and things like that." — Catherine Fossay (Moorhead, MN)

"My mother was a wonderful cook and she made all these Swedish dishes. At Christmas time especially. We had the cheese and sausage and liver *pölse*, and *gröt* and all those lovely things, so that part was Swedish." — Hazel Monson Barker (Moorhead, MN)

"We had our lutefisk, our lingonberries, and our rice. We learned to like the lingonberries with rice. We ate the two together, put the lingonberries on top of the rice. ... We ate our lutefisk the way the Swedes like it. We'd serve it with cream sauce. I think Swedish people still like it with cream sauce instead of butter. I think most Americans don't like it because of the smell. You might learn to like it yourself if you ever had it served to you that way! And some of them used to add mustard to the cream sauce. I never cared for that, but a lot of the Swedish people did. Another thing we had was pölsebröd, which is a blood bread. And I liked it very much and I'd eat it now if I could ever get a hold of it. It's baked with yeast like a regular bread only they add blood for the liquid. Then it's raised and baked like ordinary bread, but the molds are round with a hole in the middle, so that after the bread is baked it can be suspended in some way through that hole by a pole or a string or something so that it can dry. And it has to be completely dry before you can use it. And then it's boiled in salted water and of course it keeps its shape because it was dry. And then you eat it with bacon or fresh salt pork or something like that. When you boiled it the bread would soak up the water so it was kind of a spongy mass. I think that is quite a Swedish dish." — Myrtle Rundquist (Moorhead, MN)

"[*Fleske pancake*], that was Swedish. You grated the potatoes and you put salt and pepper on them. And then you thickened hat with flour so you could handle it. And then you took salt pork—I suppose you could use bacon in this day and age, but we used salt pork at our house. And then [Mother] would cut that in small pieces and then she put that in the inside and then she'd roll it again so that the meat was all inside. And then you put them in hot boiling salt water, boil for about half an hour or twenty minutes and they'd become big and brown. And you'd put butter and salt on them. And the next day, if there were leftovers, you fried them. Cut them in slices and fried them and put butter on them. That was a big dish at our house."
— Phoebe Westerholm (Moorhead, MN)

"We had lutefisk on holidays, just like everybody else. And I can remember my father buying, when he'd go to town, pickled herring, and fresh herring, because they just loved fish—*sild, sild og potaten.* My mother used to make Swedish bread, *limpa* they called it, and *pepperkake*, that would be cookies. But the candy here wasn't as flavorful as the candy back in Sweden, but we still got used to it. We ate lefse, but we liked flatbread, because that was Swedish, but we soon got used to lefse. I didn't like *römmegröt*, though, and I don't to this day. The Norwegians can have that.

We found that people ate a lot more eggs over here than they did [in Sweden]. We thought that was just great. We could eat all the eggs we wanted!" — Elsie Gale (Clearbrook, MN)

"My wife learned how to make '*klubbers*' from my mother. It's a meat dumpling, with pork inside of a dumpling and then cooked. The pork was prepared first. You cut it up into cubes and children learned to call them '*klubbers*.' Of course, lutefisk was one of the standbys, and *fattigman*, and *Berlinerkranzer*. All those goodies." — Roy Carlander (Moorhead, MN)

"Swedish foods? There was meat dumpling, *klubbkloke*, mostly pork. Then we had a sausage, beef and pork mixed with potatoes, that was *klubb*, and then we had sweet soup, that consisted of prunes and raisins and apple slices. Then we had *knakkebröd*, it was made like a dish. That would get hard and brittle, sort of like a cracker, but it was made from bread dough. In the old country they would have a hole in it and hang it on a string in the attic." — Robert Carlander (Moorhead, MN)

"My dad used to go down and buy what they called lutefisk. Well, it looked like cordwood to me. And Mother had saved up the ashes and then she would put the ashes with lye on this lutefisk when the Christmas season was coming up. So then that would eventually [turn into] the lutefisk that you can buy today. I like lutefisk, but I'm a Swede. And I've gone to where they serve lutefisk at those different places and the Norwegians have to have drawn butter. Well, we have to have cream sauce. That was our delicacy at

Christmas. Then we'd have riced potatoes and cranberries, but we had lingonberries in the old days. My mother was quite the baker and she would make this *Julekake*, but she wouldn't make it round, she'd still make it in the way they made bread. She'd make twelve loaves of bread at one time, because our stove was that big. And at Christmas we always used to have *römmegröt*." — Vic Anderson (Moorhead, MN)

"I know that one of my first impressions, at some people's house, was that they had white bread on the table every day. Just for everyday! That was something unheard of in Sweden. White bread was something that probably was seen on the table by most people only at Christmas or on some special occasion. I thought it was a luxury beyond words to be able to eat white bread every day, three times a day. It impressed me a lot! At that age [seventeen], you know, food means a lot." — Hartwig Johnard (Hawley, MN)

"I had already eaten *krumkake, fattigman, Hardangerkranser*, a Norwegian type of waffle, and sweet bread, *rullupølse*—a concoction of meat scraps put in a casing and pressed, and they were rings of meat and spice. And there was headcheese, *silta*, that was made, and blood sausage, *blødklub* and *potatoklub*, that's potato dumplings, *ekkersuppe*, that's pea soup, and *rommegrøt*, cream porridge, and *klubmelk*, that was boiled milk with some salt and dumplings, *søtsuppe*, sweet soup. And every time there was a new arrival in the family, a new baby, Mother always made sweet soup to bring to the mother. I think it was a Norwegian tradition, and it also had another value in that it was a laxative. And lutefisk, that's one thing I still haven't gotten away from. We have our lutefisk as soon as it becomes available in the fall. I used to help Mother prepare lutefisk. Dad would come home with the stock fish and we would put it in a gunny sack and we would chop a hole in the ice on the lake and drop this into the lake and leave it there four or five weeks. In the meantime, Mother would save the ashes from the hardwoods, like oak and ironwood, and maple, and she made a lye by pouring water over these ashes, in which the fish was soaked again." — John Gronner (Underwood, MN)

"We had a very Scandinavian diet, a very bland diet. We had a lot of meatballs and fishballs. [My mother] loved lefse, and the breads were highly flavored with cardamom." — Ruth Erickson (Moorhead, MN)

"We didn't use rice, because that was more, I think, Swedish. Norwegians do not use the rice as much. Like for Christmas we did have rice, but not as a rule. Lutefisk and lefse was our main [dish], and then we'd always have meatballs on Christmas Eve." — Alva Hest (Perley, MN)

"Lutefisk and baked ribs, pork I suppose it would be. And sometimes we'd have homemade sausage, pork I suppose, that my grandmother used to make. I remember my mother soaking the lutefisk in a large crock. I used to like lutefisk, but I used to like the ribs and the sausage more. We had lefse, too, of course, and flat bread. *Fattigman* we had, but I don't remember my mother making *krumkake*. But we had to have *fattigman*. That was traditional. We used to have *grøt* almost every supper. We had our meal at noon and we would have our *grøt*, and it was made with graham flour, and with some white flour, too. And I didn't like it very well. It was made with water, and salt and two kinds of flour. I think that was all. And we ate it with a dab of butter in the middle, and we drank milk with it, sometimes sour milk. I didn't particularly care for the sour milk. I used to like buttermilk, but this was regular sour milk. We kids used to put sugar on it, I don't know about the older folks. The white *grøt* was made with milk. I liked that better, 'course I had cinnamon on that, and sugar. … We'd get herring. There must have been some peddlers around who sold frozen herring. It was wintertime, you know, so that would keep outside. And *tyttebaer*, like lingonberries. That was really good. I liked that. When it came in the store it was in sort of a liquid, and then they would buy it in a little paper carton and then they made it into sauce." — Joanna Aune (Hawley, MN)

"*Lapskaus*, that's everything they put in there. Leftovers and stuff like that. We had that for supper a lot. Potatoes and cabbage and everything. And *wasgrøt*, water *grøt*, water and flour. We didn't have that much. We always had milk in ours. But there was some that didn't have much milk. We'd put cinnamon and sugar on it, and a lot of butter in the middle of the plate. And *surmelk*, *rullupølse*, *klub*, lefse, and lutefisk, we always had that."
— Henry Jacobson (Ulen, MN)

"The foods were very simple foods. Being that there was no money, everything was what you could produce at home. And, of course, a big part of it was mush, which is a kind of thick gravy, flour and milk is what it was, *grøt*, that's what it was. And bread they'd soak in milk and put sugar on it; milk, butter, cheese, and a lot of coarse flour. We had a diversified farm—grain, potatoes, and some dairy. I remember when they had the cream haulers. They hauled with horses and wagons and they would come to the farm. And then, of course, there was no real test on the cream. They would take it and dump it in the barrels. Then they would weigh it and you got an average price for it, whether it was high test or low test that was just the way it was graded. I remember when they were hauling sometimes in the fall or in the spring when the roads were very rough and sometimes the cream was already almost churned by the time it got to the creamery. A lot of this hard bread was made, because it would keep better because it was dried, and in the years back, of course, there was no refrigeration or anything for keeping products such as potatoes. We had our root cellar and it was great for that. Or by keeping things in the water, like having cream cans in cold water. ... Lutefisk we had as long as I can remember, so that's one thing we never missed. We had butter on the lutefisk, but we had white gravy on our potatoes, so now there is a mixture between Swedish and Norwegian."

— Oscar Olson (Lake Park, MN)

"At Christmas time we'd try to get a hold of lingonberries and we'd have lutefisk. At home we'd have a lot of lutefisk and we'd eat that all winter. It was cheap at that time. And probably a dish of rice, although that was more common with the Swedes than the Norwegians. And my mother would make Bohemian kolaches, which she learned to make from the neighbors. And then, of course, potatoes and lefse, and maybe flatbread. But we didn't just have that at Christmas time. We would have [those things] throughout the year." — Christian Schulstad (Dawson, MN)

"Lefse was served frequently in those days. We'd have it all the time. Mother would make it right on top of that big wood stove." — Odin Strandness (Fargo, ND)

"We had a lot of herring. They shipped that in, especially at Christmas time. And they had a lot of mush, fried mush, creamed mush. And Mom made cheese out of whole milk and skimmed milk, too. Real good cheese. That was kind of Norway special, too." — Alma Olson (Souris, ND)

"*Primost*—she used to make that from milk somehow, and it was cooked and cooked. I think it was part cream. It was fairly rich. It was more of a yellowish color. She loved it. It got more or less spreadable. I never cared for it, but she liked it." — Vern Fugelberg (New Rockford, ND)

"It was always crowded with Norwegians around there [Starkweather, North Dakota]. They had dinner together and they had card games together and they lived much the same way they did back in Norway. We had *flatbrød*, and then we had *klub* at least twice a week. And we ate mush an awful lot, at least two times a day. The evening meal was always mush. They had flour they ground themselves, every farmer had a mill of his own and they ground their own." — Kristine Svidal (Starkweather, ND)

"Lutefisk and lefse and meatballs and *spekekjøt*—dried beef. We used to make it ourselves, hang it upstairs in the attic somewhere to dry. But we salted it down, of course." — Gunhild Laske (Kindred, ND)

"And the lefse that they made was far better than the lefse now. It was not made with potatoes. Mother would sometimes make lefse with potatoes, but they weren't called lefse, they were called *potet-lompe*. But lefse was just made with flour and whatever else goes into it. They made flat bread too, and they made whatever they could out of milk, from the curd and the whey. From the curd they made cheese and from the whey they would make *primost*. Oh, things were really good!" — William Nelson (Rollag, MN)

"As far as eating, there wasn't much variety in those days. We always done our butchering and we raised some potatoes, that was all we had, meat and potatoes. Dad brought lutefisk home for Christmas. We always had to have that. We have melted butter on it. Now they usually serve it as lutefisk pudding. I think I like it best that way." — Oscar Bratlien (Hawley, MN)

"I cooked for two years in Trondheim, and to tell you the truth, we had the meat and the potatoes and the greens and carrots and for the life of me I can't see no difference in it." — Marie Tverdahl (Abercrombie, ND)

"My dad used to make *flatbrød* and *pølse*. And then, of course, lutefisk. We had to prepare it ourselves. Some used to hang it in the lake, you know, make a hole in the ice and soak it. And they cooked ashes, you know, to make the lye to soak it in for a certain length of time. It was only at Christmas, because that was quite an undertaking to prepare the lutefisk. And then if you had too much lye it got to be just like jelly after it got cooked." — Clara Johnson (Underwood, ND)

"We had cream mush, lutefisk, and lefse, flat bread and *sild*, that's herring. I still make lefse. I should have made some today. I made cookies instead." — Ellen Abraham (Villard, MN)

"We still have lutefisk and lefse. I remember my mother used to serve spare ribs or meatballs on Christmas Eve, too, besides the lutefisk. But when we have lutefisk, that's all we care for." — Mabel Enger (Oakes, ND)

"We had lutefisk and pig's feet and headcheese, *søtsuppe*, and *sild*, and of course in the sweets it was *krumkake* and *sandbakkels* and oh, I can't think of all of it. Pig's feet, I could go for that right now! Lefse, oh yah! In the wintertime we used to eat a lot of lefse." — Nilmer Bjorndahl (Hawley, MN)

"*Potet-klub*, you know, they made that with potatoes, potato dumplings. And that was stuffed with meat, pork usually. And that was boiled and you ate it warm. And afterwards you could fry it in a pan. And *grøt*, you can't forget that. They had all kinds. They had was*grøt*, *melchgrøt*, and *rommegrøt*. I don't remember how they were made. I ain't no cook!"

— William Melby (Hitterdal, MN)

"[Out on that Montana homestead] these pigs weighed about four hundred pounds apiece. Oh they were beauties! And he said, 'You're from Minnesota, I suppose you're a butcher.' 'Yup'—Never say no to anything, you know. One day he had arranged everything for butchering these pigs, he had the hot water ready and we got them peeled off and raised up in this tool shed, he had tackle and blocks and this was where he hung 'em. And right before we were going to butcher I asked what he was going to do with the blood. He was the worst one to swear I ever heard. He could swear by note! And he said a lot of swear words and then he said, 'What do you do with the blood?' 'Oh,' I says, 'We make *klub*. What are you going to do with the liver?' 'Oh, liver,' he says. So I got that and put that aside and cut the head off. A big pig like that had a big head you know, and of course I discovered that I was going to get the head so I cut it off a little bit further back than really would have been necessary. Save the head, save the liver, save the blood. Oh, he thought that was just wonderful. And a little later on he came by on horseback, he had chaps and everything, and he said 'How's that *klub*?' He was a widower, see, and he let out a lingo about a quarter of a mile long, he swore a blue streak and he said, 'The next time I get married I'm going to marry a Norwegian. Then I'll get *klub*!" — Obert Gregorson (Ulen, MN)

Chapter XIV

"It Was a Day to Live For"

THE SCANDINAVIAN-AMERICAN CHRISTMAS

Throughout the Upper Midwest it is not uncommon to meet people of Scandinavian descent who will proclaim that they have no trace of a Scandinavian heritage in their homes. They may scorn lutefisk and ignore lefse, and they may even insist that nothing Scandinavian remains of their Christmas. Nevertheless, almost all of them will admit to observing their Christmas not on Christmas Day, but on that special Scandinavian night, Christmas Eve. In many ways, it is in the observation of Christmas that the Scandinavian heritage is most strongly and securely held, and although "Merry Christmas" has replaced "*glad Jul*," Christmas is still observed in the new land in much the same way as it was in the old.

"Our big celebration for Christmas was always Christmas Eve, when we would have our big supper. And after supper there was a little program and father would do some reading and then it was time to open the presents. Christmas Day was usually a day we'd try to go to church and us or some of the relatives would have a big get-together. But Christmas in those days wasn't cut short the way it is now. They celebrated first and second and third

Christmas and it pretty well went on to New Years. … It was pretty hard to find a Christmas tree out there [on the prairie], but they shipped in Christmas trees after a while. One year we were just too hard up at Christmas time to get a Christmas tree. But we had a great big geranium. I've never seen one like that since. It was about four feet tall! And that was decorated and that was our Christmas tree. In those days they decorated Christmas trees with paper flowers and, of course, candles. We never had to eat lutefisk. I don't think it made much inroads into the Danish community. They would have fish shipped out there, though." — Philip Andersen (Fargo, ND)

"There were certain things that Mother used to make from Denmark. I know she used to make a certain Danish bread. She used to roll it and braid it and put sugar and raisins inside. Oh, it was delicious. She could bake bread! On Christmas we always had rice pudding and lutefisk and always had pork roast and spare ribs and this bologna that we made. And we had all of this on Christmas Eve. After the meal we would open our gifts and after the gifts we'd take the table cloth off and have candy and nuts. … We put the Christmas tree up on Christmas Eve and on Christmas Day we'd all go to church. And between Christmas Eve and New Year's we'd visit with all the relatives. We'd have them over to our house and we'd go to their house. And go to the neighbors for supper or dinner, and for that whole week nobody did anything except celebrate Christmas." — Phoebe Westerholm (Moorhead, MN)

"Christmas started at five o'clock Christmas Eve, and we had [our Danish] supper and that included rice and whatever else we had. And then there was always devotions before gift opening and then we sang Christmas carols and things. And then Christmas Day was just a family gathering, with usually church in the morning if we could get there. ... We always had *ebelkake*. It's plain old white bread that you've gotten dry in the oven and then you roll that into fine crumbs. And then you fry them or sort of sauté them in butter and white sugar, brown them just a little. Then on a platter you put a layer of these crumbs, then a layer of applesauce that has not been sweetened, then a layer of crumbs, then a layer of applesauce, then a layer of crumbs. It's good eaten about an hour after it's made, served at room temperature, and you cover the whole thing with whipped cream and a current jelly. It's very pretty and it's very good. I don't think I've gone through a Christmas without *ebelkake*." — Louise Andersen (Fargo, ND)

"On Christmas Eve we always went to church. We'd ride in the big sleigh with horses. And so often it was a cold, frosty, clear night and the heavens were just full of stars and the ground below was just full of diamonds in the snow and it was just gorgeous! The whole family would go to church and they would have beautiful music and the youngsters had recitations and took part and then everybody got a sack of candy and an apple. And that was no small thing, at that time it was wonderful. And if you wanted to, you could bring presents for your family to the church, and they'd put them under the tree and then distribute them. And my! That was a thrill to get a present there! They'd try to get a little doll for a girl and maybe a toy horse for a boy. But there was one thing I remember about Christmas Eve, that we were always taught that it was such a holy time. You didn't even play games then. You were supposed to concentrate on Jesus and His birth and what He stood for, and it was just too holy for mundane things. ... Santa Claus was important, but he was not from Iceland. We kids, from the very start, knew America was our country, and we were very proud of that. And they talked about Iceland having ghosts and elves and all sorts of things like that you don't ordinarily see. And I remember hearing those stories, and I thought, 'Well, in Iceland they had that, but we don't have that.'" — Kathryn Thordarson (Fargo, ND)

"At Christmas we always sang Icelandic Christmas carols and when we were in elementary school we put on plays in the churches in Icelandic. ... You always had to have candles. The Icelanders were great for having candles. They used to have them on the trees. And we always had to have *vienarterta*, a Christmas cake." — Diane Volrath (Hitterdal, MN)

"On Christmas my dad used to just go out in the woods and cut down a pine tree and we made all the decorations. And we had those little candles that you clip on the tree. And we put candles in the windows and then Mother would always read out of the Icelandic Bible on Christmas Eve."
— Freda Bjornson (Moorhead, MN)

"We liked to sing the Swedish songs and cook the way we did back in Sweden and things like that. And, of course, Christmas we always had a smorgasbord like they had back in Sweden, you know, lutefisk and *grøt*. And we'd have that every year since I come to this country. I've always seen that I get lutefisk, with white cream sauce. But the Norwegians, you know, they have melted butter on it, but the Swedes, you know, they make this really rich cream sauce. We got the fish from the barrels. I cooked up the fish with potatoes and then I cooked rice, with milk and put some cinnamon and sugar on top of it. That was the custom at home. You put all-spice on top of the lutefisk. [My husband] bought the dry fish and he sawed it up and he started on the ninth of December so it would be ready Christmas Eve. You had to soak it and then you added lye and then you had to put clear water on it every day." — Anna Lingren (Fargo, ND)

"In the early days, Christmas was always at Grandpa's place, and then we had to have rice pudding, and lutefisk, of course." — Violet Anderson (Hitterdal, MN)

"Swedish breads was what Grandma was noted for. For Christmas Eve we would have lutefisk, but not before that time. Like my sister used to say, 'Christmas Eve is a white dinner,' because it was *ris gröt velle,* which is a rice mush, mashed potatoes, mashed rutabagas, then the lutefisk, which had a cream sauce with all-spice sprinkled on the top. I don't remember what we had for dessert, but it was good. We kept this up until my sister married a German, and he didn't like lutefisk." — Amy Erickson (Moorhead, MN)

"At Christmas time we would have potato sausage, rice, lingonberries, Swedish bread with cardamom—which I dearly love—ginger cookies, and an amazing amount of things that I still remember." — Alice Oliver (Moorhead, MN)

"Lutefisk! Every Christmas Eve we couldn't be without it, with cream sauce, mustard, and butter. I didn't like it either way, so Christmas Eve was not a good meal for me. And we always had rice pudding, and I didn't like rice pudding. And Swedish *Korve*, that's kind of a sausage. We didn't have *sotsuppe*, but a lot of people did have it. They also had a big kettle and they'd have some meat boiling in it, and all day long that would be boiling on the stove and anybody who came in the house would just take some bread or whatever they had, not even take a bowl of it, just take that bread and dip it in and eat it that way. And when they did serve it at the table they'd just put it on the table. *Dippen a gruten*, they'd call it." — Gladys Westrum (Moorhead, MN)

"We had parties at Christmas. They called it *Julakolas*, and they would invite the whole neighborhood. I don't see how they had room for them all. And then the men would go upstairs and play cards and the ladies would stay downstairs to gossip. We had a big house and the men would have chairs and tables in, oh, they called it the drawing room." — Inez Holt (Chisago City, MN)

"We really didn't care about Santa Claus. Dad would go in and get that Christmas tree lit and we children would sometimes wonder if Santa Claus would have come. I don't think Mother and Dad cared much about Santa Claus. We had what they called *Tomtes*, you know. He looked like Santa Claus, he'd always have a peaked cap." — Nina Oien (Moorhead, MN)

"We celebrated Christmas until after the fourteenth of January. We didn't do that too much at Malmo [Minnesota], but we did have the traditional rice pudding, lutefisk, and boiled potatoes, and white sauce and all that. And I remember we didn't get our Christmas tree until Christmas Eve and then the boys would go to the woods and bring home a tree and decorate it and Christmas Eve was a lutefisk supper." — Amy Margaret Erickson (Wheatland, ND)

"We had a fine Christmas! Same as I do today. I don't notice any difference at all. Everything was Swedish." — Carl Elmquist (Moorhead, MN)

"We never had our Christmas tree up before Christmas Eve. That was traditional. We didn't have the Christmas tree in the middle of the room, although I can recall a neighbor who kept the tree until the Thirteenth Day of Christmas, when Christmas is supposed to be over. We celebrated at her home and I remember she had the Christmas tree in the middle of the room and everyone danced around it. We always had *Julotta*, five or six in the morning." — Myrtle Rundquist (Moorhead, MN)

***Julotta* was a uniquely Swedish tradition. It would began very early in the morning, when the winter skies were still without light, and would feature a church service illuminated with candles. At its conclusion, the first hint of morning light would appear in the east and the Swedes would go home to a Christmas breakfast.**

"One thing nice about Christmas was the *Julotta* that we would have in the morning, at six o'clock in the church. And, of course, we would have to leave quite early, because we had four miles to drive. We'd go on the sleigh and we had bells on the horses. And we'd come into town and we could hear other people coming with bells on their horses and it was really quite a thing to hear. And you'd try to get there early because, like now they try to get there early so they can park their car, but then they had sheds in town where you could put your horses in so they were sheltered some from the cold, and if you came there early enough you could get a stall for your horses, otherwise you just had to tie them up to a hitching post, you know, and put blankets on them." — Nina Oien (Moorhead, MN)

"I can remember going to *Julotta* and that was our biggest crowd. Get up at five in the morning and church would start at five thirty. We could go right straight down to Bethesda [in Moorhead, Minnesota]. It was dark when we went in and dark when we came out, and all you could see was the candles lit on the Christmas trees." — Vic Anderson (Moorhead, MN)

"The thing that I remember is the early Christmas morning services. We called it *Julotta*. We'd get up on Christmas morning at five o'clock and go to church and we'd sing the old Swedish '*Hoseanna David's Sön.*' But we'd start Christmas preparations long in advance, and make the sausage and we made ale, too. My folks didn't do any boozing, but it was sort of a homemade beer. It turned out to be quite a bit like root beer. Just at Christmas time. … We didn't set up the Christmas tree until Christmas Eve, and we would put on the candles and light them for Christmas Eve, and we heard the real Christmas story." — Roy Carlander (Moorhead, MN)

"*Julotta* was at six o'clock in the morning, and they used to have, in the olden time, barns, so that they could take the horses and put them in the barns because sometimes the services were three hours long. And then we had children's festival, or children's program. And I know that my uncle used to be in charge of the barrel of apples and the candy boxes that were given to the children. And on New Year's Eve they often had a basket social. Just before the New Year they'd have a short service and after the service, into the bobsled we'd go, jingling through the woods. And if it was a nice, bright moonlit evening, it was glorious!" — Amy Erickson (Moorhead, MN)

"They'd come with horses and sleighs and they'd drive for miles to get to a Christmas program. That was something in them days. With sleigh bells and snow, it was really pretty." — David Swedberg (Otter Tail Co., MN)

"Our home was centered around the church so much. And one of the highlights was to go to *Julotta*. Ours was always at five-thirty on Christmas morning. And we'd walk through that crisp air and it was pitch black and the stars were usually out nice and bright, and our whole family would walk to church. And when we'd get there the Christmas lights were blazing and they had candles at every window. And we'd sing '*Vi Hälsa Stjärnar Morgenstjärn*,' which means 'we're greeting the early Christmas morning.' And it was just so overwhelming. I was a child at that time, but it is just such a beautiful thing to think about." — Alice Oliver (Moorhead, MN)

"We carried over all the old Swedish customs in our home. I'm sure that we did exactly like they did in Sweden for years and years. At *Julotta*, that's when everyone went to church. It was five thirty on Christmas morning and everyone went. The church was packed. No busses or anything to ride on, each family walked. It was a beautiful service, lots of singing, and the church was lit with candles and it was the highlight of the whole year."
— Gladys Westrum (Moorhead, MN)

"I never had [Santa Lucia] in this country, I did back in Sweden when I was small. We went to *Julotta* on Christmas morning, with the horse, and the horse had bells all around him, you know. Six o'clock in the morning and we piled into the sled and went to the big Lutheran church in town." — Anna Lindgren (Fargo, ND)

"We always went to *Julotta*. In those days, you know, it was early in the morning. We only lived two blocks from church, but we'd get up early in the morning, four-thirty, five o'clock. And it got to be six o'clock, then seven o'clock, and the *Julotta* was always in Swedish, too. Whether we understood it or not, it still meant Christmas to us." — Hazel Monson Barker (Fargo, ND)

"Early morning Christmas Day they had the traditional early morning service in the church. They called it *Julotta*. That's Christmas! It was a little heartbreaking for the Scandinavians to break off and get into the English. They thought the church was going to go haywire." — Frank Alm (Christine, ND)

"I wasn't much for going to *Julotta*. I was generally too sleepy to go." — Robert Carlander (Moorhead, MN)

At the conclusion of *A Christmas Carol*, Charles Dickens urged his English readers to keep Christmas. Of the Scandinavian immigrants to America, it was perhaps the Norwegians who clung most tenaciously to their Christmas traditions.

"Christmas is a joyous time, because it is the occasion of the birth of our Savior. And from the very time you could speak, it was a day to live for. And the preparation for Christmas was not only in your home, but it was supposed to be in your heart. And you lived it! That was the beauty of it. As children you lived it. When I grew up, on the afternoon of Christmas Eve, after we all had taken our bath, cleaned up, we were given new clothing, including underwear, stockings, and everything had to be new because the Savior was coming. ... Lefse, you couldn't get along without lefse, and flatbread, and fancy cookies, and you wouldn't believe this, but out biggest treat as children was to get an orange. ... At Christmas Eve, at five o'clock, all the churches in town started ringing their bells and they rang steady for half an hour. At seven o'clock, people would go to church. ... It's a funny thing. This is something you never outgrow, even at my age. I still get homesick on Christmas Eve. I haven't been [to Norway] for a long time, but I still get homesick." — Leif Christianson (Moorhead, MN)

"My brothers would go out and milk the cows a little early on Christmas Eve, and everybody had to have a bath. And we had only an ordinary tub. We went down to the lake and cut ice and mother melted the ice so we would have soft water for our bath. And I can remember standing with one foot in the tub and one foot outside the tub when we took our once-a-week bath. But even if Saturday night had been only one day before, we still had to have a bath on Christmas Eve. ... The dishes had to be washed, and the younger kids were pretty impatient, but the dishes had to be washed before we could have our Christmas Eve together. We had our Christmas tree and the younger members of the family all had to learn a Christmas story. The girls could read a Christmas story, but we all had to do some kind of recitation, both in Norwegian and American. The gifts could not be opened until after the program. After the gifts were opened, we had lunch again. The children had mostly popcorn and apples and other cookies, and *fattigman*. We didn't have Santa Claus tradition in the early years, but after my sister went away to Moorhead Normal College she came back and then we began to have Santa Claus. But I can remember my mother talking about Nisse. ... The traditional Christmas Eve was Norwegian, and we have maintained that to this day in our family. Mother always served lutefisk, meatballs, and spareribs, all three on Christmas Eve." — John Gronner (Underwood, MN)

"We did not start celebrating Christmas early. We started only just before Christmas Eve, perhaps the twenty-second or twenty-third, when we would have sort of an introductory meal, I might call it, to Christmas, when we were just about ready with all the baking. And after that, it would continue for a good two weeks. So Christmas lasted until about the sixth to the twelfth of January." — Clara Hanson (Moorhead, MN)

"We would have the big program and we would have a tall ceiling in the church and we would go out in the woods and get the tallest pine we

could find and have it decorated with just simple things, popcorn and things, and then each one of us that were in Sunday School and on the program would get a brown bag with some candy and an apple and some popcorn in it, and that would be the greatest time of our lives. And we'd take the horses and the sled and we'd go in for church for Christmas. On Christmas Eve we had our big Christmas and then the Christmas dinner, too. And it was the greatest time of our lives, although we didn't get much for presents."
— Florence Fritz (Detroit Lakes, MN)

"My favorite Christmas, I think I must have been about nine years old, and my sister was six, and we each got a doll for Christmas. Oh my, we thought that was fine. And Mother had made a box. And she covered this box with cloth as a place for the doll to be in. And she dressed the doll, even to her shoes. My brother liked to hammer things, so my dad sawed off a log and he bought him a pound of shingle nails. So he got busy. He kept pounding and pounding until he had the log all glittery with nail heads." — Cora Kragnes (Felton, MN)

"On Christmas Eve we had a program, sometime around seven o'clock, so we had supper earlier. And we had all of the things. We had *Julekake*, and brown bread, and we had lutefisk and all the cookies. And we had lots of company, too." — Anna Hanson (Moorhead, MN)

"They never started celebrating Christmas until Christmas Eve, and then it went on for twenty days. The thirteenth of January was supposed to be the end of Christmas. In the meantime, then, we used to get together for supper here and supper there. It was kind of quiet around home, but I heard of places where they really, up north of Hawley [Minnesota], I guess, there was a lively bunch. They really got out and celebrated Christmas." — Nilmer Bjorndahl (Hawley, MN)

"The first time we had Christmas at our place [in America], of course they didn't have any pine trees to go and cut. They used to do that in Norway. You could always cut one in the woods. And here finally we got another kind of tree that looked, oh, kind of a nice little tree. And we covered that with ornaments and it was all right for the first Christmas. ... The *Nisse* was very good. He was in the home and in the barn and he was supposed to be so good for the cattle. He helped them give milk and they gave him enough to eat. He was good to the people so long as the people were good to the cattle. Oh, there were thousands of things like that." — John Klukken (Osakis, MN)

"[My uncle] had a beard and he'd dress up like Santa. He looked just like him. He had a red suit. He had the presents and he brought them in. Oh, yah, he was Norwegian. Of course he talked Norwegian. ... My dad, at Christmas time, he'd put up a big pole and he'd have a couple of big bundles of wheat wrapped around that pole for the birds, for the birds at Christmas."
— Henry Jacobson (Ulen, MN)

"We'd hang up our stockings on Christmas Eve and go to bed and then in the morning we'd get up and look in our stockings. And my mother always put a bun or biscuit that was full of raisins into the stocking, because we had long stockings in those days and it took a lot to fill. There wasn't too much money." — Mabel Enger (Oakes, ND)

"On Christmas Eve we always had lutefisk. My mother made a lot of lutefisk. And lefse, we had lefse all winter. And *fattigman*, flat bread, and *kringle*, like a pretzel, a great favorite. The whole family was very fond of that. There were other things, too." — Clarence Glasrud (Moorhead, MN)

"The Christmas tree ended up as a branch off an evergreen. We never had a real tree. It was just a branch. And we'd decorate it with popcorn, and had candles on it. We'd light 'em and stand and watch it. It was quiet, but there was always a Christmas program to go to, in the church and the school." — Ellen Abraham (Villard, MN)

"Dad had gone to town and gotten a nice Christmas tree, but we didn't have any decorations yet, you know, so Mom and Dad bought the most beautiful decorations. They had little lanterns made out of colored window glass like they have in churches, and they'd fold up flat when you put them away. And then we had those little wax candles that you had to light. And we had tinsel on it. Beautiful! And I can remember us kids holding hands and walking around it singing in Norwegian, '*Glad Jul.*' That's the first Christmas [in America] that I can remember. And, of course, we never were allowed to see the tree until it was all decorated. They'd keep us in the kitchen until they were all ready. ... We eat more lutefisk at Christmas now than we did years ago. At home a lot of times we had rice mush. And we children really liked that because we liked the rice and also because there wasn't much dishes to do so we could start opening presents earlier. But we had lutefisk, too, especially if we had company." — Alma Olson (Souris, ND)

"When we were children we had a Christmas tree that was always decorated with Norwegian flags and candles and we sang Christmas songs. None of us could speak English when we were small. And it was their tradition to hold hands and walk around the tree and that's what we did. And they always kept straw shocks from the fields in the fall and put them out for the birds at Christmas time. And they always gave the animals extra food every Christmas Eve." — Solveig Johnson (Niagara, ND)

"We marched around the Christmas tree and sang. We did that back in Norway, too." — Dagne Faust (Colfax, ND)

"In South Dakota we used a tumbleweed for a Christmas tree, there was no trees around. After we moved to Minnesota we improved things by getting a box elder for our Christmas tree." — Ole Olson (Fargo, ND)

"I don't know if it is traditional, but we had a Christmas tree and we went to church on Christmas Eve. We had a Christmas tree in our church and we spoke pieces, well, I guess maybe it was in Norwegian." — Gunhild Laske (Kindred, ND)

"We had very small living quarters during the winter because we closed off part of the house and we would have the tree in what was both our living room and our kitchen in the wintertime. We had it sort of in the corner, but we had to have it so we could walk around it." — Joanna Aune (Hawley, MN)

"I remember Mother talking that on Christmas Eve we had to give the cows a little extra hay and do something good for the chickens. It seems to me she used to put something out for the birds. She used to save out a bundle of grain from threshing and put that out near the barn and that would be for the birds at Christmas. … Early in the afternoon we'd put the tree up. We never got to put the tree up until the afternoon of Christmas Eve. We made a lot of homemade things and hung on [the tree] because we couldn't afford to have too many other things. And we saved them from year to year and they were real precious to us, little glittery things. We would maybe cut out something from paper and I think that we strung cranberries, too, and popcorn, and hung that on the tree. And then we had to have a little program. We children would have our little recitations that we learned in school and then we would join hands and walk around the Christmas tree and sing '*Glad Jul.*'" — Gertie Holm (Hawley, MN)

"There were lots of Christmas bakings. We used to have *smorgasbords* in later years—lutefisk, lefse, sweet goodies. That is one tradition that we still have, lutefisk on Christmas Eve, and lefse, *sandbakkels*, and *kringle*. ... We had something like Santa Claus. My dad used to hide behind the coal stove. He used to put the gifts out around the stove. And my brother hid behind the stove one time so he could see him. I don't know if he was Santa Claus or just what we called him." — Alpha Bowersox (Wolford, ND)

"[My wife] is very good at fixing the old traditional goodies for Christmas. She bakes *krumkake* and *Sandbakkels*, lefse, and all kinds of goodies. And the tradition at our house, her folks come from the northern part of Norway, and her traditions were a little different. We had a big frying pan, and that was fried pork for Christmas with lefse. And then we had what they called *risengrynsgrøt*—rice pudding. We had that after we had walked around the Christmas tree and sang Christmas carols. Of course, we lived during the winter months on lutefisk and potatoes, 'cause that was a poor man's diet in Norway. And it took me a long time before I could eat lutefisk after I came to this country 'cause I was so sick and tired of lutefisk that I couldn't even stand the name. It was my job to make that lutefisk because my grandfather taught me how to do it." — Sven Thompson (Willmar, MN)

"We never had a Christmas tree after my mother died, but my enjoyment was to go to [my aunt's] house, and she had an old chair, with a hole in the middle, and the tree went in there. And when I went to her place for Christmas it was just like heaven for me." — Clara Johnson (Underwood, MN)

"Christmas was the same old things as they was in Norway. The first thing we did was to bring in the wood. Wood was piled up high in the kitchen, enough to last over the holidays, and two sheaves of grain were put up on a high pole for the birds and the cattle were given extra rations, you know. And on Christmas Eve everyone had to get washed up, and then have our supper, with the fisk—cod laid down in a brine and had gone through a ripening process. You eat that raw with lefse, flatbread, and butter, and then the next meal would be a rib steak. That was a must, you know. And then cloud berries—yellow berries that grew in the swamps in Norway, and we had lingonberries, too. And we had rice pudding; that was a must. And a glass of brandy, good brandy. And then my dad would read the sermon for the Christmas Eve and that would take till midnight. I know I was awfully sleepy. It was all the evening reading until midnight. You weren't supposed to go to bed before midnight because that's the time the Christ child was born. … There was always something under the Christmas tree." — Louis Haugen (Crookston, MN)

"[Christmas] was pretty much American, because my dad thought this country was absolutely fantastic!" — Beatrice Schaefer (Osakis, MN)

"Well, we all had the same Bible, of course. And the Norwegians would have their Christmas program in the Norwegian church and the Swedes would have their Christmas program in the Swedish church. But if you were interested in Christmas programs, we'd go to see theirs and they'd come to see ours." — Lloyd Westrum (Moorhead, MN)

"Christmas was always something for us to look forward to. We always had trees. They probably weren't the fanciest looking ones, but they were trees. One year my dad didn't get in to town [Glyndon, Minnesota] to get one and us kids had been over by the church and some branches had been thrown out so my dad wired them together, put them on a little spool from a binder, and that was our Christmas tree, with three candles on it. We had popcorn strings and cranberry strings and tinsel. … We'd get together with our immediate family and we'd be together on Christmas Eve and Christmas Day. We always went to church on Christmas Day and the church was always filled—Concordia Church of rural Glyndon. The church services, when I was a kid, were in Norwegian but also in English. They alternated." — Regina Hanson (Glyndon, MN)

"Christmas was a great day for the pioneers. We had it mostly in our own homes, of course. The two-three weeks before Christmas, was there ever a busy time! In school we had to be preparing for programs and at home mothers had to do a lot of baking and fathers had to do a lot of butchering and they had to make *růllupølse*, and ham, and get the bacon ready and make sausage, and headcheese, and the greatest thing, the most important thing before Christmas, was lutefisk. It was so good. It was much better that way than what we buy now. And then, of course, Mother had to bake lefse and flatbread. Those were the standing things. And *Julekake*, Christmas bread, and *fattigman, sandbakkels, Berlinerkranzer*, and *krumkake*. Oh, that was the food for Christmas. ... On Christmas Eve, that was usually a big supper, that as a family we had, and then we children had to go to bed early because we had to put our stockings under the stove because *Julenisse* was coming and we had to get to bed early. Of course, we had been taught why we celebrated Christmas was on account of the Christ Child, but this was the gift giving part. In the morning when we got up our stockings were filled and oh, but we were happy. Sometimes we had an orange and a banana and sometimes we girls had a doll. I remember once I got a ring, and it was big enough for an old lady and that ring I have kept. ... And then we had parties. That's the time the neighbors used to gather. Sometimes we had big Christmas parties. I don't know how Mother could prepare everything. It was the dinner during the day and in the evening the young people would get together and Mother would have things for that too. And sometimes, when people knew there was a party at a place, then the Christmas Fools would come. And they were all dressed up in masks and they would have to be treated, too." — Alma Ramse (McIntosh, MN)

One Scandinavian-American tradition that was eagerly anticipated by both the Norwegians and Swedes was *Julebokking*. "Christmas fooling," as it came to be known in English, was a progressive party the combined elements of Halloween and *Marti Gras*. In most areas of the Upper Midwest, this was a totally "dry" activity that would involve the whole family. In some areas, however, the *Julebokker* would stay at the home of his sometimes unwilling host until he was provided with a drop or two of something that had alcohol in it. This tradition is not well known among today's Scandinavian-Americans, and that may be a pity. From the following descriptions, it sounds like a lot of fun!

"At Christmas time we, well we haven't done it for a number of years now, but we would put on different kinds of clothing and we went from place to place and if it was a snowy winter we went with horses and sleds and we had a lot of fun, you know, just driving around the country. We'd go to the different farm places and we'd go in and we had masks so they didn't know who we were, and often we'd frighten the children, scare the kids, and oh! I think the custom came from Norway, but we had a lot of fun. And then they'd treat us when we came to the different houses. They'd have cookies for us and some places they'd have wine. I had wine one time, homemade wine made from chokecherries, you know. I'd fill up the glasses for everyone. Some of them didn't like that wine. They didn't think it was good enough. But some of them liked it and they drank till they got stinky. I could even mention names, you know. One girl that liked it so well she drank several glasses and she got dizzy in the head. And some places they gave coffee and cookies and Christmas goodies. It was fun. But I think it's more or less going out of style now. Christmas fooling, you don't hear much about it anymore." — Alma Olson (Souris, ND)

"There was *Julebokking*. Well, they'd dress up so you wouldn't know 'em and then run around from neighbor to neighbor, and then you'd try to guess who they were. They were disguised. Some places you were welcome and some places they would jump right on you and tear your mask off. Then you'd run out. Sometimes we'd walk and sometimes we'd go by sled. Oh, I suppose we had some refreshments along sometimes. We'd use anything we had for masks, anything to cover our face. A stocking with holes cut out or something. Of course, later on some people bought masks. This went on for about twenty days at Christmas time." — William Melby (Hitterdal, MN)

"We who were young, we would dress up, we called it *Julebok*. We would dress up in all kinds of costumes and wear a mask, and we'd call on the homes. We called on the old people, especially if they didn't have a family. We'd join hands and dance around the Christmas tree. Then we'd go to the next house." — Leif Christianson (Moorhead, MN)

"At Christmas time we'd go *Julebokking*. I didn't go many times myself, but they'd get a bunch together. All would dress up in all kinds of clothing and put a mask on, and go from place to place and see if they could know you or not. I always got a kick out of it when they would come to our place. They used to come two, three times every year. Some of 'em gave coffee and something like root beer, to treat the *Julebokkers* and give 'em cake or something. Some of 'em got pretty thirsty walking. It was all walking, most of the time in them days. When they went on a long ways, well then they'd use a sleigh. Sometimes they'd start out with two couples at one place, and then go to the next place and get two, three more and then go to the next place and get two, three more of them, and pretty soon there'd be ten, fifteen people. In our territory there was very little [drinking]. I think that was more in certain other places. I think that was more with the Swedes. We were pretty strong in temperance." — Nilmer Bjondahl (Hawley, MN)

"Oh, yes, I loved *Julebokking*! People would go for miles. I suppose when they wanted to see somebody's home, that was a good excuse to get into the home. We had fun them days, of course, like we don't have now." — Clara Johnson (Underwood, ND)

"*Julebokking*? Yes we did that. Of course we had done that back in Sweden, too. I think that was one of the things that my folks enjoyed. I think they were surprised that things were so much the same over here." — Elsie Gale (Clearbrook, MN)

"At Christmas time we always went *Julebokking*. We'd dress up. The English have something like it. They call it mumming. And we'd dress up in fantastic clothing and masks and go around to houses of the neighbors at Christmas time. That was very exciting." — Clarence Glasrud (Moorhead, MN)

"It was fun. We got together sometimes when the weather was nice. We'd enjoy it. Tie the sleigh bells on and we'd go from place to place." — Oscar Olson (Lake Park, MN)

"*Julebok*. We used to go *Julebokking*. We'd go from our place to the neighbors and a couple more would join us there and on we'd go. We dressed up, you know, in different kinds of costumes with masks on, and by the time we'd get through there may be a dozen of us or more. And we'd have coffee and your ears would be frozen so we'd have to thaw them out." — Henry Jacobson (Ulen, MN)

"Oh yes, we went *Julebokking*. And if we were children it was more fun to have *Julebokkers* come to our house." — Amy Erickson (Moorhead, MN)

"And we had *Julebokking*. Everybody dressed up. They liked to dress up and you weren't supposed to know who they were and they'd wear masks and go the these dances and then you had to guess who you were dancing with, and then they'd have these big feeds. It was a wonderful time at Christmas when everybody got together." — Mabel Fynskov (Osakis, MN)

"*Julebokking*, the whole deal was just to dress up in comical things so that you would be sure they didn't recognize you. That was the big thing. And you could never talk because they could get you on that. But if they ever guessed, then you had to take off your mask. But if they couldn't guess you, well they'd just have to give up. No, we were never invited anywhere, that would take the fun out of it. Well, sometimes we'd have some refreshments, but usually we'd go to somebody's place for lunch, that was usually planned out ahead of time." — Violet Anderson (Hitterdal, MN)

"Sometime during the course of Christmas some of the neighbors would dress up and go visit some of the other neighbors. They called it *Julebok*. They'd dress funny and act funny and put on masks so they should not be recognized. And the people they'd visit would probably treat them a little bit, some Christmas cookies or something. Some of them couldn't even drink a cup of coffee because of the masks. They just wanted to visit and show themselves and maybe say something funny." — Clara Hanson (Moorhead, MN)

Chapter XV

"We Got to Be More United"

THE ETHNIC WATERSHED: WORLD WAR I

Carl H. Chrislock, in an article entitled "The Impact of World War I Nativism on Scandinavian Ethnicity in the upper Midwest," saw the First World War as "the decisive force assuring the early demise of the fragile Scandinavian subcultures that had demonstrated some vitality in the early years of the century." America would not enter the war until April of 1917, but already by that time it was possible to detect a campaign against hyphenated Americans. Waldemar Ager, following the *Syttende Mai* **celebrations of 1916, noted "We have papers that cannot express a kind word about May 17 without explicitly affirming their loyalty and devotion to the new land ... in order not to be misunderstood." After American entry into the war, these pressures increased, fueled by a "One-hundred percent American" campaign that found expression in such things as the Iowa telephone law, which forbade the speaking of a foreign language on the telephone. It was illegal, for a time, for two Norwegian grandmothers to exchange lutefisk recipes over the telephone.**

When the question of how the First World War had affected their ethnic perceptions was posed to the interviewees, their recollections of

the time centered on items that would have been common to all Americans of that era. A number reported that they or a member of their family had served in the war out of a sense of duty and with no thought of cementing their "Americanness." Most also recalled Red Cross drives and school programs that were decidedly patriotic. Upon reflection, however, a significant proportion of the interviewees did concede that the domestic atmosphere during the war had contributed to a decline in Scandinavian ethnicity and while all maintained that they experienced no coercion to become less "Scandinavian," they did admit that the era strengthened their identity as Americans. Furthermore, a number of those interviewed did recall anti-German sentiment during the war. It would seem, then, that this solid identification with America, reinforced by community ethnic homogeneity, actually hastened the assimilation process.

"I was the first to register for the army in Ransom County [North Dakota]. I was in Class 1, but then when I was farmin' they put me in Class 4, and then I got the flu in the fall of 1918 so I couldn't go. They couldn't take me because I was in bed." — Arne Arneson (Fargo, ND)

"I wanted to go in the service, because I was tall and thin. And it was a disgrace at that time if you didn't go into the service. In the Second World

War you was a hero if you didn't have to go." — Charles Westerholm (Moorhead, MN)

"I was drafted in 1917, when the First World War broke out and they passed the draft law. We were getting only thirty dollars a month in the army, but we didn't get that because they took out for an insurance. I thought I was better off than in Sweden because there they would only give you five cents a day so I figured I'd gained. I took out insurance for ten thousand dollars and I sent that to my mother [back in Sweden]." — Andrew Lindgren (Moorhead, MN)

"My uncle was in the band when he went into the army, but when he got overseas they put him in the trenches. I don't remember how long he was in the service, but when he got home he was shell-shocked and he didn't do too well after that." — Freda Bjornson (Moorhead, MN)

"They were quite patriotic. They sold an awful lot of bonds and did Red Cross work. Lots of boys went. I was one of the last ones drafted. I went with the last draft from Wahpeton to Grand Forks to the University there. We were there for two months. They started drilling us and training us there and then the flu epidemic hit. Out of two hundred and five in my unit that went into the university, only eighty-five came out alive, the rest died from flu. So that was hard on the young folks there. I had it for ten days, but I got well." — Frank Alm (Christine, ND)

"I think there was some pressure to become more 'American' during World War I. I think we felt that way before, too, because this was where we lived, and got away from Swedish things and I think my parents did too. I can remember when [the boys] went off to war. The band played 'Nearer My God to Thee.' I think that was an awful thing to play. We'd go to the county seat to see them off. I remember the day my brother left home. That was an awful sad day, and we didn't even take him to the train because Dad was sick and we had some lively horses, and Mother and we kids watched him walk off down the road carrying his suitcase." — Nina Oien (Moorhead, MN)

In the minds of many Americans, Scandinavians were just about the same thing as Germans, and therefore their loyalty was sometimes questioned. Furthermore, many Scandinavian-Americans felt closer ties with Germany than they ever did with England, and in the years before American entry they had frequently voiced their preference for the Central Powers. But American entrance into the war encouraged Scandinavian-Americans to demonstrate their loyalty. In many cases, for instance, campaigns for the sale of war bonds called more attention to the need to prove ones loyalty to their adopted country than to any impact that the bonds would have had on the war effort.

"I remember very well when I first heard about it. I was over to Rollag [Minnesota] to get the mail. ... And [the postmaster] had just heard over the telephone that the United States had declared war on Germany. And there was an older man there at the time and he said in Norwegian, but this is what he meant, 'Have they got into it now!'—the fact that we were kind of unnecessarily pushing ourselves into the conflict. And this was somewhat the attitude for a little while. You know, the Norwegians were actually closer to the Germans then they were to the English, or had been, so it took a while to see which side they were supposed to favor. But it didn't take long before they realized. And there was much more enthusiasm at the time, you know. The boys went off to war. It was a glorious thing. We had parties for them, and I was old enough to go to them." — William Nelson (Rollag, MN)

"Well, Luther came from Germany, you know. And I was confirmed during the war. And our preacher was very pro-German. He could have got into trouble because he just carried on something awful. He was quite partial to the Germans. ... But oh, did they knit stockings for the poor people in Europe!" — Carl Elmquist (Moorhead, MN)

"The thing I remember best about the First World War is that when it started, in 1914 ... we and most of the Norwegians, we leaned toward Germany more, because we were more familiar with Germany. And then, of course, Wilson was able to swing my folks around as they go so disgusted with this evil warfare. My dad got a citation for selling bonds and my mother set a record for knitting socks. The whole community was very patriotic once we got into the war." — Allan Erickson (Moorhead, MN)

"At the time of the First World War they were stricter, because they were afraid that somebody would take part with the Germans, you know. And there were lots of Germans around, so they became more strict. And we had to be more careful. And we bought bonds, and I think we did the best we could." — John Klukken (Osakis, MN)

"My dad had a Buick with yellow wheels, and yellow was a color associated with the Germans, and my dad painted those yellow wheels black." — Palmer Tverdahl (Abercrombie, MN)

"If they were Germans, you didn't want to associate with them. The war started shortly after I came over here. I remember when Woodrow Wilson got elected the second time. I went to the show and they announced it. I had a lot of young friends who had to go. Carlson and Swanson and Johnson, all had to go. A lot of Scandinavian boys got killed in the war, all right, but after they came back, those who had been in the war, then they became an American citizen. They could pick up the papers after they had fought in the army." — Anna Lindgren (Fargo, ND)

Three months after America entered the war, Waldemar Ager began a five installment essay in *Kvartalskrift* entitled "The Great Leveling." The third installment, which appeared in the April, July, and

October issues of 1919, was entitled "The Citizen and the state." In a desperate cry against the assimilation process that seemed to be accelerating, Ager wrote, "If one reaches the point where he regards himself or his nationality as the embodiment of an ideal, his development is then complete; a natural consequence is that further growth ceases, and he seeks instead to shape others in his own image."

In many respects, this is what happened to the Scandinavian-Americans in the Upper Midwest. Among those interviewed, there were none who felt that they, as Scandinavian-Americans, were less of an "embodiment of an ideal" than other Americans. Within a decade after the last part of "The Great Leveling" appeared in 1922, most Scandinavian-American Lutheran church services were being conducted in English. The second generation was conversing in English much of the time and their children spoke English all of the time. World War I, the caldron that had shaped the history of Europe, had also shaped the Scandinavians who lived in America and blurred the distinctions between them and their fellow Americans.

"We used the Swedish language almost exclusively until I was six, probably because my grandparents, when they moved off the farm and came into Fergus Falls, lived above us. I spoke no English until I started school. But somehow I think we got an idea that we should become Americanized.

This was a melting pot. We weren't too proud of the fact that we were Scandinavian. I think other nationalities, the idea was so prevalent that we must become American, that we must not just hang on to our old heritage. And maybe that came about because of the fact there were so many people who came here and wanted to hold on to it that they decided maybe it wasn't the best thing to do that. And of course the First World War had a little bit to do with this Americanization, too, but by that time they had been in the country for quite some time. We never used the Scandinavian language in our home after I started school." — Catherine Fossay (Moorhead, MN)

"By World War I, nobody gave their actual nationality. They were all Americans. They were good Americans, too, patriotic! Much more patriotic emphasis in the schools. There was a little ceremony with hanging up the flag in the morning, and the pledge, and patriotic songs. Just about everyone had someone in the war that they knew or were related to. I remember Armistice Day. We had the flu then. And we were upstairs, we were both in bed, and when the Soo train came through it whistled continuously. It went from Oakes [North Dakota] into Portland tooting all the time so we knew something was up. Then we heard the armistice had been signed. … In 1918 many people died. Just about every family lost someone [to the flu]. They would run out of oranges. They said you were supposed to eat all the oranges you wanted, and sometimes you couldn't get them because they were all sold out. And some of the oranges that came were of poor quality, you couldn't hardly eat one. And then we'd take quinine. We were supposed to take quinine until your ears buzzed, and when they started that, then we should stop for a while. So we did that. We both lived." — Mabel Enger (Oakes, ND)

"[During World War I] we sang patriotic songs and saluted the flag, and we marched, and we were very patriotic. We all tried very hard to be American, it was just the language barrier and we had to overcome that." — Bernice Schaefer (Osakis, MN)

"During World War I they taught free, to any girls, telegraphy, at the Western Union building over in Fargo. So my sister and I attended the course for about nine months and then we were ready to work. I worked there for many years. There was a shortage of men, you know. A lot of the men didn't come back. There were a lot of single girls." — Eva Thortvedt (Glyndon, MN)

"People had to be very careful what they said. … One German farmer living near Hawley [Minnesota] had a picture of the Kaiser, and people broke in there and burned the picture. … People were almost forced to buy bonds. Public opinion was so strong that if you refused then you weren't patriotic. Even if a person couldn't afford to, you were almost forced to make an effort to buy them in order to have peace in the community. [The war] had a lot to do with making everybody learn English and speak it, at least in public anyway. In my case, we really didn't have that problem, because our folks were quite Americanized by the time we came up to Hitterdal, and so I was never so conscious of it, and it took place so gradually I never did recognize or realize any definite [change]. But I think it was accelerated during and after the First World War." — Wilferd Anderson (Hitterdal, MN)

"There wasn't so much interest in [the war] around here because we were all Norwegian. It might have been different if there were some Germans. There were some Germans in Hawley. I guess there was quite a stir-up in Hawley. Somebody had gone into a house and tore down a picture of Kaiser Bill." — Nilmer Bjorndahl (Hawley, MN)

"The First World War seemed to unite the people more. It seemed like the Germans and the Norwegians and Swedes had a, I don't know what you call it, a purpose in life, when a lot of the boys were drafted and sent overseas. It seemed as though some of [the Germans] were [looked upon with suspicion] and some of them were pro-German. They had their ideas about the war and I suppose that came out and people found out about it. Some of them had pictures that the patriotic people really thought they shouldn't have. We heard that someone had gone into [a home of a German] and had taken the picture [of Kaiser Wilhelm II] down. What they did with it I don't know. I think there were two instances of that. ... My German friend had two brothers in the service. I really think it helped get more people united. ... The telephone operator in Hawley had rung one long ring on the party line and there must have been about twenty of us on the line, I suppose, and it just rang and rang and rang until everybody took the receiver down and then [the armistice] was announced. We lived out in the country about nine miles, I don't know what they did in town. ... I think there was pressure to become less Norwegian and more American and we got to be more united." — Joanna Aune (Hawley, MN)

"It was just a little tough with the old Scandinavians. I don't blame them. They wanted to hang on to their mother tongue. It was hard for a lot of them, and a lot of them have quite a dialect and some never broke it."
— Frank Alm (Christine, ND)

"We processed our own wool, yes, we used to spin it and card it and during World War I we helped to make scarves and knit stockings to send overseas." — Freda Bjornson (Moorhead, MN)

"In school it was our country, our country, U.S.A. Very nationalistic, especially during World War I. And we'd have big parades." — Borghild Overby (Moorhead, MN)

"There was a social value that said you were not socially acceptable if you maintained your Scandinavian accent or your Scandinavian brogue. That was a result of the war, World War One." — Carl Narveson (Moorhead, MN)

"There got to be a lot of emphasis on patriotism. [Before the war] many people who had come from Europe spoke of themselves as 'Norwegian-Americans,' 'Danish-Americans,' ... and so on. And then there got to be slurring remarks passed about hyphenated Americans. No one was supposed to be a hyphenated American. So in many families where they had been speaking a foreign language, they just tried their very best to stop it, and a lot of them did." — Christian Schulstad (Dawson, MN)

"I remember [during World War I] my folks even putting out the United States flag. Before we saw more of the Swedish flag, the yellow and the blue, but after that it was the United States flag. I think my folks were proud that my brother had gone to war because they had this blue star with a red and white background that they put in that window right there. Then when they got the notice that Pershing sent that my brother had been killed in France, they took the blue star down and put a gold star there. They thought it was just the thing because then they were United States citizens now and they'd better abide by it. And I never heard them gripe or say anything about it." — Vic Anderson (Moorhead, MN)

"By that time, I think the second generation people, we were Americans and didn't even think that we were Norwegians. We think much more that way now. We're much more conscious that we have a mother country than we were [in 1917]." — William Nelson (Rollag, MN)

"Before World War I, most of the children who came to the [Twin Valley Minnesota Children's] Home were like our family, where the children had been well brought up but one or both of their parents had died. After World War I, a little bit different child came into the home. They were from broken homes. And there were knife fights, because some of them brought their knives with them, and they were quick to fight." — Carl Narveson (Moorhead, MN)

"I remember the day the war ended. School was let out and they took us in trucks. We all stood up in trucks and they took us through the streets of Moorhead and we were all singing." — Gladys Westrum (Moorhead, MN)

"In Moorhead and Fargo, after the First World War, they drove up and down the streets with automobiles with washboards and tubs dragging behind the cars making all the noise they could and tooting their horns." — Ole Olson (Fargo, ND)

"On Armistice Day we went outside and I know we marched around the school and sang patriotic songs. I was just little, I was in the second grade, all I can remember was that it was a hullabaloo." — Violet Anderson (Hitterdal, MN)

"There wasn't so much pressure to become more patriotic until about 1918. Then we had to get our flags and we had to have the flag salute every morning and patriotic songs. And of course then we had to learn more history, too. And we had the sale of bonds. They were all expected to buy bonds. We were almost forced to buy bonds." — Alma Ramse (McIntosh, MN)

"Bondsales? I know the name, but I don't recall him. I heard the name all right. Bondsales. Where was he from?" — Arne Arneson (Fargo, ND)

Chapter XVI
"That's What America Is!"

SCANDINAVIAN-AMERICAN VALUES

Most of the oral histories of the Scandinavian-Americans reveal a nostalgia that was not for an old country that they had never seen, but for the way parents or grandparents remembered that old country. The pleas of those who called for resistance to assimilation were appreciated by those who had a real affection for the old country and a tempered sense of the new, but by the 1920s a new generation of American-born Scandinavians existed. They could love the Old Country because their parents loved it, but there was, for them, no question of a divided heart.

Assimilation proceeded more rapidly than most could have imagined, but as with other ethnic groups, pride in Scandinavia remained. Virtually all of the oral histories reveal the maintenance, consciously or unconsciously, of certain customs in their homes, and the mere mention of lutefisk evoked an expression of affection that reached beyond a recollection of the taste. There was a pride in holding on to the heritage, as represented among the Norwegians by the *bygdelag* movement in America and by the other Scandinavian groups in their celebrations of national days. With the turn of the century Norwegian ethnic societies, organizations, fraternal lodges, mutual aid groups and reform associations proliferated, especially in the cities. The *bygdelag* movement, which featured the organization of emigrants from a particular region in Norway, eventually numbered more than fifty societies. Their summer reunions gave their members the opportunity to feast on traditional foods and beloved memories. Chicago alone had more than seventy different Swedish clubs and societies during the 1870s, from temperance lodges to choral societies, gymnastic clubs, and fraternal orders.

Perhaps one of the better expressions of how the Scandinavian immigrant viewed his presence in America is to be found in the 1902 "Statement of Purpose" of the Icelandic Association of the University of North Dakota. The society did not "aim to maintain a foreign nationality segregated and ancient in custom and in speech. It believes that the first duty of the foreigner is, above all others, to become an American citizen."

This pride could be overt, as is everywhere evident during the Nordic Fest held annually at Decorah, Iowa, or the Hostfest held in Minot, North Dakota, or it could just be there, inconspicuously a part of everyday life. There are still numerous Finnish saunas in use, although some of the rituals have been abandoned, and one can still find Finnish flatbread, rice pie, sweet soup, and fish pie. And long after the children

had stopped using Norwegian in the home, when the Hitterdal High School Vikings played the Ulen High School Panthers in a basketball game in Western Minnesota, the Hitterdal cheerleaders would lead their supporters with the rousing yell, "Lutefisk and Lefse, *Fattigman* and *sild*! Ve'll beat Ulen, You Bet Ve Vill!"

"Grandma Johnson's biggest wish, to her dying day, was to go back to Iceland sometime, but moneywise, they couldn't afford it." — Diane Volrath (Hitterdal, MN)

"I remember my mother always said she missed so much the scenery in Iceland, the mountains and the glaciers. The mountain streams, the rivers all came flying down and the water is so clear and lovely. She was fifteen when she left and she said she always missed the scenery of Iceland. But I never heard any regrets from any of them. There were people that wished they were back in Iceland, but none of my people felt that way. They were so individualistic, and some of them were very poetic. They'd read poetry to you, and I didn't always relish that because I didn't always understand it as a kid. The stories, though, I used to like. … There was this old man that my mother took care of, and we had this old gray horse, and he was fixing an old clock for us, and he said, 'It would be best to destroy us, the old gray horse, the clock, and me.' There was the poetic element in him, you see. He saw himself in the class with the old clock and the old horse. There was that

appreciation for that kind of thing. And there was also sort of a sport where somebody would start a couplet. They'd give the first line and then you'd have to finish it. And that was quite an interesting thing. We had people from our community who went into various fields of endeavor and many of them did very well in their work, and most of them went to college. Although there were many who did not go to college who excelled. My husband's uncle was reputed to have the best private library in the country and he gave it to the University of Wisconsin and that raised the reputation of the library."
— Kathryn Thordarson (Fargo, ND)

"I think among all these people of Finnish background the background lives with them, and not as a language or anything else, but the fact that they are interested in things Finnish. And we find among these young people now that there is a tremendous interest, even those of the third generation … that might not have spoken much Finnish at home. But they know a little bit of it, and they're studying the Finnish language. … The young people are interested in learning Finnish because their grandparents or great-grandparents came from Finland, and they want to know who they are, and what they are and why." — Russell Parta (New York Mills, MN)

"I don't think any of our relatives ever went back to Sweden. I remember Dad saying he never wanted to go back. The oldest son inherited everything and that seemed so unfair because they had quite a bit of acreage." — Roy Carlander (Moorhead, MN)

"I can see why they weren't too enamored with their life [in Sweden] at that time. There was no money there. The population was growing and really no place for them to get enough land so that it would pay for them to stay there. Their hard times over there were things that they came over here to forget. Their fun times were family associations, and those were things they brought with them." — Catherine Fossay (Moorhead, MN)

"Each time that I've gone back to Norway, I've come back with a stronger appreciation of my family heritage than I ever dreamed I could have. On this last trip, I uncovered one hundred and thirty one relatives, including nine living first cousins." — John Gronner (Underwood, MN)

"They used to talk to us about the Old Country. That was their favorite topic of conversation. The Old Country and all the relatives that they had there. And they went back in 1946, and stayed a year. And they went to see everybody. But what was most important to them to go back to Norway was to visit their parent's graves. Because when they left Norway, they never saw their parents again. That was important to them to visit their graves and to be able to bring flowers, and to make a donation to the old home church that was standing, just an old building, but if they could make a donation to that, that was important." — Solveig Johnson (Niagara, ND)

"I always liked America, and I've never been lonesome or homesick. You know, there were some that came from Norway who were so homesick, but I ain't never been homesick. Yah, I went back in 1954, but you know how it is. After forty years there wasn't very many left. So if you plan on going back, if you ever leave here, don't stay away that long. Because it isn't anything to come back to a grave." — Marie Tverdahl (Starkweather, ND)

"[My parents] just thought the world of Norway, but they never told us a lot." — Inga Moore (Moorhead, MN)

"There is one thing I'd like to mention and that is about the early pioneers as I remember them. It was something that was stressed in our home and in every home around us. Honesty and dependability! We could depend on each other's help, and could depend on every neighbor's honesty. If you lost anything, it was brought back to you, and if they owed you anything, they paid you what you had coming and if they couldn't pay you, they came back and did something for you. They worked very much like true friends and neighbors should work. That's the beauty of the old recollections that I have from my childhood and my youth, and even from my early years of marriage. And for that I thank God for all the good memories I have."
— Clara Hanson (Moorhead, MN)

"Our children, our two sons and their families, they still hold true to tradition. They have lutefisk and lefse and sweet soup, meatballs and those things for Christmas Eve. And this is tradition." — Alva Hest (Perley, MN)

"The Norwegians are the first to tell the Norwegian jokes. Whereas before it was 'don't tell Norwegian jokes.' But, you see, there's a security now, and they can tell the Norwegian jokes. And they can tell them with a flat accent, they can tell them any place. I think that's very interesting, the change that has come. Before you didn't mock, you didn't laugh at, you didn't ridicule. But now they can stand up to these, whatever it is, the 'dumb Swede,' the 'dumb Norwegian,' and they can laugh and I think that's important. … I heard an interesting comment from a woman who came from Norway only ten or twelve years ago. She said 'The good people of Moorhead ought to go back and be missionaries to Norway, because the standards here are so much more rigorous than those in Norway! They are carrying here the moral attitudes or social attitudes of their forbears and it didn't change, whereas in Norway and Sweden it changed extraordinarily." — Delsie Holmquist (Fargo, ND)

"I don't think there are any [old world customs that remain today], unless it's that we eat lutefisk and bake lefse." — Edwin Markestad (Maddock, ND)

"It's wonderful now compared to what it was. It's really changed from what I remember." — Alma Olson (Souris, ND)

"I think most of the traditions sort of petered out." — Amy Margaret Erickson (Wheatland, ND)

"The thing that struck me, and the thing I remember most vividly, is that whenever anyone Norwegian did anything notable, that was worth some kind of points. 'Look what the Norwegian had done.' There was sort of a feeling that Norwegians were not quite first class citizens because they spoke with an accent and stuff. But they felt extremely proud to be Norwegians. There was no apology for being Norwegian. Norwegians were obviously the best people in the world. No question about that! And yet, going along with it was the feeling that the rest of the world didn't know it. It hadn't been proved conclusively the rest of the world, and you ought not to overlook any chance to prove it." — Clarence Glasrud (Moorhead, MN)

"Whenever there was an old Norwegian song sung or played, well, she would get a very sad look in her face or eyes because I think she really loved the country there." — Florence Fritz (Detroit Lakes, MN)

"We still talk Norwegian around here when we take a notion, just for the fun of it." — Gertie Holm (Hawley, MN)

"I still know the language. I know the words, but I can't find them because English words come ahead of them. Because for sixty-two years I've used almost exclusively English, trying to get as much command of the English language as I possibly can get, you know. The words are there, but I can't recall them fast enough, because I think in English." — Sven Thompson (Willmar, MN)

"It was in the forties, I suppose, when people stopped talking Norwegian all the time. But you can go out to Rollag today and you can always find someone who can speak Norwegian with you." — Nilmer Bjorndahl (Hawley, MN)

"My children actually have a stronger Scandinavian background and heritage today than I did as I was growing up, and I guess I'd have to say I'm happy for the experience. It's something that I missed on my own, and it was nice to be able to learn those skills that my past would have normally generated for me and I think that it's probably one of the benefits of being in an American culture. You can see your past heritage and other people's heritage and how they meld and work together. It makes us all more interesting." — Maureen Christianson ((Kenmare, ND)

"I consider it a very good heritage. We had to learn to fear God, and we had to learn to love our country and love our fellow man and work and respect and love our neighbor. We brought that with us to America and we think that's good for America and we think that's what America is." — John Klukken (Osakis, MN)

BIBLIOGRAPHY

THE PRAIRIE VOICES

Preserved at the Northwest Minnesota Regional History Center, Livingston Lord Library, Moorhead State University, Moorhead, Minnesota.

Abraham, Ellen, April 3, 1990, S4918-5012.

Alm, Frank, May 19, 1976, S733.

Andersen, Louise, April 16, 1976, S753.

Anderson, Carl Axel, undated, 1975, S735.

Anderson, Lynn, October 19, 1982, S835.

Anderson, Victor, January 21, 1976, S723.

Anderson, Violet, August 19, 1990, s4946-5086.

Anderson, Wilferd, December 14, 1975, S719.

Arneson, Arne, May 14, 1976, S767.

Askegaard, Oscar, April 14, 1976, S750.

Aune, Johanna, April 9, 1976, S747.

Barker, Hazel Monson, April 27, 1976, S752.

Bjorndahl, Nilmer, February 4, 1976, S752.

Bjornson, Anna K., May 15, 1976, S799.

Bjornson, Freda, January 26, 1976, S724.

Blumer, Matilda, December 6, 1978, S2631.

Bowersox, Alpha Jacobson, April 28, 1990, S4918-5031.

Bratlien, Oscar, January 30, 1976, S726.

Burgess, Henrietta, April 30, 1976, S755.

Campbell, Rosa, May 10, 1976, S800.

Carlander, Robert, March 3, 1976, S739.

Carlson, Minnie, September 9, 1975, S734.

Christiansen, Maureen, April 22, 1990, S4918-5013.

Christianson, Leif Livar, April 29, 1976, S780.

Dinusson, Wayne E., June 14, 1976, S798.

Elmquist, Carol C., May 22, 1976, S788

Enger, Mabel, April 4, 1976, S788.

Erickson, Allen, April 14, 1976, S789.

Erickson, Amy, April 27, 1976, S732.

Erickson, Amy Margaret, May 8, 1990, S4918-5014.

Erickson, Ruth Dahl, May 6, 1976, S787.

Faust, Dagne, May 10, 1976, S763.

Fossay, Katherine, May 25, 1796, S778.

Fritz, Florence, May 8, 1990, S4918-5016.

Fugelberg, Vern, April 14, 1990, S4918-5016.

Furcht, Clara Euren, January 19, 1976, S722.

Fynskov, Mabel, May 8, 1976, S769.

Gale, Elsie, March 18, 1976, S743.

Glasrud, Clarence, May 7, 1976, S785.

Gregorson, Anna, January 17, 1976, S720.

Gregorson, Obert, January 17, 1976, S720.

Gronner, John, May 14, 1976, S760.

Hanson, Anna, May 5, 1976, S758.

Hanson, Clara, May 17, 1976, S777.

Hanson, Norman, November 16, 1976, S2607.

Hanson, Regina, November 16, 1976, S2607.

Haugen, Louis, June 17, 1976, S805.

Hegland, Lela, May 7, 1976, S776.

Herfindal, Bernice, April 15, 1990, S4918-5017.

Hest, Alva, March 1, 1977, S839.

Hillman, Esther, May 5, 1990, S4918-5031.

Hillman, Leo, May 5, 1990, S4918-5031.

Hitterdahl, Clifford, January 17, 1976, S721.

Holm, Gertie, April 9, 1976, S747.

Holmgren, Henry, Undated, 1975, S737.

Holmquist, Delsie, April 14, 1976, S771.

Holt, Inez, May 14, 1990, S4918-5018.

Iverson, Gale, March 6, 1976, S741.

Jacobson, George, March 1, 1977, S838.

Johnard, Hartwig, May 13, 1976, S792.

Johnson, Clara, June 16, 1976, S804.

Johnson, Solveig, April 18, 1990, S4918-5019.

Johnson, Tora Jeppesen, April 6, 1978, S899.

Kaeding, Helene, April 28, 1976, S775.

Kivi, Karen, July 20, 1973, S241.

Klokseth, Edythe, November 15, 1978, S2608.

Klukken, John O., May 26, 1976, S774.

Kragnes, Cora Klokseth, November 13, 1978, S2606.

Kromarak, Eloise, April 16, 1990, S4918-5020.

Laske, Gunhild, May 14, 1990, S4918-5021.

Lien, Marlene, April 7, 1990, S4918-5022.

Lindgren, Andrew, May 6, 1978, S833.

Lindgren, Oscar, May 7, 1976, S766.

Lundgren, Svea, June 7, 1976, S795.

Markestad, Edwin, April 14, 1990, S4918-5023.

Melberg, Anna, March 1, 1977, S840.

Melby, William, March 6, 1976, S740.

Moore, Inga, May 19, 1976, S783.

Narveson, Carl, May 27, 1976, S790.

Nelson, Judith, April 15, 1990, S4918-5024.

Nelson, Norman, February 3, 1776, S728.

Nelson, William, February 3, 1976, S727.

Norman, John, November 19, 1978, S2619.

Oien, Nina, June 2, 1976, S796.

Oliver, Alice, May 19, 1976, S786.

Olson, Alma, April 22, 1990, S4918-5025.

Olson, Ole, January 10, 1979, S2632.

Olson, Oscar, March 11, 1976, S742.

Overby, Borghild, May 20, 1976, S782.

Overby, Nels, May 20, 1976, S782.

Parta, Russell, August 9, 1973, S243.

Ramse, Alma, May 2, 1976, S761.

Rundquist, Myrtle, April 29, 1976, S754.

Schaefer, Beatrice, April 18, 1976, S722.

Schulstad, Rev. Christian, October 9, 1978, S2626.

Simonson, Ralph, April 16, 1990, S4918-5020.

Strandness, Lillie, May 5, 1976, S759.

Svidal, Kristine, May 3, 1990, S4918-5027.

Swedberg, David, August 14, 1974, S736.

Thompson, Rev. Sven, April 13, 1990, S4918-5028.

Thordarson, Kathryn, January 31, 1979, S2634.

Thortvet, Eva, August 7, 1974, S707.

Tiedeman, Minnie, November 4, 1979, S2609.

Tverdahl, Marie, May 8, 1976, S764.

Tverdahl, Palmer, April 25, 1976, S762.

Volrath, Diane, May 6, 1990, S4918-5029.

Waldon, Arthur, April 20, 1976, S781.

Westerholm, Charles, April 9, 1976, S748.

Westerholm, Phoebe, April 12, 1976, S749.

Westling, Louis Emil, November 12, 1984, S2779.

Westrum, Gladys, February 9, 1976, S730.

Westrum, Lloyd, February 19, 1976, S731.

SELECTED BIBLIOGRAPHY

Anderson, Arlow W. *The Norwegian-Americans*. Boston: Twayne Publishers, 1975.

Babcock, Kendric Charles. *The Scandinavian Element in the United States*. Urbana, Illinois: University of Illinois, 1914.

Benson, Adolph B. *America of the Fifties: Letters of Fredrika Bremer*. New York: The American Scandinavian Foundation, 1924.

Blegen, Theodore C. *Norwegian Migration to America, 1825–1860*. Northfield, Minnesota: The Norwegian-American Historical Association, 1931.

———. *Norwegian Migration: The American Transition*. Northfield, Minnesota: The Norwegian-American Historical Association, 1940.

Christianson, J. R. (ed.) *Scandinavians in American Literary Life*. Decorah, Iowa: Symra Literary Society. 1985.

Fridley, Russell W. "Debate Continues Over Kensington Runestone," *Minnesota History*. Saint Paul: Minnesota Historical Society, 45/4. Winter, 1976.

Friis, Erik J. *The Scandinavian Presence in North America*. New York: Harper's Magazine Press, 1976.

Furer, Howard B. (ed.) *The Scandinavians in America, 1986–1970*. Dobbs

  Ferry, New York: Oceana Publications, In., 1972.

Grele, Ronald J. "It's Not the Sound, It's the Singing," *Envelopes of Sound*.

  Chicago: Precedent Publishing Company, 1975.

———. "Movement Without Aim: Methological and Thematic Problems in Oral History,"

  Envelopes of Sound. Chicago: Precedent Publishing Company, 1975.

Harris, Alice Kessler. *Envelopes of Sound*. Chicago: Precedent Publishing

  Company, 1975.

Hasselmo, Nils. *Swedish America: An Introduction*. New York: Swedish

  Information Service, 1976.

Holmquist, June Drenning (ed.). *They Chose Minnesota: A Survey of the*

  States's Ethnic Groups. St. Paul: Minnesota Historical Society, 1981.

Lindberg, Duane Rodell. *Men of the Cloth and the Social Cultural Fabric of*

  the Norwegian Ethnic Community in North Dakota. New York: Arno

  Press, 1980.

Ljungmark, Lars. *Swedish Exodus*. Carbondale, Illinois: Southern Illinois

  University Press, 1979.

Lovoll, Odd s. (ed.) *Cultural Pluralism versus Assimilation: The Views of*

  Waldemar Ager. Northfield, Minnesota: The Norwegian-American

  Historical Society, 1977.

———. *The Promise of America: A History of the Norwegian-American People*. Minneapolis: The University of Minnesota Press, 1984.

Moberg, Vilhelm. *The Emigrants*.

———. *Unto A New Land*.

———. *The Settlers*.

———. *The Last Letter Home*.

Nelson, David T. (translator and ed.). *The Dairy of Elizabeth Koren, 1853–1955*. Northfield, Minnesota: The Norwegian-American Historical Society, 1955.

Nelson, Helge. *The Swedes and the Swedish Settlements in North America*. New York: Arno Press, 1979.

Nielsen, George R. *The Danish Americans*. Boston: Twayne Publishers, 1981.

Okihiro, Gary Y. "Oral History and the Writing of Ethnic History: A Reconnaissance into Method and Theory," *The Oral History Review*. Volume 9, 1981.

Qualey, Carlton C. *Norwegian Settlement in the United States*. Northfield, Minnesota: The Norwegian-American Historical Association, 1938.

Rolvaag, Ole E. *Giants in the Earth*. New York: Harper and Brothers, 1927.

Runblom, Harold and Hans Norman, (eds.) *From Sweden to America: A History of the Migration*. Minneapolis: University of Minnesota Press, 1976.

Semmingsen, Ingrid. *Norway to America: A History of the Migration.* Minneapolis: University of Minnesota Press, 1978.

Sherman, William C. and Playford V. Thorson, (eds.) *Plains Folk: North Dakota's Ethnic History.* Fargo: North Dakota Institute for Regional Studies, 1986.

Skardal, Dorothy Burton. *The Divided Heart: Scandinavian Immigrant Experience Through Literary Sources.* Lincoln: University of Nebraska Press, 1974.

Smemo, I. Kenneth. "Norwegian America's Golden Age." *The Norseman.* Oslo: Nordmanns Forbundet, No. 1. 1989.

Thernstrom, Stephen (ed.) *The Harvard Encyclopedia of Ethnic Groups.* Cambridge, Mass.: Harvard University Press, 1980.

Wefald, Jon. *A Voice of Protest: Norwegians in American Politics, 1980–1917.* Northfield, Minnesota. The Norwegian American Historical Association, 1976.

Made in the USA
San Bernardino, CA
16 June 2015